Bullspotting

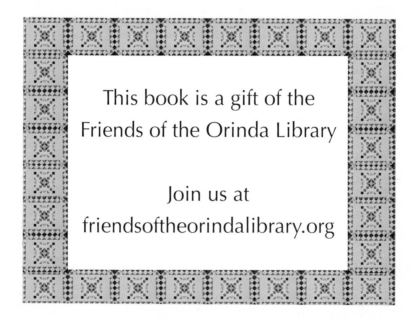

This book is a gift of the
Friends of the Orinda Library

Join us at
friendsoftheorindalibrary.org

LOREN COLLINS

Bullspotting

FINDING FACTS
in the Age of
MISINFORMATION

 Prometheus Books

59 John Glenn Drive
Amherst, New York 14228–2119

Published 2012 by Prometheus Books

Cover image © Jamie Grill/Media Bakery
Cover design by Jacqueline Nasso Cooke

Inquiries should be addressed to
Prometheus Books
59 John Glenn Drive
Amherst, New York 14228–2119
VOICE: 716–691–0133
FAX: 716–691–0137
WWW.PROMETHEUSBOOKS.COM

16 15 14 13 12   5 4 3 2 1

Library of Congress Cataloging-in-Publication Data

Collins, Loren, 1978–
    Bullspotting : finding facts in the age of misinformation / by Loren Collins.
        p. cm.
    Includes bibliographical references and index.
    ISBN 978–1–61614–634–4 (pbk. : alk. paper)
    ISBN 978–1–61614–635–1 (ebook)
    1. Critical thinking. I. Title.

BF441.C565 2012
001.9—dc23

                                                                    2012023390

Printed in the United States of America on acid-free paper

 CONTENTS

INTRODUCTION

For all their differences, one thing the skeptic and the conspiracy theorist often have in common is the conversion experience. The motivating event that caused each to reevaluate his or her previous beliefs and, like the religious convert, adopt a new worldview. It is the autobiographical origin story.

In my case, the way it started (or at least the way I like to tell it) was with the Confederate flag.

Throughout the 1990s and early 2000s, a major controversy in my home state of Georgia centered around the state flag. Since 1956, the Georgia flag had featured, in addition to the state seal, the battle flag of the Confederate States of America. Some argued that this was representative of a racist past. Others felt that this was a display of Southern heritage and was no more offensive than the flag's use on the roof of the Duke brothers' Dodge Charger.

I fell into the latter camp. I was, after all, a dyed-in-the-wool Southerner. My Southern credentials were (and still are) impeccable. I am a seventh-generation Georgian. The Collinses have lived in Georgia since the 1830s; other branches of my family tree can be traced back to the 1700s Carolinas. The only branch of my family that didn't live in the antebellum South was the branch that immigrated to America in the late 1800s . . . and settled in the South. I am descended from not one, not two, but five Confederate soldiers. And I was raised in Stone Mountain, home to the world's largest memorial to the losing side of a war.

So, naturally, I grew up defending the Confederacy, which I saw as synonymous with defending the South itself. It was an extension of regional pride and was unsurprising, given my influences. Such influences included the accepted "fact" that the Civil War was fought not over slavery but rather over a series of legitimate Southern grievances. To suggest that the Confederacy was motivated primarily by slavery or racism was nothing more than an anti-Southern smear campaign.

And so, when it came to the state flag, I saw the inclusion of the Confederate battle flag as a symbol of pride, not prejudice. I wanted to defend it from those who saw it as an opportunity to demean my ancestors and to destroy my heritage. Having heard for years that the South had fought over states' rights, I thought that a good defense strategy would be to document and summarize the South's "real" motivations—to draw from contemporary source material the Southern states' unanswered complaints of oppressive tariffs, unfair regulation, and more.

That was what I expected to find. What I found instead changed me.

The contemporary sources didn't support my thesis; they outright contradicted it. Confederate leaders in 1860 and 1861 were not threatening secession over tariffs or regulations. Rather, all secession rhetoric at the time was centered around a single issue: slavery.

Jefferson Davis, the future Confederate president, proposed a constitutional amendment that he argued would avert secession. Its terms were simple: it would have protected the legal status of slavery. Forever. Four Confederate states issued declarations of cause, detailing their reasons for seceding; all four identified the protection of Negro slavery as their primary motivation. Alexander Stephens, the Confederate vice president, proudly bragged that the Confederate government was the "first, in the history of the world, based upon this great physical, philosophical, and moral truth" of black inferiority.[1]

Other contemporary sources told the same tale. When taxes were cited in support of secession, they were taxes related to slavery. When regulations were cited, they were regulations related to slavery. To the extent secession proponents spoke of states' rights, they appeared to be concerned with but one right: the right to own slaves.

This was not what I had always believed. But there it was, in the Confederate leaders' own unambiguous words. And my efforts to find more positive sources were fruitless. Every contemporary argument for secession made slavery either its primary focus or its exclusive focus. Any other concern was plainly inferior to slavery and was not, by itself, a driving force of secession.

I had set out to gather support for a conclusion I already had scripted. I had wanted to justify the belief I already held. But the evidence I found was so universally against my position that I could not even pick and choose my sources; any source that even mentioned a nonslavery grievance mentioned slavery far more prominently.

I had a choice to make. I could look past this evidence and find other ways to justify my existing belief, or I could change my belief. I chose the latter.

I am sure that to some readers, this sounds like a perfunctory decision. Like it was nothing more than being corrected on what year James Garfield was assassinated. But this was not a mere factoid; it was a cultural truth. Remember, it was at the center of a major debate over the state flag.

Accepting that I had been wrong meant acknowledging that I and others I trusted had been advancing a false argument for a long time. Moreover, given the nature of this new truth, it also meant that my five ancestors had fought on the wrong side of that war. It meant realizing that my hometown prominently honored the leaders of that wrong side.

It did not make me ashamed to be a Southerner. But it did make me ashamed to have believed for so long that the Confederacy was an aspect of my heritage to be proud of. Accepting the truth was difficult because it was an uncomfortable truth. Conceding the evil of the Confederacy's ways gives me little satisfaction. And yet, there is no shortage of Confederate apologists who seem to have made the opposite choice from me. They object to the presentation of slavery as the South's motivating interest, and they have their own ways of justifying their belief.

What makes my argument more compelling than theirs? I like to think that it comes down to the nature of the evidence presented. When I set out to defend the Confederacy's honor, I immediately set my sights on what I believed would be the most determinative and elucidative enumerations of the Confederate cause: the words of the Confederate leaders themselves, as they were promoting the creation of the Confederacy. Perhaps this wouldn't be unimpeachable evidence; perhaps they might paint a rosy portrait of themselves. But it is certainly a logical starting point, for the same reasons that any discussion of America's founding starts with the Continental Congress and the Declaration of Independence.

Confederate defenders don't take this approach. They find their justification in other places. They quote what Confederate leaders said after the war was over, after the Confederate States of America had lost, and once slavery was illegal. They look to the beliefs of the foot soldiers in the Confederate army rather than to the political leaders who orchestrated the secession and founded the Confederacy. They shift the focus onto the North's motivations or onto Lincoln's beliefs and then try to reverse engineer the South's motivations from that. Because they seek justification, they find places to mine it from, and then they reject the more straightforward evidence.

When I published an editorial in the university paper criticizing the idolization of the Confederacy and citing numerous sources in support of my position, I received only one response that disagreed with me.[2] And even he chose not to address the facts I presented; his only mention of my writing was to object to my use of the word *shame.* He couldn't overcome the words of the Confederate founders, so he could only ignore them.

As much as I tend to see this as the central turning point in my critical thinking, it was truthfully more of a tentpole moment along the way. It was a sudden shift in opinion, away from a belief that I then realized I had rationalized for far too long. In that sense, it was new, but I already had a history with skepticism.

Having attended a private Christian school during my teenage years, I'd been exposed to my fair share of creationism, including young-earth creationism. I was even partial to intelligent design for a time, before eventually rejecting it as well. I've leaned toward libertarian politics since high school as well, and for a time in college I supported the total legalization of drugs (despite being a teetotaler myself). When I set out to write a persuasive talk on the subject for a public speaking class, the sources I discovered did not support my beliefs. I ended up tempering my beliefs, and my speech changed.

Throughout college, I was repeatedly the person on my church mailing list who would share a Snopes® article after someone e-mailed a hoax or a chain letter. And it was also in college that I discovered Carl Sagan—specifically, his second-to-last book, *The Demon-Haunted World: Science as a Candle in the Dark.*

Over the past decade and a half, Sagan's book has become one of the primary tomes of the skeptical movement, and for good reason. Whereas Sagan had made a name for himself communicating science to the general public, here he turned those same skills toward educating against pseudoscience. *Demon-Haunted World* is filled with examples, impeccably researched, demonstrating the history of pseudoscientific thinking.

Amid the chapters on alien abductions and crop circles is one that stood out to me: "The Fine Art of Baloney Detection." In it, he writes:

> In the course of their training, scientists are equipped with a baloney detection kit. The kit is brought out as a matter of course whenever new ideas are offered for consideration. If the new idea survives examination by the tools in our kit, we grant it warm, although tentative, acceptance. If you're so inclined, if you don't want to buy baloney even when it's reassuring to do so, there are precautions that can be taken; there's a tried-and-true, consumer-tested method.

> What's in the kit? Tools for skeptical thinking.

What skeptical thinking boils down to is the means to construct, and to understand, a reasoned argument and—especially important—to recognize a fallacious or fraudulent argument. The question is not whether we like the conclusion that emerges out of a train of reasoning, but whether the conclusion follows from the premise or starting point and whether that premise is true.[3]

Sagan later warns, "Like all tools, the baloney detection kit can be misused, applied out of context, or even employed as a rote alternative to thinking."[4]

I always loved the idea of the baloney-detection kit. For reasons I'll return to in the next chapter, it's neither practical nor effective to curb the flow of misinformation simply through rebuttals and debunkings. Trying to correct wrong ideas not only takes time and effort, but persuasion is often not effective. Instead, the better approach is to instill in people the practices of critical thinking and skepticism. Arm individuals with the baloney-detecting tools to prevent false and supported beliefs so that such beliefs can be better contained.

And that's what I hope to do with this book. It is, in fact, the product of my own ill-fated attempt to kill off one of modern politics' more bizarre conspiracy theories: the Obama "Birthers." Skeptics often have a particular subject matter they enjoy debunking: anti-vaccine hysteria, or creationism, or faith healers. In my case, for the last three years, I've made a hobby of the Birthers, and not for the same reason as others who've followed the same course.

For readers unfamiliar with the term or with the conspiracy theorists it represents, in mid-2008, just after Barack Obama clinched the Democratic nomination for president, an online rumor gained wide circulation claiming that Obama had been born in Kenya and was therefore ineligible to be president of the United States. Within three days of the rumor going viral, Obama's campaign published his birth certificate online, confirming his birthplace as Hawaii. Rational Americans moved on.

But there was a small subset of fringe Republicans and Hillary

Clinton–supporting Democrats who weren't convinced. They argued that the document seen online was forged or inconclusive. A well-known 9/11-conspiracy theorist attempted to sue Mr. Obama, and a handful of other attorneys followed. Even with no measurable media attention, either on television or in print, the conspiracy theories began to flourish online.

New permutations of rumors began being created. It was claimed that Mr. Obama was born in Canada; or that he was adopted in Indonesia; or that he was actually, but secretly, the son of civil rights leader Malcolm X. Shortly after Obama was elected in November 2008, a novel legal theory began spreading, claiming that President-Elect Obama was ineligible for the presidency by virtue of his Kenyan father. That the existence of Obama's Kenyan father had been a widely publicized fact in his biography for the entire two-year campaign did not make these nascent Birthers question why Obama's parentage was suddenly constitutionally critical after his election.

It was at this time, in November 2008, that I began encountering Birther claims on Internet forums, even nonpolitical ones. I adopted a posture of debunking the claims I saw, saying "this is the sort of easily disproven conspiratorialist hoohah that needs to be nipped in the bud *now* before it's allowed to fester for the next four years."

Looking back, I was somewhat right about the necessity of timing. Birthers have indeed continued to fester since 2008, eventually driving the president to publicly release a copy of his so-called long-form birth certificate in April 2011. They have also taken the 2012 primary season as an opportunity to file lawsuits in states across the country, attempting to bar the president from his own reelection ballot based on their unreasonable suspicions and unsupported legal theories.

What I was wrong about in 2008 was my own inability to stem the tide of the Birthers' conspiracism. I first tried to debunk false claims on a Birther website but was banned within a couple of weeks. I started a blog, and although some of my writing got some attention across the web, it seems to have done little to change the opinions of any Birthers themselves.

After a couple of years, I decided to channel my investment in the Birthers into a book. In searching for an angle to tell the story of this utterly silly bit of political ephemera, I realized that Birtherism served as a concentration of virtually every kind of failure of critical thinking. Birthers began as denialists, growing into conspiracy theorists as they attempted to defend their doubts. Their founding myth was nothing more than an Internet rumor, but they built on it over time through anomaly hunting and cherry picking. They dabbled in pseudoscience, created pseudohistory, and dove headfirst into pseudolaw. To engage a Birther in debate is to confront a continuing stream of logical fallacies until they resort to name calling and changing the subject. Birtherism was large enough to be occasionally newsworthy but small enough to actually trace the evolution of its beliefs. In so many ways, Birthers were the ideal anti-skeptics, and I could use their mistakes to illustrate the practice of critical thinking (or the lack thereof) in a myriad of ways.

Eventually, though, I realized that the value of such a baloney-detection book went well beyond the Birthers themselves. To build such a book around one particular political conspiracy theory, even one with underappreciated variety, was to pigeonhole it unnecessarily. And so that book transformed into this one. Instead of using aspects of Birtherism exclusively to illustrate the lack of critical thinking, the canvas is much broader. Holocaust deniers, Truthers, anti-vaccinationists, creationists, anti-Stratfordians, JFK-assassination-conspiracy theorists, pseudoscientists, sovereign citizens, moon hoaxers, and even followers of David Icke . . . all of them and more are included here to let the reader see where each goes wrong.

While I may not be able to make a dint in Birtherism as it already exists, I hope that I might be able to help arm readers with baloney-detection kits of their own and to introduce the art of skeptical thinking to an audience of those who may not have known what they were missing. I must admit upfront that I'm no Carl Sagan, but I can only hope that I might do justice to his vision.

CHAPTER 1
BALONEY DETECTION

Every man should have a built-in automatic crap detector operating inside him.
—Robert Manning,
"Hemingway in Cuba," 1965

Ernest Hemingway said this in 1965.[1] He was talking specifically about the art of writing at the time, but his advice is worthwhile on a far larger scale. Crap detection is not only a valuable tool; it's an essential one. We're constantly bombarded with information, much of it unreliable, from every source imaginable. Television, radio, print, news, word of mouth, and especially the Internet, are continuous founts of misinformation. Of crap. Operating in the world efficiently depends on one's ability to identify that crap, to spot bull, to know what to trust and what to be suspicious of. But how does one go about making those distinctions as automatically as Hemingway would suggest we should?

When I told a friend that I was writing a book on recognizing misinformation, his response was, "You only need one thing: common sense." This was not an undereducated friend; he is a lawyer with a master's degree in business. But he's dead wrong. It's immediately tempting to agree that common sense is all that's needed to tell fact from fiction, but it's common sense that's driving that sense of agreement.

Common sense is, unfortunately, often unreliable. Indeed, it's so unreliable that humanity has developed a mechanism to try to overcome the common errors of common sense—a means by which we can cut through the morass of prejudices and blind spots and unconscious assumptions, and discover the true reality underneath. And we've given that antidote for common sense a name: science. Or, to put it more broadly, the scientific method. A question is posed. Research is conducted. A hypothesis is constructed. The hypothesis is tested. Analysis is done, and a conclusion is drawn. And that conclusion can then be validated or invalidated through further iterations of the scientific method.

It's not perfectly suited to all aspects of life, but the success of the scientific method of thinking is evidenced by its own successful results. Within less than sixty years, humanity went from putting the first man in flight to putting the first man on the moon. In fewer than fifty years, we went from discovering the makeup of DNA to successfully cloning a large mammal. Common sense, by contrast, told us for most of human history that the world was flat. That the stars moved, but not the earth. That the world was composed of but four elements: earth, fire, wind, and water. That life had existed for only a few thousand years. That illness was caused by supernatural forces. That certain races of people were inferior. That women were inferior to men. That magic exists.

For millennia, these were our accepted truths. Humanity's knowledge was largely governed by common sense, and progress was slow. It was science—and its tools for rationally examining our universe and uncovering its undiscovered truths—that propelled the rapid change of the last few hundred years.

That's not to say that common sense is useless or that it leads only to false answers. Common sense is frequently helpful and does sometimes aid in making legitimate observations about the world. For instance, common sense might recognize that the consumption of certain natural plants tends to be followed by helpful (or harmful) aftereffects and might thus conclude that the plant is medicinal or poisonous. Identifying that pattern can help lead to the discovery of an underlying truth. Still, it's no guarantee. Hypotheses, after all, are essentially the operation of common sense. We look at existing data and patterns, and we draw a tentative conclusion. Some hypotheses turn out to be correct; many don't. Common sense is the same way.

Perhaps the biggest change that science has provided in the past century has been the introduction of the Internet. It's often said that such developments make the world smaller, but on the individual level, this has made the average person's world immensely larger. Historically, people tended to have local friends, read local newspapers, follow local events. Our lives are no longer so insular.

Our access to information has grown exponentially, and so, simultaneously, has our access to misinformation. Entire libraries of scholarship are available online, but so are innumerable amateur blogs. Legitimate and respectable news sources are ever-more convenient, but ideological and agenda-driven websites offer up factually questionable propaganda posing as news. Video archives preserve the past, but inexpensive cameras and editing software now permit even the nuttiest conspiracy theorist to produce a polished video presentation that can be visually compelling.

Unfortunately, most of us are not conditioned to distinguish between trustworthy and untrustworthy information, particularly given the avalanche of new facts we're presented with each day. So we turn to logical shortcuts. We favor information from people or sources we like. We distrust information that's inconsistent with our personal biases and beliefs. We accept information when it supports a conclusion we like, and we deny it when it supports the opposite. We fall back on common sense.

Using such shortcuts is not necessarily wrong. Indeed, it's often necessary, given the sheer volume of information we're confronted with each day. One can hardly be expected to research and validate every new piece of information encountered; life would be a perpetual series of mundane research projects on insignificant subjects.

Still, there are ways that misinformation can be spotted and singled out for further review. A properly trained skeptical eye is always on the lookout for suspect information and is possessed of the tools to evaluate it. Then, even if a firm answer cannot be easily found, the skeptic knows to keep an open mind as to the validity of the new fact and can avoid treating it as a confirmed truth or a proven falsehood. He or she can avoid being a duped participant in the further spread of misinformation.

Indeed, while the Internet has facilitated the spread of misinformation, there are simultaneously ever more resources that examine, challenge, and debunk false claims. Barbara and David Mikkelson founded the website Snopes® in 1995, with the original mission of addressing urban legends that circulated the web, particularly through e-mails. Today, with a scope that is far broader than just urban legends, Snopes remains the web's go-to source for the lowdown on the latest popular rumors. And despite the site being an independent operation, the Mikkelsons are regularly attacked by cranks for their debunking. Similar websites, such as TruthOrFiction.com and About.com's Urban Legends page, are also good resources that have been challenging false claims since the late 1990s.

It wasn't until the 2000s that new websites were devoted to a field where misinformation is not only endemic but also has the potential to be far more influential than a simple chain e-mail: politics. Elected officials, political commentators, interest groups . . . they all regularly spin the truth to suit their agenda, and during election years, that spin gets broadcast directly into the public's homes as part of every campaign. FactCheck.org was created to evaluate the claims made by candidates and officials, and in 2004, it garnered national attention by being cited in a televised vice-presidential debate. In 2007, it was joined by PolitiFact.com, which graded political claims on its "Truth-O-Meter" scale, ranging from "True" to "Pants on Fire."[2]

Debunking even made its way onto television with the popular Discovery Channel show *Mythbusters*. Premiering in 2003, each episode of the show takes on a handful of rumors or myths, and the hosts conduct experiments to see if the claims stand up to scrutiny. Depending on the result, the myth is declared to be either Busted,

Plausible, or Confirmed. And while the show's experiments are not scientific in the strictest sense, cohost Adam Savage has noted that the show roughly follows the scientific method: they take a claim, develop a hypothesis, make a prediction, conduct some tests, and evaluate their findings. It's condensed and formatted for broadcast purposes, but the end result is that *Mythbusters* can make skepticism and critical thinking into enjoyable entertainment. (Having regular explosions doesn't hurt, either.)

The show's methodology also illustrates a critical point: "debunking" may be a result, but it shouldn't be a goal. That's why the word *debunking* is sometimes frowned upon by the skeptical community, since it implies that one begins with the intention of proving a claim to be false. Such firm commitment to a particular result is not scientific; starting with a preconceived outcome is, rather, the pseudoscientist's approach to evidence.

The scientific approach is to begin with a hypothesis. For most purposes, it's sufficient to use what is called a "null hypothesis," a default proposal that two phenomena are not related, or that a proposed process will not work as promised, or that a speculated fact is not accurate. A null hypothesis could be that crop circles were not created by aliens, that TWA Flight 800 was not felled by a missile, or that the president was not born in Kenya. From that starting point, one evaluates the evidence to see if the null hypothesis can be rejected—if there's not enough evidence to reject it, then the question remains open for further investigation.

Unfortunately, the human mind doesn't operate this way automatically, and even when it tries, it is prone to making errors. Not only that, but the human mind is conditioned to make very particular kinds of errors when evaluating questions, and those errors lead to incorrect beliefs.

Prehistoric humans had no concept of science or any sort of organized system of reasoning. But they were observers of the world around them, and they were capable of recognizing patterns in their environments. The sun would rise and set. The seasons changed in a predictable fashion. Clouds would appear in the sky before it rained. Certain animals might migrate and return at the same times during the seasonal cycles. Poisonous plants and animals could be identified by detecting the morbid pattern of when someone fell ill or died after eating them. Food could be located by identifying the patterns of where certain plants were likely to grow, or where certain animals were prone to live. Making these simple and basic associations helped ancient humans live and better understand their world.

But while we were evolving to recognize valid patterns, we weren't evolving the equivalent skill of rejecting invalid ones. If a man heard a suspicious sound and believed it was a tiger instead of a rodent, he did not particularly suffer if he responded as if it was a tiger. On the other hand, if he failed to sense a pattern between "sound" and "tiger" and he was wrong, then he was cat food. The man who saw a false pattern lived to spread his suspicious genes; the man who failed to see a real pattern won the Paleolithic equivalent of a Darwin Award. People thus evolved to spot patterns, even when they weren't there, and so began our love affair with misinformation. Out of our predilection for making associations, even false ones, came superstitions and some of the earliest forms of pseudoscience, like astrology.

Michael Shermer, founder of *Skeptic* magazine and author of *The Believing Brain*, termed this phenomenon *patternicity*, which he defined as "the tendency to find meaningful patterns in both meaningful and meaningless noise."[3] Shermer further named another psychological phenomenon inherited through the practices of our ancient ancestors. *Agenticity*, as he called it, is "the tendency to infuse patterns with meaning, intention, and agency." He illustrates this by using the same "cat in the grass" illustration: when the ancient wanderer heard the rustle, it was advantageous to his survival when he assumed that there was a conscious agent behind the sound (a predatory cat) rather than an inanimate force (the wind).[4]

We thus developed the tendency to draw associations not only between physical events but also between physical events and perceived motives behind those events. Superstitions were imbued with supernatural elements, invoking the existence of intelligent forces outside our sight that could be credited as the causes of the effects we observed. There came to be supernatural powers that caused the seasons to change, or caused crops to die, or brought famine. Special rituals could please the gods and earn their good favor, like dances that could bring rain or shamanic practices that could heal the sick. Animals and trees, the sun and the moon, even the earth itself were imbued with spiritual powers.

From these supernatural beliefs, then, grew bodies of myths. Humans are narrative creatures by nature; professor Walter Fisher coined the term *Homo Narrans*, the storytelling man.[5] As generations of superstitious practice and observations accumulated, they were assembled into narratives. Impersonal natural spirits became pantheons of gods with names and personalities and individual histories unto themselves. Over time, humanity's tendency toward agenticity did not merely ascribe anonymous agency to worldly events; it also personalized those events. To the ancient Greeks, lightning and thunder were the works of Zeus; the seas were controlled by Poseidon; and so on.

These same tendencies toward pattern seeking and myth making underlie much of modern misinformation as well. Conspiracy theories are deeply rooted in the desire to find agenticity in accidental events, or to reassign agenticity to a more comfortable source, thereby creating their own tiny mythologies. Rumors are created when false associations are made, either in drawing incorrect conclusions from one's own observations or by misinterpreting information provided from some other source. Pseudo-scholarship is built on a foundation of faulty patterns and conclusions, and on a willingness to believe myths offered up through poor research rather than accepted truths that are backed by better and broader information.

Since evolution did not provide us with a crap detector that works to counteract our worse tendencies for misinformation, we have to train ourselves to spot misinformation as it presents itself. We have to hone our own crap detectors to learn the skills of proper skepticism and of critical thinking.

Spotting misinformation in advance is essential in avoiding it, for the same reason that we're so susceptible to it. The human mind is prone to a multitude of cognitive biases that influence how we think. We will view information differently depending on how it's framed; survey questions can get different results based on nothing more than how the questions are worded. We tend to give more weight to recent events over older events. The phenomenon of pareidolia causes us to see or hear messages in random data, allowing the image of Jesus to appear on a taco or satanic messages to be heard when a record is played backward.

But according to Shermer, the king of all cognitive biases is the confirmation bias.[6] Once we believe something, it is not in our nature to equally seek out all new evidence as it comes along and evaluate it neutrally. When we do look for new information, we put our best efforts toward finding information that supports the things we already believe. We make little or no effort toward discovering whether there is credible evidence that contradicts our beliefs. When we're confronted with information and evidence that undermines our already-held beliefs, we try to undermine the value of that information. We question its credibility, we interpret it in the least favorable light, or we just ignore it entirely. And at the same time, we're prone to give every benefit of the doubt to each tidbit of evidence that seems to support our existing beliefs, no matter how questionable its credibility may be or how much we have to bend it to suit our needs.

This bias toward confirmation of our beliefs drastically hinders our ability to dispel ourselves of false beliefs. A 2005–2006 study on political beliefs produced the discomfiting finding that subjects presented with corrective information did not have their beliefs corrected. In the first study, subjects were presented with a mock news article suggesting that Saddam Hussein had stockpiles of WMDs prior to the 2003 invasion of Iraq, with a correction appended to the article's end saying that no such stockpiles were found to exist. Not only were conservative subjects not persuaded by the correction;

there was a "backfire effect," as the study authors called it, by which the conservative subjects who read the correction became *more* likely to believe the WMDs were real.

The researchers found this effect among its liberal subjects as well. In another study, they used a mock article stating that President George W. Bush had banned stem-cell research, with a correction that stated he had not done so. Conservatives were positively influenced by the correction, but liberal subjects did not change their beliefs in response to the correction (although they did not display any "backfire effect" in the study).[7]

When we cannot trust ourselves to be neutral arbiters of information, when we're primed to contort evidence to fit our beliefs rather than adapting our beliefs to fit the evidence, it's in our best interest to spot misinformation before we adopt it into our belief system. If our crap detectors can weed out bad information before it becomes ingrained, then that's less time and effort that has to be devoted to freeing ourselves from that information later. And even when something slips by, if you're aware of your own biases and limitations, and schooled in the signs of misinformation, then you'll be better equipped to reevaluate it and dismiss it later on.

ANOMALY HUNTING

Truther is the term often given to persons who don't believe that the World Trade Center attacks of 9/11 were an al-Qaeda terrorist attack but rather that they were the result of some grander conspiracy, usually involving the United States government and frequently (but not always) claiming that the true cause of the towers' destruction was explosives planted in the buildings. Over the past ten years, 9/11 Truthers have produced multiple books, papers, and websites promoting their arguments, and they even host conventions to discuss their speculations.

But if you were to peruse some of those Truther papers, you

would begin to notice something they have in common: they don't often point to any significant positive evidence of their claims. By "positive evidence," I mean concrete pieces of evidence that directly support their theories. They don't prove the existence of explosives in the Towers; at best, they might dwell on isolated details that they argue may be consistent with explosives. They don't demonstrate any conclusive proof of government complicity; again, at best they might mention quotations or actions that they deem to be suspicious.

What Truthers do instead, and what they do a *lot*, is try to "poke holes" in the accepted version of the events of 9/11. This often involves asking a lot of open-ended questions with sinister implications or simply speculating on matters with insufficient information. Why were the planes not shot down? Why did the buildings collapse so quickly? They can't produce any proof of the tons of explosives they claim existed, so instead they'll try to build an argument around microscopic dust at the scene that they pretend is indirect proof of explosives.

This tendency is in no way unique to Truthers. A primary feature of virtually every form of creative misinformation, from denialism to conspiracism to pseudo-scholarship, is anomaly hunting.

Science likes positive evidence. So do historians and researchers of all types. In the evaluation of evidence, anomalies are like pictures of UFOs. They're called "unidentified flying objects" because they're unidentified. The blurry photo doesn't provide enough information to make a clear determination of *what* it is. But just because it can't be conclusively identified as a weather balloon or a military aircraft doesn't mean that it should instead be assumed to be an alien spacecraft.

Anomalies can be useful in science and research as a means of directing investigation. When one researcher finds an anomaly he can't explain, and which is inconsistent with other evidence, further research may be done to see if that anomaly signals some larger truth. In 2011, scientists at the CERN (European Organization for Nuclear Research) research facility in Europe clocked neutrinos at a speed that appeared to be faster than the speed of light. Meanwhile, Einstein's theory of special relativity says that nothing can move faster than the speed of light, and it is one of the most well-proven aspects of physics. For months, the CERN neutrino findings were anomalous, with speculation that confirmation of the results could require special relativity to be modified. Others suspected that something might have simply been overlooked in the experiment, and that the neutrinos didn't actually exceed the speed of light at all. The latter, more cautious interpretation proved to be correct: subsequent tests showed neutrinos traveling at acceptable speeds, and the anomalous results were eventually attributed to a faulty connection in the equipment's wiring.

Misinformation agents use anomalies in a different way. Instead of stumbling across anomalies in the pursuit of positive evidence and then attempting to explain them, denialists, conspiracists, and pseudo-scholars seek out anomalies directly. Having been confronted with a consensus view that they wish to undermine, they gather up anomalies and then attempt to use the collective weight of those individual unanswered questions as part of their argument that the consensus view is wrong.

The problem with this approach is that it doesn't tend to produce a cohesive alternative theory that they can argue explains the facts better. All too often, the anomalies don't add up to a cohesive theory at all. This is why the focus is so often on the individual anomalies themselves; to pull back and look at this "evidence" as a whole, it's all too easy to realize that they may not even be internally consistent. JFK-assassination-conspiracy theorists have done this for decades, dwelling on every supposedly "suspicious" thing about the events of November 22, 1963, in Dallas. They have found multiple little anomalies, some more interesting than others, which they argue prove that Lee Harvey Oswald was not a lone gunman or that a larger conspiracy was behind him. But apart from dismissing Oswald, their evidence splinters from there, and they'll gladly argue that anyone from the Soviet KGB to Vice President Lyndon Johnson was behind

Kennedy's murder. Evidence that points in all directions does not make a compelling case that any one of those alternate theories is true. To the contrary: the fact that their evidence points in so many different directions undermines that their anomalies mean anything significant at all.

Creationists play a similar game with the sciences. They don't conduct research and experiments whose results point to the earth being six thousand years old; for the most part, they just single out anomalies that they say science hasn't explained yet. They point to rocks from volcanoes that test as older than they really are. Or the erosion caused by Niagara Falls. Often, these "anomalies" actually *do* have scientific explanations, but they're ignored. Moreover, creationists' interest in anomalies is sufficiently strong that they are overly susceptible to hoaxes. The Calaveras Skull, a supposedly prehistoric human skull found in California in 1866, was long ago proven to be a hoax.[8] And yet some creationists, such as members of the Center for Scientific Creation, continue to cite it as an anomaly that they say undermines evolutionary theory.[9]

Not all evidence underlying every misinformation campaign is made up of anomalies, but anomalies are a common feature among many of them. Conversely, compelling arguments in science or history are not built on a foundation of anomalies. If they have achieved a consensus opinion, then they have something more to offer. Recognizing that a specious argument is heavily reliant on small and unrelated anomalies—and if the arguer doesn't attempt to tie them together in a strong cohesive whole—can be incredibly useful in spotting a misinformation campaign.

Another common feature that is related to anomaly hunting is the logical fallacy of proof by verbosity. Denialist and conspiracist arguments are often just aggregations of anomalies and can thus grow to surprising lengths. Strong evidence may be able to be summarized and condensed, but promoters of weak evidence frequently use quantity as a substitute for quality.

One of my earliest confrontations with Birthers, conspiracy theorists who deny that President Obama was born in Hawaii, involved a pseudonymous self-proclaimed "expert" named Ron Polarik who claimed to have proven Obama's birth certificate was a forgery. He once said, "Frauds do not produce 160-page reports with 140 images," because he had produced such a 160-page "report."[10]

Except he's wrong. Frauds regularly produce tremendous volumes of material. Another Birther wrote a rambling thirty-one-thousand-word blog post.[11] James von Brunn, the Holocaust museum shooter (and part-time Birther) wrote an entire *book* that was supposed to document the Jewish conspiracy.[12] Denialists and conspiracy theorists produce far more content than one could ever want to read, much less respond to.

And that becomes their argument: failure to address each and every one of their claims and anomalies is a concession that they're right. Polarik used this argument regularly, confident that no one would ever waste the time necessary to rebut, point by point, a 160-page screed by an anonymous online conspiracy theorist. Meanwhile, the opposite argument is used when promoting anomalies as proof: only one detail of the consensus view need be undermined to render the entire consensus unreliable.

Seeing either of these arguments advanced provides, again, a good means of spotting misinformation. Researchers and scientists deal with bodies of evidence, not discrete pieces. An outlying data point or curious fact does not, alone, bring down a supported body of work. If it's truly inconsistent, it must be confirmed as accurate and validated by other research. It's possible that the CERN neutrino experiment might lead to a change to special relativity one day, but it hasn't yet. Or it could be an error. Few subjects, however, have rules as firm as relativistic physics, and thus anomalies or oddities in the evidence in other fields may be nothing more than irrelevant curiosities.

When faced with such questions of anomalous evidence, Occam's razor is a classic tool for evaluating hypotheses. It is a guiding principle that says if you're presented with two or more competing hypotheses, the best and most plausible hypothesis is the one that makes the fewest new assumptions. Denialists and conspiracists typically rely on mountains of assumptions. Assumptions of covered-up or hidden evidence. Assumptions of false experimental results. Assumptions of secret agreements and conspiracies. Assumptions of inexplicable behavior on the part of the actors involved.

No one predicted that Birthers would still be active in 2012, probably because their hypothesis fails at Occam's razor so badly. Birthers propose that the president's nineteen-year-old mother left Hawaii to travel ten thousand miles to Kenya to give birth in a country she'd never visited while surrounded by people she'd never met, for reasons that even the Birthers themselves can't agree on. She then snuck her newborn baby back into Hawaii soon thereafter, procured a birth certificate from the state, and managed to get birth notices published in the Honolulu paper a week later. Then they say that Obama spent decades claiming to be foreign-born, until he changed his biography to say he was born in Honolulu. They insist that all the birth certificates and 1960s-era documents testifying to Obama's Hawaiian birth are forged or the result of fraud and that all the evidence of his foreign birth (such as supposed instances of him claiming to be born overseas) have been miraculously scrubbed from existence. They find this muddled mess of motivations to be a superior hypothesis to the consensus view: that Barack Obama was born in a Honolulu hospital eight miles down the street from his mother's home.

Not all competing hypotheses are as dramatic as this one, but employing the razor is helpful in laying out those claims for consideration, particularly because denialists and conspiracists are unusually reticent about actually laying out their preferred hypothesis. To commit to a single view of "this is what I believe" is to open themselves up to a concise refutation. By listing anomalies, by "just asking questions" instead of proposing answers, by expressing more interest in tearing down a well-established theory than constructing a cohesive and superior alternative, they avoid having to admit just how sparse or silly their underlying hypothesis may be. Or they may have to admit that they have no hypothesis at all, apart from "I think the experts are wrong."

Such a pronouncement may seem presumptuous, that one's homegrown Internet research is more credible than the shared view of the world's educated professionals in a given field of expertise. But again, the human mind is prone to various shortcuts and fallacies that allow us to make these otherwise irrational assertions. An insightful one here is the Dunning–Kruger effect, which was proposed as recently as 1999. This cognitive bias causes unskilled individuals to fail to recognize their own skill level and instead to overestimate their personal competence and to underestimate the legitimate competence of others. In other words, we're incompetent at recognizing our own incompetence. This phenomenon allows the crank in his basement to think that he has overturned Einsteinian physics or the Internet commenter with a high school diploma to insist that he understands American jurisprudence better than the Supreme Court.

The fight against misinformation is a continual battle against all these sorts of mental biases and fallacies. In day-to-day living, such shortcuts are essential, allowing us to draw conclusions without questioning and investigating every action we take. But in a world where we are going to be bombarded with more information than ever, it's crucial to hone our skills at spotting misinformation and not letting those cognitive biases lead us down the path of believing comfortable but false things.

That's where we need the tools of critical thinking. That's where we need the scientific method. How can we best skeptically approach the claims we're confronted with and spot the spurious ones?

CHAPTER 2
DENIALISM

Modern science was born over many years, but the first half of the seventeenth century might well be considered the turning point in our scientific understanding of the universe. Galileo defended the heliocentric model of the solar system in a 1632 best-seller, René Descartes was largely responsible for coining the scientific method in 1637, and Isaac Newton was born in 1643. Some point to Descartes' book *Discourse on the Method* as the starting point for the Age of Enlightenment.

Concurrent with these birth pangs of modern science, Ireland's archbishop James Ussher produced one of the most significant works of research of the pre-Enlightenment era. Ussher's *Annals of the World*, published in 1650, chronicles the history of the world from the destruction of the Jewish Temple in CE 70 all the way back to man's creation in Genesis. It was Ussher's calculation of this latter date that has given him lasting fame and notoriety, as he pronounced the precise date of the biblical Creation to be October 23, 4004 BCE.

This conclusion, setting the earth's age at just over six thousand years at present, has long been respected by young-earth creationists and ridiculed by scientists and skeptics. Noted paleontologist and evolutionary biologist Stephen Jay Gould, however, actually defended Ussher's work as "both honorable and interesting," noting that Ussher was in fact one of the best scholars of his time and that his efforts should be viewed through the context of the prescientific era in which he lived. Ussher's scholarship was premised on the accepted notions of his day, and Gould argues that he can hardly be blamed for failing to anticipate the discoveries of future generations.[1]

But as respectable as Ussher's efforts may have been, that doesn't change the fact that his conclusion was wrong. Just as modern science has debunked such long-held prescientific notions as alchemy, geocentricism, and spontaneous generation, so, too, has science consistently and repeatedly disproven the young-earth hypothesis. Rather than six thousand years old, our best estimate of the age of the earth now stands at 4.54 billion years old. Yet there are those who stand by the belief that our planet is less than ten thousand years old. Joseph Farah, creator of the conservative website WorldNetDaily, has repeatedly proclaimed his belief in a six-thousand-year-old earth, consequently implying that he himself has lived through a full 1 percent of the planet's existence. Farah also believes that humans and dinosaurs lived side by side, having apparently taken *The Flintstones* to be historical fiction.[2] The WorldNetDaily site proudly sells Ussher's *Annals of the World*, as well as a variety of other young-earth literature.

Farah and company's continued belief in the young-earth movement is deeply rooted in a tradition of biblical literalism and the Creation account from the book of Genesis, and their strident opposition to contrary evidence is most directly tied to their opposition to the theory of evolution. But their denial of the science on the earth's age goes much further than merely evolutionary biology.

Many, many fields of science touch on the subject of the age of the earth or of the universe at large. Chemistry provides the estimate of 4.54 billion years, a figure derived from analysis of the half-life of uranium isotopes. Physics tells us that the light from the stars in the sky has been traveling for far longer than ten thousand years. Astronomy and astrophysics point to a universe that began approximately 13.7 billion years ago. Geology demonstrates how the continents have moved over the millennia, and mineralogy and petrology explain how minerals and rocks formed over time. Genetics and biology find links in the building blocks of life that extend back more than millions of years. Paleontology, the favorite science of every third grader, puts the extinction of the dinosaurs at sixty-five million years ago. Even social sciences, like anthropology, chronicle human history as being older than ten thousand years. The famous Chauvet Cave paintings in France are estimated to have been created by ancient humans between 23,000 BCE and 32,000 BCE.

In other words, the belief in a young earth and the denial of an ancient earth is not merely a denial of evolutionary science. It is the denial of virtually *all* science—science that has, for the last four hundred years, proven itself to be increasingly predictive and credible. And, as evidenced by everything from medicine to microchips, science works. Young-earth believers inevitably find themselves forced to invent their own brands of pseudoscience, such as flood geology and Creation geophysics.

Denialism blinds those who fall into it. Denialism takes a person whose quality of life is exponentially better than Ussher's due to scientific advances and makes that person simultaneously believe that all that science is nonetheless wrong and adopt the outdated beliefs of centuries past—to ignore reams of evidence, even whole fields of study, in favor of debunked and disproven notions that they simply find more comforting.

The denialists' approach to contrary and contradictory evidence is straightforwardly simple: they deny it. They deny its efficacy, its authenticity, or even its reality. They may put any number of rationales on their denials, but their rejection is ultimately rooted in their absolute commitment to their a priori beliefs. If some piece of evidence conflicts with their belief, that is not an indication that the belief is flawed. Rather, it means that the evidence is.

The world is filled with untrustworthy information; this is especially true of the Internet. But how can you tell when it is good information that is being rejected? It helps considerably that denialism, by and large, is not a very creative endeavor. Conspiracism is intensely creative, and that often plays a role in rationalizing the consequences of denialism. The rhetorical use of logical fallacies usually carries at least some choice of strategy; should you respond with an ad hominem or a changing of the subject or a moving of the goalposts? But denialism is simple and, often, predictable.

Denialism may seem like a strange place to begin a treatment of misinformation. As a field, it's relatively young, its use as a label can often be controversial, and it's a term that's far less well-known than pseudoscience or conspiracy theories. But denialism is a more basic form of misinformation that often serves as the foundation for other, more conspicuous errors in judgment. Most popular conspiracy theories require the believer to first reject the accepted, or "official," explanation for an event. Thus, JFK-assassination-conspiracy theorists deny the evidence that Lee Harvey Oswald acted alone. 9/11-conspiracy theorists deny that al-Qaeda agents brought down the World Trade Center with hijacked planes. Moon hoaxers deny that the Apollo 11 mission took place. Anti-Stratfordians deny that William Shakespeare wrote the plays attributed to him. In all these cases, their alternative explanations for these events are secondary; first, they must be willing to reject and deny what the history books say.

The same pattern holds for pseudoscience. Proponents of perpetual-motion machines must deny the proofs that such machines are impossible according to the laws of physics. Alternative-medicine advocates regularly must deny the myriad of studies that show their treatments are no better than placebos. And the aforementioned creationists must very nearly deny the conclusions of almost all fields of scientific study.

Thus, where denialism is a prerequisite for other wrong ideas, it is useful to be able to recognize the signs of denialist thought before falling further down the rabbit hole. So what are the symptoms of denialism; what are the warning signs?

First and foremost is the belief in a minority view or even in a fringe view. Denialism, by its very nature, concerns the rejection of accepted truth. Whether it's the preference for alternative medicine over science-based medicine or belief in a historical Atlantis over the consensus of serious historians, the denialist favors a view of reality that has been explicitly rejected by experts in the relevant field.

It's important to recognize what actually constitutes a consensus by relevant experts. According to a 2010 Gallup poll, some 40 percent of Americans believe humankind was created in our present form less than ten thousand years ago.[3] There is surely no *popular* consensus on the reality of evolution versus supernatural creationism, but popular opinion is not the arbiter of scientific truth. Scientific fact is not determined by majority vote. Scientists in biology, in anthropology, in paleontology, and so on all universally concur, based on myriad lines of credible evidence, that humans are much older than ten thousand years and that the earth is far older than that. The question is a scientific question, and thus the rejection of the consensus of scientific experts constitutes denialism.

At the same time, it is also critical to remember that, while a denialist view is necessarily a minority view, that does not mean that any minority view is automatically denialist. Many areas of history are matters of legitimate scholarly debate, and science is premised on the testing of new hypotheses and the challenging of unproven beliefs. The practice of law necessarily involves competing interpretations of cases and statutes. It is only when the facts weigh so heavily on one side of a "debate," when experts themselves stop disagreeing and all share the same conclusion, that the continued belief in a minority opinion becomes denialist.

The denialist justifies his rejection of a consensus opinion by concocting reasons to reject the underlying facts that others accept as true and decisive. One of the primary tactics of denialism in this exercise is anomaly hunting. Evidence is scrutinized for any feature the denialist perceives as odd. Once an anomaly is identified, it is used to spin an argument as to why that particular isolated piece of evidence should be doubted, and even why the whole of the evidence should be viewed with suspicion.

A notorious example of this approach is how moon hoaxers deal with photographs of the Apollo moon missions. They look at pictures of astronauts standing on the moon and focus on the length and direction of shadows cast by the rocks on the moon's surface or on the visibility of stars in the moon's sky. They argue that these details are inconsistent with what real moon photos "should" look like and conclude that NASA's photos must therefore be fake.

Anti-Stratfordians apply a similar analysis to the works of William Shakespeare. Small details about Shakespeare's life and his writings are singled out and speculated about. Shakespeare occasionally spelled his last name differently. There seems to have been little popular interest in his death. He wasn't high-class or widely traveled, but his plays dealt extensively with cultured society and foreign locales. These curiosities are treated as reason to doubt Shakespeare's authorship, in contrast to the rather well-documented history of attribution to him.

The reliance on anomalies as evidence in turn explains another tendency among denialists, and that is the inability to advance a cohesive alternative theory. Legitimate science and legitimate history work by assembling data and building a conclusion based on that data. Hypotheses are what are initially advanced, but they are scrutinized through testing and further research, and they may be rejected if the evidence fails to support them. Over time, this process is what creates consensus.

Denialism doesn't operate the same way. It is not primarily interested in determining a truth; it is concerned with rejecting one. The focus on anomalies rather than on positive evidence leads to the creation of multiple competing theories, and denialists don't tend to prioritize reaching any sort of consensus among themselves as to which of those theories might be true.

For nearly fifty years, JFK-assassination-conspiracy theorists have rejected the Warren Commission's conclusion that Lee Harvey Oswald was the lone gunman responsible for the president's death. They've written volumes, libraries even, on the anomalies they see in the Oswald explanation. And so, who do they say the evidence points to as the responsible party? The Soviets. The Cubans. The Israelis. The Mafia. The CIA. The Federal Reserve. The vice president. The father of *Cheers* actor Woody Harrelson. And many more. The Warren Commission found that the evidence, taken together, pointed decisively to Oswald acting alone. The conspiracy theorists find "evidence" pointing in a thousand different directions and not toward a single, compelling alternative. Vincent Bugliosi's book debunking JFK-conspiracy theories, *Reclaiming History*, was over sixteen hundred pages long precisely because there were so many competing theories to address.

Those who doubt Shakespeare's authorship of the plays bearing his name have advanced over seventy different alternative candidates, including Francis Bacon, Edward de Vere, Christopher Marlowe, and even Sir Francis Drake—all of whom are premised on a sampling of anomalies and details, and none of whom are supported by a clear and determinative body of evidence. Much of the evidence for any one alternative author is shared by other alternatives as well, because the supposed evidence doesn't point at a particular individual so much as it is simply "consistent" with the preferred author. (Consistency is a weak form of proof. If I were to describe a particular person as being a wealthy but eccentric bachelor and millionaire playboy who lives in a mansion, is associated with nightlife, and who uses an animal logo for himself, I could be talking about either Hugh Hefner or Batman.)

Proposed sites for a historical Atlantis have been placed all over the world. Creationism doesn't provide a testable alternative to evolution so much as it focuses on poking holes in evolutionary theory. Conspiracy theorists who question the Apollo 11 moon landing are capable of agreeing on little more than a generic reaction of "NASA faked it."

This splintering of opinions was standard in the pre-Internet age, but with the development of the World Wide Web, denialists have demonstrated an increased ability to reach some form of consensus on some issues.

This is also not a matter of there simply being different factions of JFK-conspiracy theorists who advocate for different theories. Many may have a preferred conspiracy, but rare is the conspiracy nut who is committed to just a single theory to the exclusion of all others. A discussion might begin with a focus on one particular alleged culprit, but if the arguments for that theory start getting shot down as inaccurate, then the conspiracy nut often won't hesitate in retreating to blaming some other culprit.

Whereas the JFK assassination has become the poster child for conspiracy theories, and whereas David Icke and his "reptoids" have become the poster child for the fringiest of fringe thought, the defining illustration of denialism is the same one that practically coined the term: Holocaust denial. Between 1933 and 1945, some six million European Jews were murdered by the German Nazi Party under the leadership of Adolf Hitler. It was genocide of a magnitude and calculated depravity that history has rarely witnessed, and its effects continue to shape international relations to this date. Yet there is a movement of persons who deny that the Holocaust ever happened, at least not the way it is told by historians. According to them, the Holocaust killed merely thousands, not millions. There were no gas chambers used for mass murder. And Hitler never ordered the deaths of the Jews; the blame should instead be placed on the overzealous Nazi middle management.

Naturally, to make these sorts of denials requires that one reject reams of historical evidence that supports historical reality of the Holocaust. The physical evidence from the camps. The documentary evidence from the Nazi regime. The testimonial evidence from the Nuremberg Trials. And, of course, the thousands of firsthand witness accounts from those who lived through the camps while seeing their friends and family murdered.

The Nazis themselves laid the foundation for subsequent deniers, couching the orders and objectives of the "Final Solution" in bureaucratic terms that avoided the blunt language of murder and genocide. A common argument from deniers is that there is no memorandum from Hitler flatly saying "Let's kill all the Jews." When the German government did not wish to acknowledge the true nature of its operation, it is perhaps only natural that others would try to do the same in later years.

The first notable denier, at least in America, was Harry Elmer Barnes, a Columbia University historian who had already demonstrated

German sympathies following World War I. After World War II, Barnes continued to defend Germany and began to argue that the Holocaust was little more than Allied propaganda, created to justify the war against Hitler's Germany. By the 1960s, Barnes had intellectual company. He helped arrange for the works of French author and Holocaust denier Paul Rassinier to be translated into English and published in America. Another follower of Barnes, the historian David Hoggan, would write a book of his own in 1969, *The Myth of the Six Million*. Both Rassinier's and Hoggan's books were published by Noontide Press (Hoggan's book was published without his consent), a company founded by anti-Semite Willis Carto that specialized in the publication of anti-Semitic literature. Today, Noontide continues to publish such books as *Mein Kampf* and *The Protocols of the Learned Elders of Zion*.

In 1978, these individual efforts at Holocaust denial finally gave way to an organized campaign with the creation of the Institute for Historical Review. Founded by David McCalden and Willis Carto, the IHR attempted to make Holocaust denial into a "respectable" view through the utilization of pseudo-academic "experts" and the publication of its own non-peer-reviewed *Journal of Historical Review*. With the IHR's resources, Holocaust deniers have been able to publish a considerable amount of propaganda over the past three decades. Thankfully, their efforts have mostly been for naught, as they continue to be identified with anti-Semitism and as Holocaust denialism continues to be the gold standard for the inexcusable rewriting of history.

Of course, Holocaust deniers don't particularly care for the label *denier*. Instead, the IHR and others of its ilk prefer the term *historical revisionism*, but this self-initiated attempt at rebranding is roundly rejected by historical scholars. As will be discussed in more detail in a later chapter, historical revisionism is a real and legitimate area of historical study, but Holocaust deniers are attempting to appropriate a term that doesn't apply to their work.

Holocaust deniers are not alone in their disdain for the *denialist* label. Most denialists of any stripe make the same objection. They argue that their data is factual, that their conclusions are justified, and that their concerns are real. A favorite trope to this end is the "Galileo Gambit." The seventeenth-century Italian astronomer Galileo Galilei concluded, based on his observations of the bodies of the solar system, that the earth revolved around the sun. This was contrary to the teachings of the Roman Catholic Church at the time, and in 1633, the Inquisition put Galileo on trial, where he was found guilty of heresy, and his book *Dialogue Concerning the Two Chief World Systems* was banned. The book remained banned for over a century, and it was not until 2000 that Pope John Paul II apologized for the church's error in trying Galileo and rejecting the heliocentric view of the heavens.

Denialists love Galileo, and they love analogizing themselves to him, because he was rejected by the authorities of his day but was ultimately recognized as being correct all along. A similar sentiment is expressed in a popular quote among denialists: "First they ignore you; then they laugh at you; then they fight you; then you win." This fallacy is dubbed the Galileo Gambit, with the fallacious underlying notion being that if one is vilified or ridiculed or attacked for holding a given belief, then it follows that that belief must be correct! The fallacy here, which is obvious the moment you step back to take a wider look, is that there is no positive correlation between being rejected and being right. People are regularly vilified and ridiculed and attacked for believing things that are, in fact, wrong. Wrong ideas may often merit ridicule, and the presence of such ridicule does not miraculously increase the likelihood that the idea is correct.

The ignore/laugh/fight trifecta is particularly shrewd in its own way, as it succinctly covers virtually every response one can have to a wrong idea. Thus the quote can be trotted out in any circumstance, whether the response is to take the idea seriously, to not take it seriously, or to ignore it entirely. For instance, Obama eligibility Birthers vacillate through these stages depending on the news cycle. If the media isn't reporting on Birthers, then they're being ignored. If the media is making fun of Birthers, then they're being ridiculed. If the media is explaining why Birthers are wrong, then they're being attacked. From the denialist point of view, it's a win-win-win scenario. Or, as Carl Sagan said of the Galileo Gambit: "The fact that some geniuses were laughed at does not imply that all who are laughed at are geniuses. They laughed at Columbus, they laughed at Fulton, they laughed at the Wright brothers. But they also laughed at Bozo the Clown."[4]

Denialists wish to identify themselves with Galileo, but they miss the mark on what made him right. It was not the fact that he was rejected by the authorities of his day and recognized as correct only by later generations; it was that his theories, as revolutionary as they were in the day, were borne out by facts.

Still, the most committed conspiracy theorists or the most diehard denialists will insist that they do have facts on their side. Even the followers of David Icke, who believe that world leaders are secretly shape-shifting reptilians, claim to have proof of their beliefs; a search of YouTube® produces dozens of videos claiming to show the color-changing eyes of presidents and prime ministers. Denialists are so confident in their "facts" that they aren't afraid to issue public challenges for debates and promises of rewards for being proven wrong.

SPOTTING DENIALISM

Mark and Chris Hoofnagle, who run the *Denialism* blog, define denialism this way: "Denialism is the employment of rhetorical tactics to give the appearance of argument or legitimate debate, when in actuality there is none. These false arguments are used when one has few or no facts to support one's viewpoint against a scientific consensus or against overwhelming evidence to the contrary. They are effective in distracting from actual useful debate using emotionally appealing, but ultimately empty and illogical assertions."[5]

Distinguishing denialism from legitimate debate is not necessarily easy at first glance. It requires the ability to tell good information from bad information and to recognize whether a dissenting opinion is making a potentially valid argument worth considering, or whether it is relying on fallacious logic and poor reasoning. Indeed, it requires knowing what the scientific consensus actually is, and it helps immensely to know what facts and findings underlie that consensus. The Hoofnagles suggest five tactics that denialists regularly employ, which distinguish them from legitimate controversies: "selectivity (cherry picking), fake experts, conspiracy, impossible expectations (also known as moving goalposts), and general fallacies of logic."[6] To that list I would separate out a sixth feature, which they seem to group under selectivity: unscientific evidence (including anecdotes and anomaly hunting).

Selectivity/Cherry Picking

Denialists are defined, first and foremost, by their willingness to deny evidence that the rest of the world finds compelling and conclusive. How they go about rejecting or dismissing the conclusive value of the evidence is both predictable and representative of how denialists in general approach matters of evidence. These approaches can be broadly grouped into three categories.

Denialist Response 1:
Deny the Veracity of the Evidence

After Obama's certification of live birth was first posted online on June 12, 2008, the news spread quickly around the web. FreeRepublic posters started two different threads about the newly released certificate that day. It took less than twelve minutes in the first thread for a poster to explicitly allege fraud: "I'd bet $100 that this one is a blank that some OBAMA RAT who works in HI took and forged!"[7] In the second thread, it took less than ten minutes, courtesy of poster "RaceBannon," whose immediate reaction was "There is NO WAY this is real!"[8]

People put their trust in paper all the time. Contracts, checks, receipts, and records. The modern world has also provided us with an array of recorded and digital documentation, including e-mail, audio, and video. When someone asks for proof of a claim, it's practically a given that documentary proof is what's desired. Thus whenever Obama's birth is discussed on a television news program, it should come as no surprise that the first two pieces of evidence always cited are the birth certificate and the newspaper birth announcements. Such documentary evidence is powerful, both visually and rhetorically, and most people are willing to accept such evidence as authentic. They don't tend to question whether the documents might have been the product of elaborate forgery schemes.

Denialists approach documents differently. Their reaction to documentary evidence isn't just filtered through their own biases and beliefs; it's governed by them. If a document supports the Birthers' worldview, they will extend it every benefit of the doubt. If it contradicts their worldview, then they will readily deem it a forgery.

The Birther does not want to believe that Obama was born in Hawaii. But Obama's certification of live birth plainly states that he was born in Hawaii. Therefore, either the document or the belief must be faulty. So, as RaceBannon demonstrates, the denialist concludes that the document must not be authentic, and thus the belief survives unscathed.

Moon-landing denialists are infamous for this sort of rationalization. There is, after all, a famous piece of footage of Neil Armstrong stepping onto the surface of the moon. In fact, there's quite a bit of film footage of Armstrong and other astronauts on the moon, taken from six different missions. How does the moon hoaxer respond to this evidence? By claiming it's faked. This would necessitate faking a moon landing six times, involving dozens if not hundreds of people, and producing a finished product that managed to fool not only scientists but also our national rivals. If the United States faked a moon landing at the height of the space race, it's surprising the USSR didn't make an issue out of it. The Soviets even had their own spacecraft, Luna 15, which arrived at the moon at the same time the Apollo 11 astronauts lifted off.

So when there are documents, the denialist is prepared to declare them to be forged. When there's video or audio or photographs, they're deemed fake. Even when there's physical evidence, such as the moon rocks that were brought back by astronauts, that, too, is considered suspect. Easier than any of that is the denialist response to testimonial evidence: the person is lying. Neil Armstrong lied about walking on the moon. President Obama is lying about being born in Hawaii. Scientists are lying when they say that vaccines don't cause autism.

There's also a common exercise in circular reasoning when a denialist attacks the veracity of the evidence he opposes. Once he's concluded that the evidence has been faked or forged, he then uses that conclusion to bolster his own doubts. According to the denialist, if someone has been actively manufacturing evidence, he then has something he's trying to hide. Denialism becomes a self-justifying belief system.

Denialist Response 2:
Deny the Conclusiveness of the Evidence

If you can get past the hurdle of getting a denialist to concede that a piece of testimonial evidence is credible and trustworthy, you can expect that the very next response will be that it's still not dispositive.

Holocaust deniers can't get around the fact that concentration camps existed, that many people were sent to them, and that fewer people left them. The physical buildings are there for inspection, and many people lived through being relocated to the camps. Arguing that concentration camps aren't real is a complete nonstarter. So instead, Holocaust deniers claim that the camps and the firsthand experiences of Holocaust survivors aren't actually proof that genocide took place there. The survivors, naturally, never witnessed the gassing firsthand, so their testimony is deemed insufficient. Deniers argue that the gas chambers were used for purposes other than mass-killing humans, even as they admit that the furnaces were used to dispose of bodies. And while they can't deny that people died in the camps, they instead claim that they died from mistreatment, not from calculated mass murder.

Moon hoaxers typically don't claim that moon rocks are normal earth samples. They will often admit that the rocks originated from the moon, but they'll claim that they were collected on the earth, having fallen in Antarctica as meteors millennia ago. That phenomenon is real enough (even though it produces meteorites that don't look the same as natural moon rocks, and it doesn't explain the number of moon rocks), and so it becomes moon hoaxers' preferred alternate explanation for how NASA procured rocks from the moon.

Pseudoscientists and alternative-medicine advocates regularly use this response to deal with the umpteenth scientific study that establishes that a given treatment doesn't work as promised. The standard reply is that "there needs to be more testing done." They'll never concede to being wrong, but they can perpetually insist that the existing research is insufficient in their eyes.

Denialism Response 3: Ignore the Evidence

When evidence can't be called fake and can't be labeled inconclusive, the denialist falls back on his last resort: pretending that the evidence isn't there. This can be harder to do when debating someone outside the denier camp, but when interacting with each other, it can become a comfortable fallback position. If some discovery or study is detrimental to their belief, and if it can be ignored, then they'll gladly ignore it.

The two towers weren't the only buildings to fall on 9/11. Another building that fell was 7 World Trade Center, a forty-seven-story red building that sat adjacent to the taller towers. 9/11 Truthers who deny that the buildings were brought down simply by the plane impacts like to point to this third building as proof of their speculation that the towers were felled by controlled explosives. They highlight photos of WTC7, which appear to show it to be relatively undamaged. And an undamaged building, they say, wouldn't fall on its own.

What they don't show in their arguments is that photos and video from other angles plainly show the building to be quite damaged. When confronted with such evidence, the Truther may try to downplay it as insignificant, resorting back to attack its conclusiveness. It's not the conclusiveness of the evidence that defines him as a denialist, though; it's his willingness to cherry-pick the photos that support his theory that WTC7 was not damaged, and to just ignore the photos that contradict that theory.

JFK-assassination-conspiracy theorists play a similar game. One infamous picture shows the dead president lying on his back, undressed for an autopsy. Because of the lighting in the room and from the camera, the head is dark. The lone-gunman denialist will point to this photo as proof that Kennedy wasn't really shot in the head, because no head wound can be seen in this particular photo. What he will ignore is that other photos from the same autopsy, photos taken directly of the head, show the wound plain as day. Those photos, however, don't help his denialist arguments, and so he singles out the one photo that suits his arguments the best and pretends that the others don't exist.

Pseudoscientists rely heavily on cherry picking evidence, bypassing all the studies and research that disagree with their beliefs and instead heaping attention on the isolated study that seems to help them, even if that outlier study is inferior work, having been poorly controlled or subject to researcher bias, or if the study hasn't been replicated by further research. But pseudoscientists can be far more subtle by cherry picking data that is then used to manipulate studies to produce the results they prefer. They'll keep the "hits" and ignore the "misses," and the result is that a study may reach a completely novel conclusion because half the data has been thrown out. Investigators of the paranormal are notoriously bad about doing this, documenting all the times they think they found a paranormal event and then glossing over all the times they didn't for one reason or another.

Fake Experts

In spite of their common rhetoric of questioning and rejecting the opinions of experts and authorities, denialists still love to trot out their own experts in an attempt to make the same appeal to authority that they claim to be reacting against. The difference is that denialist experts generally lack one thing that sets them apart from recognized experts: actual expertise in the relevant fields.

The creationist Discovery Institute rejects the consensus view of the evolution of species, including humans, and instead promotes intelligent design as an alternative to evolution. The institute was cofounded by Bruce Chapman and George Gilder, neither of whom are scientists. Chapman has worked in journalism and politics, and Gilder was a speechwriter and Republican activist. As of 2012, the Discovery Institute website listed eleven senior fellows as part of its organization; only one of the eleven (Stephen Meyer) is indicated as having a science degree of any kind, and it was an undergraduate degree in physics and geology, two fields that are completely unrelated to the study of the biological origins of humans. The other ten primarily have degrees in politics, law, and theology.

The credentials of intelligent-design proponents outside the Discovery Institute are not much better. William Dembski is one of the more prolific proponents of intelligent design, but his degrees are in psychology, mathematics, and philosophy. Michael Behe may be the movement's best-known name, and his degree in biochemistry does sound authoritative at first blush, but biochemistry has relatively little to do with the study of evolution.

The men responsible for the Holocaust-denying Institute for Historical Review were, despite their organization's name, not actually historians. They included a classics teacher, an engineer, a graphic artist, a political activist, and a professor of French literature. David Irving, perhaps the most widely known Holocaust denier, is a writer with no scholarly credentials to speak of at all. The one exception is Mark Weber, who earned a master's degree in European history the year before the IHR was founded, and who is currently the director of the IHR. But whereas Weber may have a degree, his other credentials discredit him as an authority even more. The year after finishing his master's, Weber became the news editor for the neo-Nazi magazine *National Vanguard*. His postcollegiate career has been almost exclusively devoted to anti-Semitic causes, including sending graduating high school seniors copies of an anti-Semitic and racist book.

As befits their low status even among denialists, Obama Birthers have struggled to find even fake experts. For years following the initial release of Obama's certification of live birth, Birthers' claims that the document was forged rested largely on the shoulders of supposed experts who were simply anonymous Internet commenters claiming to possess credentials. One, "Ron Polarik" (mentioned in chapter 1) was ultimately revealed to have a doctorate in instructional systems but no expertise whatsoever in computer forensics or document examination. The other, "TechDude," simply vanished from the web after it was discovered that he had been borrowing the credentials of another man.

When Obama released his long-form birth certificate in 2011, the Birthers produced a longer list of supposed experts, this time with real identities, who claimed the new document was forged as well. Several of these individuals at least had computer-related jobs, but they, too, turned out to be printer salesmen, or typographers, or writers of Photoshop® handbooks—again, no experts in any sort of forensics. And it wasn't for a lack of trying; a handful of legitimate forensics experts were consulted for their opinions as to whether the document was forged. They consistently found no distinguishing evidence of forgery, but per the denialist practice of selectivity, these experts were promptly ignored.[9]

In support of their constitutional theory, by which they deny that the native-born children of noncitizens can grow up to be president, Birthers have managed to be even less successful in locating experts. The closest to a legal scholar they've managed is Herb Titus, a Christian fundamentalist and former law professor, who was terminated from his last law school position in 1993. By and large, Birthers rely simply on their own amateur reading of the law, gleaned from cases and books they can read online, after which they write their own legal treatises that they hold up as superseding the consensus view of the law.

Income-tax deniers regularly tout the same sort of pseudo-legal scholars, citing not to the research of law professors or legal historians but to non-attorneys who have done their own amateur investigations. William J. Benson is one of the most well-known tax protesters, having popularized the argument that the Sixteenth Amendment was not ratified and that income taxes are thus illegal. Benson's background was not as a constitutional scholar; he was a disabled former employee of a steel company, and his closest affili-ation to legal history was spending a few years in the 1970s assisting the Illinois Department of Revenue with their investigations. But in releasing his 1985 book *The Law That Never Was*, Benson cemented himself as one of the biggest "experts" in tax denialism.

The legal system long ago grew tired of attorneys trying to inject fake scientific experts into cases for various reasons, and so it created what is called the Daubert standard, named for the case that intro-duced it. The standard was eventually codified in federal law: "If scientific, technical, or other specialized knowledge will assist the trier of fact to understand the evidence or to determine a fact in issue, a witness qualified as an expert by knowledge, skill, experi-ence, training, or education, may testify thereto in the form of an opinion or otherwise, if (1) the testimony is based upon sufficient facts or data, (2) the testimony is the product of reliable principles and methods, and (3) the witness has applied the principles and methods reliably to the facts of the case."[10]

Denialists, needless to say, do not apply this level of scrutiny to the experts they promote.

Conspiracy

Denialists may not have to acknowledge reality, but they do have to confront it. Cherry-picked evidence and fake experts can be used to fabricate the illusion of a legitimate argument, but it's very difficult to make them appear to support a strong argument. Critics will inevitably point out that there is considerable evidence, indeed overwhelming evidence, against them. How does the denialist explain the lack of more compelling evidence and the lack of recognized experts willing to switch sides of the debate? This is when denialists begin to fall back on the crutch of conspiracy theories. The next chapter will deal with conspiracy theories in more detail, but they play an integral role in any denialist's worldview.

Denialism is not fundamentally conspiracist at the start, but it is inevitably conspiracist in the end. As the denialist learns more facts, and is exposed to more and more evidence that contradicts his preferred belief, he appreciates just how fringe his belief is. And if he sincerely considers his cherry-picked evidence to be compelling, then he has to rationalize why others don't find it so compelling. Why won't the world believe what he finds to be so obvious?

That's the function that the conspiracy fills. Because the denialist is confident in his evidence and in his own sincerity, he concludes that everyone else must be rejecting his evidence for insincere reasons. The more universal the rejection, and the more educated the ones doing the rejecting, then the more it becomes obvious to the denialist that such widespread insincerity cannot be accidental but must be the result of some kind of mutual collusion. And so the conspiracy is born.

This justification for the popular rejection of their beliefs can take the form of an active conspiracy, one that has faked and hidden evidence that the denialist claims would otherwise support his theories. Moon-landing deniers necessarily invoke such a conspiracy from the start to explain away the ample physical, documentary, and testimonial evidence that NASA sent six missions to the moon's surface.

There's no way to deny the Apollo 11 landing without simultaneously claiming that many, many people went to a lot of trouble to fake a moon landing.

Or the denialist could theorize a more passive conspiracy, one where the world's elite have simply decided to unilaterally turn a blind eye to the denialist's evidence. Maybe out of self-interest, such as when vaccine denialists and alternative-medicine advocates claim that Big Pharma wants to keep people sick in order to sell them medicine. Maybe out of political pressure, such as accusations that climatologists around the world support the theory of global warming only because they support liberal politics. Maybe out of fear of the consequences, such as when UFO believers say that the government is covering up alien visitations because it would cause global panic if the world were to know the truth.

Whatever the reason, the injection of a conspiracy into the denialist's worldview lets him explain why he finds himself standing alone. It then provides an emotional ballast as well, as he sees himself as the honest man standing up to the conspiracy, the lone voice speaking truth to power. That feeling of self-importance is what then drives denialists and conspiracists to continue their efforts and to resist the pressures to concede that they're simply wrong.

Impossible Expectations

All fields of research confront questions of fact that must be resolved. Questions are posed, evidence is collected, and conclusions are drawn. The scientific method.

Stephen Jay Gould, the renowned evolutionary biologist and paleontologist, once said, "In science, 'fact' can only mean 'confirmed to such a degree that it would be perverse to withhold provisional assent.' I suppose that apples might start to rise tomorrow, but the possibility does not merit equal time in physics classrooms."[11] We reach scientific conclusions not because we are absolutely certain that we have discovered how the universe works, but because the evidence supporting those conclusions is overwhelming enough that any other conclusion can be safely ignored.

A common and seemingly reasonable denialist characteristic is the veil of sincere skepticism. It is the admission that all the evidence currently available is more or less trustworthy, but that the denialist needs just a little more evidence to be convinced. Just produce one more designated piece of evidence, they say, and they will be satisfied and walk away. This seems to carry the air of reasoned analysis at first glance, and there may be the occasional critic who would be satisfied with a single additional piece of evidence. In practice, however, this ostensibly innocent request inevitably reveals itself to be a never-ending cycle of unscientific scrutiny. In skeptical parlance, this is termed Moving the Goalposts. Once a previously established goal is met, the goalposts are simply moved a little further away. The denialist may claim that he needs just one more thing to quell his doubts, but he will forever need just "one more thing."

Moon-landing denialists have made this a tentpole argument for decades. They argue that if NASA would simply point a telescope at the moon and photograph the landing sites, then that would finally prove the reality of the moon missions. In July 2009, NASA's Lunar Reconnaissance Orbiter did exactly that. The LRO sent back photographs of all six lunar landing sites, showing the lunar modules, the astronauts' walking paths, and even the American flags planted on the surface. On the anniversary of the Apollo 11 mission, NASA had given denialists the exact evidence they had demanded for forty years.

What was the response from moon-landing denialists to receiving their ultimate evidence? It wasn't enough. The photos, they said, were too grainy. Too distant. Inconclusive. Or just fake Photoshopped images created by NASA. In short, they applied the same irrational level of skepticism to the new evidence as they had to the old evidence. Despite receiving exactly what they had said for decades would resolve their doubt, they continued to doubt nonetheless.

Evolution deniers have played this game even longer in their demand for a "missing link," the evolutionary intermediary between modern humans and our primate ancestors. Paleontologists have located multiple such transitional fossils, tracing human evolution through history. Before *Homo sapiens* there was *Homo erectus*; and before that, *Homo habilis*; and before that, *Australopithecus*, and so on. But while deniers claim that they just want to fill the "gap" in human evolution, they are never satisfied because each new discovery within a gap merely creates two smaller gaps. The denier doesn't even need to create a new argument; he simply needs to repeat his old one.

In January 2009, I penned a satirical dialogue predicting that Birthers would engage in exactly this practice themselves.[12] And they have. The pinnacle of this process came in April 2011, when after nearly three years of denialist demands to see his long-form birth certificate with the hospital name and doctor's signature, President Obama requested the document from Hawaii and held a press conference to release it to the public. Did that satisfy the denialists who had been specifically asking "Where's the birth certificate?" and saying that the only thing the president needed to do to end the speculation was to release that document? Of course not. They immediately called it a forgery, or they said that it wasn't actually proof Obama had been born in Hawaii, or they shifted their argument to assert that he was ineligible for entirely different reasons.

It was, in many ways, the perfect example of goalpost moving. Birthers had been demanding this exact single document, specifically saying that it alone would end their dissent. And when that exact single document was produced, they just changed their expectations and plugged along.

Some denialists may not be so willing to offer up even a practical possible resolution to their doubts. They may set the burden of proof so high from the start that it can't possibly be reached. The easiest way of doing this is for the denialist to avoid setting any objective, measurable standards for the evidence; he insists that he will concede only when he is "convinced." This is quite common in rewards offered by denialists. They will offer a million dollars for proof that their belief is wrong. But the standard for winning the reward is never a test that can be conclusively satisfied or failed; it is always to convince the denialist based on his vague and unstated evidentiary standards. It's impossible to win such rewards, because the denialist only needs to be stubborn and stingy.

General Fallacies of Logic

General fallacies of logic are the lifeblood of all forms of misinformation, and denialists allow these erroneous ways of thinking to lead them to equally erroneous conclusions. They will also use logical fallacies to defend their beliefs. They will cite a famous name and rely on the argument from authority to suggest that that person should be trusted, whether or not they're informed. They will utilize the argument by verbosity, claiming that an argument should be trusted simply because it's long and wordy. And in debates, there is nothing the denialist loves more than the non sequitur. Having been forced into a position where he might have to admit a mistake, the non sequitur response is to change the subject of discussion and start all over again.

The list of logical fallacies is extensive and could easily command a book of its own. Familiarizing oneself with the common methods of fallacious reasoning is an essential part of a baloney-detection kit, and while this book singles out some of those methods, there are many more worth knowing. Two very good resources for learning about the most common logical fallacies are provided by the Nizkor Project and the Skeptics' Guide to the Universe.[13]

Unscientific Evidence

The practice of selectivity covers the denialist's tendency to pick and choose what facts and findings he will acknowledge, creating the illusion that there is serious evidence to support his beliefs. But denialists aren't always satisfied with limiting themselves to cherry-picked data; they occasionally branch out and try to find supporting evidence on their own. Unfortunately, when a belief is objectively wrong, such evidence has an overwhelming tendency to be flawed and unreliable from the start. Denialists thus trade not only in carefully chosen pieces of serious evidence; they simultaneously rely on other information that more serious minds would barely acknowledge as evidence.

Anecdote, or an account of personal experience, is a particular favorite. There may be controlled studies and professional research consistently reaching one conclusion, but the denialist puts more trust in his own subjective experience and his recollection of that experience. Proponents of alternative medicine and vaccine denialists rely heavily on anecdote: mothers who claim that their children acted differently after being vaccinated; patients who claim that their illnesses improved with acupuncture; people who claim that homeopathic drugs had any biological effect at all.

But, as they say, the plural of "anecdote" is not "evidence." Controlled and blinded studies exist to protect against the kind of first-person accounts that anecdotes are. Anecdotes would suggest that faith healers like Jim Bakker can heal the sick, but no serious researcher would accept that as good evidence.

Denialists may even cite rumors or completely false information as support for their rejection of an accepted belief. 9/11 Truthers still falsely claim that 7 World Trade Center wasn't damaged, when it was. Some denialists even still repeat the rumor that thousands of Jewish people failed to appear for work that day. When the first Birther lawsuit was filed, it actually cited Internet rumors as part of its argument.[14]

As discussed in the last chapter, anomalies are another favorite of denialists. And while anomalies can be useful in guiding research, good research is more than an accumulation of unrelated anomalies. It's different if they all point in the same evidentiary direction, or if they serve as the starting points for further investigation. On the other hand, they could just be errors or stray data or unimportant curiosities. As evidence in and of themselves, they're weak.

Worse yet, denialists can be prone to treating doubt itself as if it were evidence, similar to the way accusations of forgery get turned into "proof" of malicious intent. Denialists will trot out an unending stream of questions, and then when they fail to be satisfied with the answers they receive, they claim that the "unanswered questions" justify their denialist attitude. It's incredibly circular, but it allows the denialist to create the illusion of a factual controversy, when, in fact, he is attempting to cite his own stubbornness and undue skepticism as reasons for why he's right to be stubborn and unduly skeptical.

The ultimate effect of this approach to evidence is for denialists to adopt an attitude of incredible, overriding skepticism in relation to evidence that supports the consensus, while simultaneously treating claims that support their own position with an attitude approaching total credulity.

CHAPTER 3

CONSPIRACY THEORIES

At 2:56 a.m. Greenwich Mean Time on July 21, 1969, Neil Armstrong became the first man to set foot on the moon. Video and audio of the momentous step were beamed the quarter-million miles back to earth, where some six hundred million people watched in real time as humankind reached out and touched the final frontier.

If any singular event in human history could be deemed to be incontrovertibly true, this should have been it. The Apollo 11 landing was experienced and witnessed firsthand by two credible men of unassailable character. It was achieved through the work of thousands of scientists, conducted over the course of a decade. It was videotaped for posterity and broadcast live. Over half a billion people worldwide, nearly 20 percent of the planet's population, witnessed it via those live broadcasts. The men involved returned to earth with physical evidence of their trip. And that trip was replicated five more times over the next three and a half years, with another ten men walking on the moon's surface.

Yet one of the prototypical denialist movements contends that this was nothing but a lie: that Neil Armstrong and Buzz Aldrin are liars, that NASA is a front for fraud, that the video was faked, that six hundred billion people (including our Soviet adversaries) were fooled by this fake, that the physical evidence is bogus, and that NASA conducted this whole farce a total of half a dozen times without the scientific community ever catching on.

Conspiracism and denialism are, in many ways, flip sides of the same coin. Whereas denialism is primarily concerned with tearing down an accepted truth, conspiracism proposes alternate theories of truth to take its place. And just as denialism is a perversion of skepticism, conspiracism is an exaggerated variation of legitimate thinking, because conspiracies between people are a real phenomenon.

A conspiracy is simply what occurs when two or more people orchestrate an unlawful action. The Columbine High School massacre of 1999 was effectively the product of a two-man conspiracy. The participants in a conspiracy can even be government actors. In 2006, Atlanta police officers raided the home of ninety-two-year-old Kathryn Johnston under the false belief that drugs would be found there. Johnston was shot and killed in the no-knock raid, and the ensuing investigation revealed that the offending officers attempted to plant drugs in her house after the raid and that they orchestrated the false testimony of a confidential informant to retroactively justify their raid. Three officers eventually pleaded guilty to federal charges of conspiracy to violate civil rights resulting in death.[1]

Conspiracies can even be responsible for the significant, world-changing events that attract conspiracy theorists. The World Trade Center attacks of 9/11 were the product of an al-Qaeda terrorist conspiracy, made up in part by nineteen conspirators on the four planes, whose aim was hitting the World Trade Center, the Pentagon, and some third target in Washington, DC. The Watergate break-in and ensuing cover-up led to the first resignation of an American president. And while theories of the JFK assassination may run rampant, it was the assassination of Abraham Lincoln that was part of an actual criminal conspiracy.

John Wilkes Booth was not the only hopeful assassin on the evening of April 14, 1865. Booth, in fact, had three coconspirators: Lewis Powell, David Herold, and George Atzerodt. Their intention was to kill the top three federal officers simultaneously and hopefully leave the Union in disarray. But while Booth succeeded in shooting and killing Lincoln, the others failed.

Powell was supposed to kill secretary of state William Seward, who was bedridden at the time, recovering from a carriage accident. And yet, despite Powell gaining entry to Seward's house, his plan went awry, and he managed only to scar Seward's face before fleeing. Herold, who had been waiting outside to serve as Powell's guide in his escape, abandoned Powell upon hearing the screaming from inside the house. Atzerodt never even made it that far in his attack on vice president Andrew Johnson; he got drunk in Johnson's hotel and abandoned the scheme entirely.

Booth and Herold met up as planned and fled to Virginia, where Booth was eventually shot and killed, and Herold was arrested. Atzerodt went to Maryland, where he, too, was located and arrested. Powell never even made it out of Washington, DC; being unfamiliar with the city, he was lost for three days until he returned to a coconspirator's home and found investigators already there.

There is a level of irony in the fact that Kennedy's assassination by one man has spawned myriad theories about secret conspiracies, but Lincoln's assassination, which actually was the product of a conspiracy, is widely remembered as being the act of a lone gunman.

In addition to illustrating the reality of criminal conspiracies, the other crucial lesson imparted by these examples is that criminal conspiracies are not the impeccably crafted plots detailed in popular fiction. Plans have unexpected hiccups, participants don't follow the script, third parties get involved, and conspirators confess. The officers' conspiracy in the Kathryn Johnston case fell apart when one policeman told investigators that he couldn't lie anymore, not with a woman dead. Similar confessions were what brought down President Richard Nixon, and the central offense of the Watergate scandal was nowhere near as morally objectionable as murder.

The attack on Secretary of State Seward should have been straightforward: shoot the injured man lying in the bed. But Powell got nervous and tried to shoot one of Seward's family members first. Then his gun misfired, and it was damaged when he used it as a bludgeon. Powell attempted to stab Seward to death, but Seward was saved by the medical device he was wearing because of his carriage injuries. And because of all that ruckus inside, Powell was left to fend for himself when Herold ran away. Meanwhile, Azerodt simply got cold feet. He had initially gotten involved with Booth when the plan was to kidnap Lincoln, and he told Booth that he had no interest in murder. Still, he took the assignment, only to let fear or his conscience or some other instinct make him fail to follow through. Indeed, even Booth's part of the plan might have failed as well if Lincoln's bodyguard had acted predictably. But the bodyguard had retired to a tavern across the street at intermission, leaving the president's box unprotected when Booth arrived and let himself in.[2]

Even the terrorist attacks of September 11, as well orchestrated as they were, did not play out entirely as planned (though in this instance, what was "planned" requires some degree of speculation, given that the conspirators died). Flight 93 was hijacked and redirected to Washington, DC, but it crashed in rural Pennsylvania. Although the US Capitol was a favored target of al-Qaeda leaders, the plane's precise intended destination is still unknown. The Pentagon was successfully hit, but the effect was more symbolic than disabling; out of 18,000 people in the Pentagon, the crashed plane killed 125.

It's similarly not certain what al-Qaeda's expectations were for the World Trade Center towers. The 1993 bombing of the World Trade Center had been intended to bring the towers down by causing the North Tower to fall into the South Tower, but though the bomb went off as planned, it failed to destroy either tower, and it killed only six people. Even if the al-Qaeda conspirators' hopes included the possibility of both buildings being destroyed, that still does not mean that they themselves would not have been surprised by how effectively two planes caused the towers to collapse.

Being able to recognize conspiracism is helpful because there is very little that conspiracy theorists have in common demographically. Young and old, rich and poor, liberal and conservative, religious and secular, educated and uneducated, all are attracted to various conspiracy theories. It may be that a particular conspiracy theory attracts certain people more than others (for example, Birthers are overwhelmingly, but not universally, white people over the age of fifty), but conspiracist thinking in general affects all groups.

There appears to be just one trait that is strongly associated with believing in a given conspiracy theory: believing in *other* conspiracy theories. In his research for his book *Among the Truthers*, Jonathan Kay found that nearly every 9/11-conspiracy theorist he interviewed also had conspiracist beliefs about who assassinated John F. Kennedy. In my own research on the Birthers, I regularly found that people who questioned President Obama's birth also often believed in at least one other discredited theory, whether it was creationism or 9/11 Trutherism or the missing Thirteenth Amendment or a world-wide scientific conspiracy on global warming—and to clarify, this last was not merely a dissenting view on climate-change research but the belief that scientists the world over are actively conspiring to create a false crisis.[3]

It is thus possible to encounter conspiracy theories from all manner of sources, even persons one might otherwise consider trust-worthy, making it all the more important to be skilled in spotting the flaws in conspiracy thinking and not just in the thinkers themselves. If all conspiracy theorists wore tinfoil hats and talked like David Icke, it would be easy to avoid their influence; since they don't, it's essen-tial to know more.

In *A Culture of Conspiracy*, political scientist Michael Barkun pro-posed three types of conspiracy theories categorized by the scope of the supposed agenda.[4]

Event Conspiracies

The first, and most widely recognized, are event conspiracies. These propose that a particular, discrete event did not occur as popularly believed but was instead the product of a conspiratorial effort. Events of great import, like assassinations and wars and moon landings, shock and fascinate the public at large. When a wrong is committed, there is an emotional demand for a culprit, and sometimes the true villain is not emotionally satisfying or does not feel equal to the crime. President Kennedy was the most powerful man in the world, a beloved family man with a beautiful wife and an influential family, and he was taken out by a twenty-four-year-old with a bolt-action rifle. On September 11, 2001, two of New York City's most prominent buildings were destroyed and over 2,600 were killed because a handful of extremists armed with box cutters hijacked two airplanes.

These were events of huge historical significance, and they affected the course of history in very real ways. That they were carried out by mere hate-filled young men is not comforting. We like the world to be orderly and for things to happen for a reason. And so there is the understandable instinct to believe that a presidential assassination must have been the work of the Russians or the Mafia or the CIA. Or that the 9/11 attacks were engineered by the Israelis or giant corporations, or that they were a false-flag operation by the US government itself. *Those* are villains equal to the crimes.

Sometimes the unfortunate truth may be that there is no culprit at all. When TWA Flight 800 exploded in 1996 and killed all 230 persons onboard, it was natural and important to ask "Why?" When the investigation concluded, and the answer was "Probably fuel vapors ignited by a short circuit," there was no one to single out for blame. A passenger jet exploded? Surely that must be the work of an orchestrated attack, whether by terrorists or the government or *somebody*. And so conspiracy theories continue to circulate, blaming any and all "somebodies" for the disaster.

Event conspiracies are often denialist in nature, in that by their nature they tend to deny the accepted explanation for an event. People who deny that Lee Harvey Oswald shot JFK or that Neil Armstrong walked on the moon are interchangeably referred to as conspiracists and denialists; when they begin to explicate their ideas for what *really* happened, that is when the conspiracism comes to the fore.

Because they are so often rooted in denialism, event-conspiracy theories are almost never consistent across an entire event. Real scholarship collects evidence and builds a case around what is known; event conspiracies tend to tear down an accepted belief based on anomalies and then try to build an alternate theory around their interpretation of those anomalies. The result is that their "evidence" rarely converges on a single preferred alternate explanation; if it did, such beliefs might not be considered conspiratorial.

Thus, while JFK-conspiracy theorists agree that Lee Harvey Oswald was *not* responsible for Kennedy's death, they fracture from there in saying who *was*. Everyone from vice president Lyndon B. Johnson to Charles Harrelson (actor Woody Harrelson's father) has been implicated over the decades. The same is true of virtually every assassination-conspiracy theory: the standard gunman is rejected, but no viable alternate is agreed upon.

In the context of 9/11, Truthers contend that al-Qaeda did not act alone, but then they splinter. Some take the "Let It Happen" position: the Bush administration learned of al-Qaeda's plans and consciously kept US intelligence from stopping the attack. Others take the "Made It Happen" approach: Bush officials (including vice president Dick Cheney) were the actual planners, and al-Qaeda's role was secondary, if it was involved at all. Many, but not all, have come to subscribe to the theory that the towers were loaded with explosives to bring them down. Some argue that the Pentagon was never hit by a plane but was instead struck by a missile. Some argue that the towers themselves were never hit by planes and that the jets seen over New York City were nothing more than giant holograms.

Systemic Conspiracies

The second type of conspiracy theory identified by Barkun is the systemic conspiracy. These types of conspiracies are less concerned with the *what* of a conspiracy's agenda than with the *who* that is behind it. Whereas an event conspiracy is focused on the responsibility for a discrete action or occurrence, systemic conspiracies posit that there are actors with much broader and more sweeping goals in mind. However, these are not the all-powerful overlords that are the subject of super-conspiracies, as discussed below. Rather, as Barkun defines them, systemic conspiracies have interests that are not so all-encompassing. They wish to control the world's oil supply or its money. They want to promote the spread of communism. Or, more recently, they hope to advance an Islamist agenda. The agencies advancing these agendas are shadowy and secretive, but they are still largely recognizable as singular organizations with an identifiable interest. Monied interests. The military-industrial complex. The Catholics. The Communists. The Islamists. The Jews.

The most infamous example of a systemic conspiracy is the international conspiracy of bankers and/or Jewish people; the close and interchangeable relationship between the two being the result of the historical prominence of Jewish individuals in banking. Overt anti-Semitism was still prevalent well into the twentieth century in America, but like overt racism, such blunt bigotry is no longer publicly tolerated. The specter of "international bankers" carries much of the same sentiment, however, much as how a polite racist may attempt to substitute the word *urban* for *black.*

The central tome of the Jewish conspiracy is *The Protocols of the Learned Elders of Zion,* a 1903 Russian book that purports to document a secret meeting by Jewish leaders as they expounded on how their control of the world's economies and the press would allow them to mold the world into a Jewish image. The book was a complete fraud, heavily plagiarized from an 1864 French satirical novel, *The Dialogue in Hell between Machiavelli and Montesquieu,* and it was exposed as a fraud within just a few years. Despite that, it has continued to be held up by anti-Semites as "proof" of an international Jewish conspiracy.

While anti-Jewish sentiment is no longer acceptable, the same cannot be said of anti-Muslim sentiment, which is reflected in a more recent religious systemic conspiracy focused on Islam. An afternoon spent perusing posts at the conservative web forum FreeRepublic will turn up numerous allegations of Islamist agendas intent on subjecting Americans to sharia law. The grain of truth that allows such claims to flourish is that there are Islamist agencies, like al-Qaeda, that wish to harm America, and there are countries that ground their civil law in Muslim religious law. That, however, is a far cry from the fear that there is a conscious and organized Islamist effort to subvert the US Constitution, or that President Obama and the Democratic Party secretly support the Islamist takeover. The noncentralized structure of Islam means that conspiracy theorists of this stripe cannot single out a discrete Islamist organization as their villain, but the same was true of Judaism until the *Protocols* manufactured one.

Other popular modern bogeymen are the Bilderberg Group, the Trilateral Commission, the Council on Foreign Relations, and the men who gather at Bohemian Grove. Each of these groups is alleged to be made of world elites who gather in secret to plan world events. Unlike the Learned Elders of Zion, these organizations are quite real, their meetings are a matter of record, and the members have varying levels of privacy surrounding their activities. Far from being secretive cabals, the Trilateral Commission and the Council on Foreign Relations even have official websites featuring publications and membership lists.

SUPER-CONSPIRACIES

While systemic conspiracies may be far-reaching, they still tend to operate on the presumption of self-interest on the part of the conspirators and within a scope of influence that, while not realistic, is at least comprehensible. The Bilderberg Group doesn't control international relations, but one can at least see that the group does hold meetings—and one can then speculate wildly about what happens behind closed doors.

Super-conspiracies take it one step further and start merging event conspiracies and systemic conspiracies into an ever-more complex theory of everything. They are the secret puppeteers who pull the strings behind the world's curtain. Indeed, some of the actors in super-conspiracies aren't human at all. David Icke has preached for decades that the world is secretly run by shape-shifting reptilian aliens who have infiltrated the highest levels of government around the world. They are nearly indistinguishable from ordinary humans, except that video footage occasionally shows a flicker in their eyes that betrays their true nature. Naturally, YouTube® has provided an ideal outlet for hundreds if not thousands of videos of this supposed flickering. It's unlikely that someone who believes in a super-conspiracy will be easily persuaded out of that belief, but it takes a certain mindset to be willing to buy into a super-conspiracy to begin with. It is an all-encompassing worldview, so sweeping that any possible evidence is necessarily within the control of the conspiracy itself.

So when conspiracies can and do exist, what is it that distinguishes real conspiracies from "conspiracy theories"? What makes the Lincoln assassination conspiracy an accepted historical fact, while allegations of secret conspiracies surrounding the Kennedy assassination are dismissed? Why are 9/11 Truthers branded as paranoid conspiracy theorists when the accepted explanation of the events of September 11 (thoroughly detailed in the *9/11 Commission Report*) implicates a terrorist conspiracy on the part of al-Qaeda? There are differences, of course, and those differences are useful in spotting the signs of conspiracist thinking.

SPOTTING CONSPIRACY THEORIES

Logical Fallacies

Logical fallacies were discussed in chapter 1, and they are the backbone of conspiracist thinking, as well as being the source of many erroneous conclusions. The list of logical fallacies is far too varied to examine in detail, but there are a few that often play significant roles in the creation and propagation of conspiracy theories.

The conspiracist mantra is that history happens intentionally; there are no accidents. This is the theme of a quote commonly attributed to President Franklin Roosevelt: "In politics, nothing happens by accident. If it happens, you can bet it was planned that way." This, however, was not a real quote from President Roosevelt. Rather, it appears to have first appeared in print in a 1971 conspiracist book ironically titled *None Dare Call It Conspiracy*.[5] Conspiracy theorists claiming FDR as one of their own, it seems.

This attitude is not unique to conspiracy theorists; it's just exaggerated. People have a common tendency to commit what is called the fundamental attribution error. Actions that you take yourself can be explained through the situations you find yourself in. For actions that you observe others take, however, you are more likely to attribute those actions to the personality of the other person. You had to make that last-second lane change because you were distracted by the traffic, whereas the other guy cut you off because he's a jerk. This sort of attributional bias can then be combined with the tendency toward agenticity, also discussed in chapter 1. When an event happens, there's an impulse to conclude that there was intent behind it. And if an identity can be attached to that intent, such as a distrusted political figure or corporation, then that intent can be presumed to be malicious.

Diana, Princess of Wales died in 1997 in a car crash, not unlike thousands of people who die each year in car crashes. Most such crashes are accidents, but because of Diana's stature, many people refused to accept that her death could have been so random. Conspiracy theories promptly emerged, speculating that Diana had not simply perished in an automobile accident; she had been murdered. The conspiracy theories then expanded as people began speculating as to who would have had a reason to kill Diana, and they began seeking out anomalies that they could use to justify their doubts.

Part of the reason people were driven to this sort of speculation about Diana is the result of another cognitive bias, the just-world hypothesis. There is an instinctive desire to believe that the world operates on equal levels of good and ill, that justice and injustice should be balanced somehow. Beloved princesses don't die in mere automobile accidents. Beloved presidents aren't murdered by twenty-four-year-old lone gunmen. Two of America's tallest buildings aren't toppled by a handful of angry zealots armed with box cutters.

Those kinds of imbalances aren't comforting in the just-world view. World figures ought to die with meaning, not because they weren't wearing seat belts. If the leader of the free world is killed, it's because powerful forces wanted him dead. When TWA Flight 800 falls out of the sky, killing everyone aboard, it's because someone wanted that plane destroyed. Believing, then, that there was some greater cause that is being hidden from the public, the conspiracy theorist seeks out supporting evidence. If there actually was a conspiracy, then some good evidence is liable to present itself. The 9/11 hijackers had a conspiracy between themselves, and that conspiracy has been thoroughly documented since.

Conspiracy theorists are far more likely to fall back on anomalies, and, as previously discussed, their presentations are frequently just aggregations of anomalies, with little concern for whether they hold together. They are more concerned with proving the existence of a conspiracy, any conspiracy, than with identifying the actual conspirators or focusing on specific actions undertaken by the conspiracy. It doesn't matter if the anomalies aren't even consistent with the existence of a conspiracy. Birthers discovered that Obama's mother moved to Washington to attend college after he was born. They're quite proud of this discovery and mention it regularly, but it doesn't remotely support their claims that Obama was secretly born in Kenya. Indeed, Birthers will question where Obama's mother got the funds to travel to Washington even as they simultaneously accept that she made a secret trip to Africa while pregnant.

Another cognitive bias common to conspiracy theorists is the hindsight bias. Whenever one is reviewing the evidence surrounding a historical event, there is always going to be more evidence available than there was in the midst of the event itself. There is also the certain knowledge of what ultimately transpired, as opposed to the uncertain speculation when one looks at the future. Conspiracy theorists are prone to forget these uncertainties and to impose the information they have in the present onto actors in the past. Why, they ask, did the US military not shoot the planes down on September 11 and save the towers? It seems like a reasonable enough question, until you realize the unmerited assumptions that are implicit. We know now that the planes hit the Trade Center towers, but the government didn't know that the morning of the attack. Officials knew the planes had been hijacked, but they didn't know that the intention was to use the planes as missiles or to hit the World Trade Center specifically. Because three of the planes had turned off their transponders, air traffic control hardly knew where the planes were or where they were headed.

After a catastrophe, it's all too easy to look back and single out the individual warning signs that could have been noticed. But those signs, at the time, were among a much larger body of warning signs of things that never happened. By ignoring the context in which information is received, a possible future event can be made to look like an eventuality.

Size of the Conspiracy

Many of the schemes postulated in conspiracy theories would necessitate huge operations to execute them, if they were real. But conspiracy theorists typically ignore the large number of people—as well as the time, effort, and money—needed to successfully execute a complex conspiracy.

Faking a moon landing (much less six moon landings) demands a lot more than the participation of the astronauts themselves. It requires the involvement of filmmakers, set designers, artists, and engineers. People would have to create fake launches and fake splashdowns. Even the accountants would have to fake the books to cover up the lack of an actual mission. Hundreds of people would be involved, and they would all have to be sworn to secrecy. Plus, there's the implicit cooperation of the worldwide scientific community, including those in rival nations, who would have to agree not to expose the hoax.

For the World Trade Centers to have been destroyed by controlled demolition, it would have been necessary to transport tons of explosives to the towers and install them in advance. Security would have to have been compromised, both before and after. It would have required the cooperation of the terrorists themselves and the expectation that they could not only hit the buildings but hit the buildings at the proper height. Again, hundreds if not thousands of people would have to have had some degree of involvement, and this would not be complicity in a mere space-race hoax. This would be participating in mass murder. That is a lot of people to trust to keep their mouths shut.

Some conspiracy theories operate without even seeming to consider the number of people necessary. Conspiracy theories abound about the explosion of TWA Flight 800 in 1996, often with the suggestion that the plane was shot down by a missile. Missiles, however, demand the involvement of some agency with access to missiles and the means to launch them. Any such organization would have a chain of command, both to give the order to fire and afterward. The cover-up would involve everyone from the person who hit the "fire" button to the person responsible for counting the missile stores.

The number of people involved in systemic conspiracies or super-conspiracies dwarfs even those numbers, requiring organizations with wide influence operating over decades or even centuries. Super-conspiracies in particular often find themselves forced into invoking the existence of wholly hypothetical or imaginary organizations because no recognized group of people would have the necessary manpower or resources. Such conspiracists may try to extrapolate from a historical example, such as the Illuminati, but credit that source with near-superhuman capabilities. Or they might pretend that an unorganized people are actually a unified and singular entity with a shared vision and agenda, such as "the Jews" or "Big Medicine." Or they might forego reality entirely and point the finger at shape-shifting aliens or some other wholly fictional conspirator.

Some conspiracy theories may seem, at the outset, to suggest a limited number of actors and may thus seem more plausible. But any conspiracy theory concerning a major event necessitates the participation of not only the original conspirators but also of all persons who would be involved in the subsequent cover-up.

Assassinations would seem to be a ripe opportunity for possible conspiracies, since they sometimes do involve individuals conspiring together to carry out the kill. But with any assassination of significance (and assassinations are, almost by definition, significant), the murder itself is sure to be investigated thoroughly afterward. The failure to identify additional conspirators, and the failure to recognize that a conspiracy existed at all, would mean either that the participants were phenomenally good at covering their tracks, or that the investigation itself was shoddy or, worse, complicit in the cover-up. For Lee Harvey Oswald to have been working with any entity of note, the Warren Commission and all other investigators must be assumed to have ignored the evidence. Depending on the scope of the assistance, the number of Oswald's coconspirators could also quickly multiply.

Purpose of the Conspiracy

Such extensive conspiracies also start to have muddled motivations, to the point where their intent is more or less that of a fictional super-villain group. They want to control the world, or at least to control its money/oil/religion. Even supporters of event-conspiracy theories may have difficulty delineating exactly what they think the conspiracy was hoping to accomplish. Motivations end up being reverse engineered, as theorists look for someone who could have conceivably benefited and then finger them as the conspirator. Who would want to kill Princess Diana, it has been asked? Well, Queen Elizabeth may not have been happy with her new romantic interest, so, sure, why not? So let's say Queen Elizabeth did it. Then it's simply a matter of seeking out anomalies in the queen's behavior or comments to support that theory.

Real conspiracies have defined agendas and goals. People don't usually commit elaborate crimes for vague and undefined reasons or just "because"; they do it because they want something specific, and the crime can accomplish that. John Wilkes Booth wanted to hurt the Union and avenge the South. Al-Qaeda wanted to attack symbols of American power. Even those conducting the Tuskegee syphilis experiments, with their decades of cover-up, were motivated by scientific curiosity in studying the disease.

But why would President Bush want to destroy the World Trade Center? Any rationale for that is unnecessarily complicated at best and insane at worst. What would be the purpose of shooting down a passenger plane like TWA Flight 800? What would FEMA hope to accomplish by setting up prison camps for American citizens? Why would the world's scientific community lie and claim that HIV causes AIDS if it doesn't?

Conspiracy theorists try to work around this problem of purpose by employing the adage of *Cui bono?* or "To whose benefit?" Whatever the event in history, if one looks at it from a future perspective, there will always be someone who can be said to have reaped some benefit. Once the conspiracist has identified a possible beneficiary, he can then suggest that the purpose of the conspiracy was to create that benefit. It's a worldview where events are as straightforward as an episode of *Columbo,* in which the killer is the beneficiary of a life insurance policy on the deceased.

And so it's through this logic that Holocaust deniers will say that the Jewish people and Jewish sympathizers are responsible for exaggerating the Holocaust because it helped to justify the State of Israel. Alternative-medicine proponents will claim that medical scientists are hiding cures and spreading false information because they want to protect the income streams of doctors and pharmaceutical companies. It's proposed that President Bush brought down the towers as justification for invading Iraq, ignoring that a full year and a half passed between the 9/11 attacks and the United States' entry into Iraq.

That kind of lapse in time illustrates another common problem with conspiracists' post hoc rationalizations for supposed conspiracies. History, as it happens, is not always orderly. There are many actors, working for many interests, each with different agendas and methods and goals. Elaborate conspiracies to produce an outcome cannot be assured to actually do so. Conspiracists often prefer to analyze an event from the present, pretending that the past sequence of events was inevitable and, thus, predictable—that someone could orchestrate the destruction of two New York skyscrapers, knowing that it would lead to the occupation of an unrelated Middle Eastern country some eighteen months later. World history is not an intricately plotted David Mamet play, where all the actors can be assumed to behave in very specific ways to keep the conspiracy's agenda moving forward.

Any plausible conspiracy theory must, instead, be considered from the viewpoint of the persons involved. What could they have reasonably expected to accomplish in the moment they acted? The more elaborate and long-term a supposed conspiracy is, the more opportunity there is for it to fall apart.

There are also conspiracy theories in which the conspiratorial purpose is as fictional as the conspiracy itself. Ever since fluoride was added to the water supply to fight tooth decay, conspiracy theorists have protested, arguing that fluoridation is part of a sinister plot to do something—usually involving some theory of mind control or drugging the public or even grandiose theories of world domination. Either way, these side effects are wholly imaginary and completely unrelated to actual fluoride. The same can be said of the similar theories about "chemtrails," the conspiracist label for airplane condensation trails in the sky. To the conspiracist, such trails are chemical in nature, left behind to poison the public or to control our minds or further some other evil agenda. When a conspiracy theory cannot even advance an actual, real-world purpose, it should destroy any credibility it might otherwise have. Nonexistent poisons and impenetrable theories of world conquest do not make for credible theories of reality.

Motive of the Conspirators

Beyond the aim of the conspiracy itself, there's also the related matter of the conspirators involved. Conspiracies cannot be orchestrated and executed by robots; they must be carried out by people (or, at least, by shape-shifting aliens posing as people)—people with families and friends and jobs and ideologies and belief systems. People with hopes and fears and desires.

People who engage in real conspiracies do so because they hope to gain something from it. It doesn't just accomplish a goal; it will hopefully accomplish a goal that they have a stake in. Booth sympathized with the Confederacy. The 9/11 hijackers saw themselves as fighting an enemy of Islam. Malcolm X's assassin said that the conspiracy to kill the civil rights leader was a reaction to X's criticism of another Muslim leader whom they followed. The Watergate break-in and cover-up was built on a foundation of partisanship, protecting fellow party members and the party reputation.

The actors in conspiracy theories, on the other hand, rarely have such realistic and personal motivations. They often behave more like villains in old comic books or movie serials, being evil for evil's sake. They want to rule the world or start wars or make the public sick. They're willing to kill people, even large numbers of people, for relatively minor goals.

And those are just the people at the top of the conspiracy. As the proverb says, "Three may keep a secret if two of them are dead." Conspiracy theories require not just that the chief orchestrators be unusually single-minded in their evil, but also that every other knowledgeable participant be willfully complicit as well. Chemtrail conspiracies, for instance, presuppose the knowing participation of virtually every airline pilot in the world. The size of a supposed conspiracy is problematic not only because of its unwieldiness but also because the more people are added, the more people exist who can expose the truth—people with conflicting political ideologies or moral beliefs or simply guilty consciences. Or it could be something less idealistic and more selfish, like acting out of a desire for profit or fame or spite toward the persons being exposed. Criminal conspiracies commonly fall apart because one party simply gets cold feet or fears punishment. The *Washington Post*'s investigation into Watergate was aided tremendously by Mark Felt, an FBI director whose inside information was passed along via the pseudonym Deep Throat. Some critics of Felt have suggested that he acted not out of truly altruistic motives but because of personal vendettas. That may or may not be true, or it could be a combination of both, but it shows how conspiracies cannot control the attitudes of every person with privileged information.

Conspiracy theorists sometimes try to address this flaw by doubling down on the power and evil of the conspiracy itself, proposing that the conspiracy will kill or intimidate any person willing to expose the truth. In 2012, a Fox News anchor briefly made headlines by tweeting a Birther story that claimed that the Obama campaign had threatened to kill former first daughter Chelsea Clinton if her father went public with Birther-friendly information about Obama being ineligible for the presidency.[6] The implication was that the junior senator from Illinois was capable of threatening a popular two-term president into silence, both about the information and the threat itself—and, moreover, that the Secret Service apparently didn't care. Conspiracies are commonly credited with such superhuman ability to command silence and obedience because that is frequently the only way to explain why they don't have their own "Deep Throats."

Competence of the Conspiracy

As indicated above, by the capability of the conspiracy to compel silence, conspiracy theories typically presuppose that the agencies and people involved are preternaturally good at what they do. They are capable of executing schemes perfectly, of covering their tracks, and of destroying the evidence that would incriminate them. One of the difficulties in debating a conspiracy theorist is that the lack of evidence to support the conspiracy theory is so often treated as evidence in support of the conspiracy theory. The void of credible evidence is treated as proof of the conspiracy's own power and competence.

Real organizations, of course, are hardly so perfect. People leave evidence behind, if only because of their internal blind spots for what might point to them. Conspiracies, meanwhile, are credited with having the ability to silence witnesses, to erase newspaper records, to scrub video footage, and more. Except when they're not. Sometimes the anomalies that conspiracy theorists love are interpreted to be plain demonstrations of incompetence. A flag flapping on the moon. Hidden messages on the president's birth certificate. In these cases, the conspiracy theorist manufactures reasons for why his super-competent conspiracy has suddenly become utterly ridiculous.

Thus, the conspiracy is always exactly as competent and powerful as the conspiracy theorist needs it to be. If there's no good evidence, that's all part of the conspiracy's plan. And if there's evidence that even an amateur wouldn't have allowed through, then that's also part of their plan.

Lack of Narrative Hypothesis

Conspiracy theories are not usually constructed from evidence the same way that regular theories of history are. They're constructed from doubts and questions and rumors and anomalies, often reverse engineered to create the appearance of a sinister agenda at work. Any conversation or debate with a conspiracy theorist will involve a never-ending barrage of these questions and rumors and anomalies, with associated demands for explanations and answers for each individual one.

Science involves the proposal of a hypothesis, followed by research and testing to evaluate whether that hypothesis stands up to scrutiny. Conspiracy theorists have difficulty advancing such a singular hypothesis to test, focusing instead on discrete details and anomalies, treating each one as its own independent hypothesis. Explain away one anomaly or answer one question, and they'll simply move on to the next one that they claim supports their conspiracy theory. This approach, however, rarely produces a cohesive larger narrative that can be treated as an alternative to the accepted view. If a number of anomalies all point to a single interpretation or conclusion, then there might be something there worth investigating. But if the anomalies are just random oddities, evidencing no larger pattern, then they don't add up to much in terms of proof.

This is why JFK-assassination conspiracies are so varied; conspiracy buffs have collected innumerable anomalies, but they don't converge on a single new suspect. Instead, the conspiracy theories have as many suspects as they do questions. Birthers are largely incapable of laying out what they believe is the truth about President Obama, because to do so would either lay bare the silliness of their belief or open that delineated theory up to rebuttal.

Because of that latter problem, more sophisticated conspiracy theorists will often avoid spelling out their preferred narrative. If they proposed a singular and specific alternative narrative, then that would be open to being broken down and discredited. One could see the unfounded assumptions and leaps of logic, the poor evidence that's being treated as credible, and the good evidence that's being ignored. 9/11-conspiracy theorists are happy to assume that explosives for a controlled demolition are a given; they'd rather avoid explaining exactly when and how the explosives were actually put into place.

Less sophisticated conspiracists, on the other hand, might be willing to spell out what they believe actually happened, but they will also commonly be willing to retreat into secondary and tertiary hypotheses when the first one is punctured. Such an approach to evidence and proof is not terribly scientific; it displays an end-oriented belief that is willing to contort the available evidence to support a preferred conclusion. There is a sort of faith in the existence of the conspiracy, and no matter how many individual arguments may be rejected, there will always be another backup or another justification.

Denialism and Goalpost Moving

Finally, being that their rejection of the accepted view makes them denialists, conspiracy theorists demonstrate all the denialist features previously discussed. In building the case for their theories, they cherry-pick evidence and blindly accept less-than-credible information. They'll move goalposts and set impossible expectations.

And because they often fear the conspiracist label, they will insist that they don't necessarily believe the things they say and that they're only "asking questions." What ultimately defines a conspiracy theorist is that he doesn't want to hear the right answer; he already knows the answer he wants, and he'll keep "asking questions" until he hears it.

CHAPTER 4
RUMORS

W ithin days of the attacks of September 11, 2001, a rumor began circulating that four thousand Jews (or, alternatively, four thousand Israelis) had failed to report for work at the World Trade Center on the last day the towers were open. The claim was repeated and spread by Islamic and anti-Semitic media outlets, as it served both to call into question the allegations of Muslim terrorism and to bolster a conspiracy theory that it was instead Israel that was somehow complicit in the attacks.

The rumor was, of course, utterly false. It had its beginnings in a September 12 article in the *Jerusalem Post*, which said, "The Foreign Ministry in Jerusalem has so far received the names of 4,000 Israelis believed to have been in the areas of the World Trade Center and the Pentagon at the time of the attacks."[1] For the *Post*, this was nothing more than a local-interest angle on a story, reporting how many fellow countrymen lived in the general vicinity of a major international catastrophe. Within a matter of days, Syria's government-owned newspaper, *Al-Thawra*, was reporting that four thousand Jews "remarkably did not show up in their jobs" on September 11.[2] By the end of September, the story had already been repeated by Lebanon's Al-Manar television, by Pakistan's *Business Recorder*, and by Russia's *Pravda*.[3]

There was never any substantive evidence to support the rumor. Indeed, 10 to 15 percent of the New York victims that day were Jewish, in line with the demographics of the local population. Whether intentionally fabricated or not, the false rumor took on a life of its own, and it continues to be repeated even now, nearly a decade later.

False rumors and fictional "facts" are the lifeblood of conspiracy theories and denialist movements. Pointing out perceived inconsistencies and missing information can help to create doubt in the accepted truth, but building up an alternative approach to reality requires alternative evidence. And in the absence of any reliable evidence, conspiracists readily resort to the unreliable variety, such as the story about the four thousand Jews. It is a mistake, however, to assume that false information is always created with malicious intent. Malice may be why it spreads or why it refuses to die out in the face of overwhelming evidence, but it is too simple and easy to pretend that all rumors are the brainchildren of imaginative rumormongers who take glee in fabricating lies that they foist on gullible conspiracists.

More importantly, recognizing that false rumors may have mundane origins means that, just as with the four thousand Jews, with some effort that original source might be located. And often, the best means of deflating a false rumor is not to attack it in the present but to attack it at its source. Pointing out that a rumor began as sheer speculation, or that it was first introduced by a disreputable individual, can do far more to undercut that rumor than can pages of counterarguments.

Generally speaking, the different kinds of false information and rumors can be divided into three categories:

1. facts that were misinterpreted
2. facts that were misremembered
3. "facts" that were manufactured

The distinctions between these categories lie in the availability and access of the underlying evidence on which they are based. When facts have been misinterpreted, there is still an identified source that is being cited, which can then be easily evaluated and compared to the purported fact to see if it is an accurate reflection of the truth. When a fact has been misremembered, an originating source does exist, but the person sharing the false information is unable to point to it. It has been lost or forgotten. Manufactured evidence, by contrast, has no source; it is nothing more than the creation of someone's imagination, and no amount of searching will produce a validating account.

Any of these can be innocent or malicious, but making a firm judgment on that distinction demands at least some capacity to evaluate a person's internal motives. Manufactured evidence is the variety most likely to be maliciously inspired, but even it can be inadvertent. And I consider it better to distinguish based on the relationship of the false rumor to a factual source than on the mental motivations of the rumor creator. Identifying the source of the rumor you are faced with is more useful in evaluating and combating it than making judgments about others' intentions.

1. Facts That Were Misinterpreted

Misinterpreted evidence can be the easiest misinformation to debunk, as the source is readily identifiable and available for comparison and review. But as with all debunking, whether it actually succeeds in persuading the conspiracist himself is less than certain. If the misinterpretation was an innocent mistake, it might be possible to persuade the mistaken party. This is most likely if the mistake was one of simple, factual details, like recorded quotations. But if it involves interpretation in the broader sense, like legal or literary interpretation, then you can expect to find heels that are dug in and minds that are resistant to counterargument, even in the face of superior experience and education.

Misinterpretation is a particular problem with professional papers and scientific studies that are written for a specific, educated audience but that can be drastically misunderstood by the casual reader or by someone with a motivating interest. The news media itself can be prone to this, delivering a hyperbolic account of a study's findings. An initial, small-scale study that shows promising results for a particular hypothesis is not the same as "proof" of that hypothesis. A study that shows that acupuncture works as well as a placebo in relieving pain is not proof that acupuncture "works," and it's certainly not proof that the underlying theory of acupuncture and bodily meridians has any merit. And yet studies finding that acupuncture performs no better than a placebo are often wrongly reported as "acupuncture works."[4]

The Internet is also replete with instances of people who have misinterpreted humor for fact. Satirical stories, hoaxes, April Fools' gags and the like may not even be intended as factual claims to be taken seriously, but when that intent is lost on the reader, the joke is misinterpreted as actual news. And instead of inspiring laughter, the joke sparks outrage. A greater obstacle to combating misinterpreted evidence is if the faulty interpretation is not genuine and sincere. It may be driven by a conscious desire to reach a certain result. In those instances, the information may not be considered misinterpreted so much as misconstrued.

In 1871, Congress passed An Act to Provide a Government for the District of Columbia. As the name might suggest, the act was to create a city government for Washington, DC, and to grant it, in the act's own words, "all powers of a municipal corporation not inconsistent with the Constitution and laws of the United States."[5] At some point after 1871, someone looked at this act, saw the word *corporation*, and erroneously concluded that Congress had turned the nation's capital into a privately owned company. Out of this was then borne a grand conspiracy theory, as will be covered in more detail in a later chapter. And even though the act itself is easily reviewed, conspiracy theorists who have been primed with the wrong spin continue to see it as evidence that they're right, rather than as plain proof that they've misinterpreted what Congress wrote.

Identifying a misinterpreted source is thus not the same as convincing someone that the source has been misinterpreted. Confirmation bias will stand in the way, resisting the "new" interpretation while finding reasons to justify the one that has already been accepted.

2. Facts That Were Misremembered

Within days of rumors about Obama being born in Kenya reaching a wide audience in June 2008, an anti-Muslim blogger named Alan Peters was already reporting that Obama's Kenyan birth was not only a fact but that there were witnesses. At the end of a June 14, 2008, post titled "Obama's Half-Brother Confirms Obama Grew Up a Moslem as Does His Sister Maya," Peters closes with this exclamation: "AND HIS KENYAN GRANDMOTHER *INSISTS* HE WAS BORN IN KENYA!"[6]

It took only a week for the number of witnesses to triple. On June 22, 2008, Peters wrote, "Obama's brother, sister and Kenyan grandmother all insist he was born in Kenya."[7] This claim of multiple family witnesses is something that Birthers have continued to cite for four years as justification for their doubts.

Despite my best efforts, I was unable to find a single report or even a single mention of a blood relative vouching for a Kenyan birth prior to these posts of Peters. Attempts to glean an earlier source from Peters himself were also fruitless. Thus, by trying to repeat his own comments from a week earlier, Peters was responsible for making fake witnesses out of Obama's relatives. Because, while there's no discernible source for Peters's claim about the grandmother, it seems very likely that the source of the brother and sister's testimony was nothing more than Peters's own dysfunctional memory. When presented with an opportunity to cast doubt on Obama's birth, Peters elected to repeat the grandmother myth, and in the course of so doing, misremembered the comments from Obama's siblings about his upbringing as being instead about his birth.

Perhaps this is an overly generous interpretation of events; it is possible that Peters consciously chose to make up the sibling witness testimony. But I prefer not to allege malice where I can blame incompetence, and Peters's mangling of information serves to illustrate how new rumors can be born through misremembered evidence.

The difference between misinterpreted evidence and misremembered evidence may seem hazy, and it is possible for a given rumor to fall somewhere on a spectrum between the two (or between either and manufactured evidence). But the key distinction is in the relationship between the rumor and its purported source.

The creator of misinterpreted evidence is still cognizant of the source of his information. By contrast, the creators of misremembered evidence usually can't point to the source of their claim. If they could, they wouldn't be misrepresenting it. They saw a comment on a blog or read something in a newspaper or heard a story on the radio; and when they later repeat it, they mangle the details or leave them vague enough for others to further misrepresent. It may be the events that change, the players, the context, or even the essential nature of the original story. And so a satirical story becomes a real event. A legal hypothetical becomes a rumor. And siblings who commented on their brother's exotic youth become witnesses to an exotic birth.

If it can be determined that a false rumor is premised on a piece of misremembered evidence, the easiest way to combat the rumor is simply by pointing to the original, sourced story. But that is only possible if the identity and the location of the original story can even be discerned. People who spread rumors are often not interested in vetting their information, even when challenged on it, and they are typically unhelpful in identifying their source. They may claim to be interested in learning the "truth," but they display little interest in verifying the origins or truthfulness of the information they spread. And even if you can establish a probable or certain source, that is still no guarantee of stopping the spread of the misinformation. The true believer may simply insist that there exists, somewhere, a similar but real story that supports his version of the facts—a version that has been lost or suppressed.

3. "Facts" That Were Manufactured

Manufactured facts are often the conspiracist's dream and the debunker's nightmare, because they can be tailored to suit the conspiracy's precise needs and to evade easy skeptical analysis. The upside to the debunker, however, is that once evidence can be shown to be manufactured, it not only has a greater tendency to defeat the rumor entirely, but it can also destroy the credibility of the person who created and introduced it.

In 1998, the British medical journal *Lancet* published a paper by Dr. Andrew Wakefield that claimed to have found a causal relationship between the MMR (measles, mumps, and rubella) vaccine and autism disorders. The paper concerned the study of twelve children with developmental disorders, eight of whom had parents who believed their children's conditions were related to the MMR vaccine. The conclusion of the paper was that a link was possible and that further research into a vaccine-autism link was recommended.

Wakefield's paper was the genesis of what subsequently became an international backlash against childhood vaccination. Vaccination rates fell as parents feared that they were risking their children's health. Further studies were unable to confirm Wakefield's findings; instead, the studies consistently failed to find any such link. As time went by, Wakefield's study proved to be a distinct outlier.

British investigative journalist Brian Deer began to delve into Wakefield's work, and some of the things he found resulted in a formal investigation of Wakefield by the UK General Medical Council. The end result was that Wakefield was stripped of his medical license to practice and his paper was fully retracted by the *Lancet* when it was discovered that he had falsified significant parts of his study.[8] Wakefield's "research" is obviously much grander than a rumor, but its legacy is a rumor that refuses to die: that vaccines cause autism. Because of Wakefield's falsified work, this rumor has motivated well-intentioned parents to expose their children to the very real risks of contagious disease.

The Birther movement has also been replete with manufactured facts, some of which have found longer lives than others. For example, an associate of Alan Peters attempted to start a rumor about Obama's mother, saying that she had registered his birth with the address of a "seedy hotel." This was a story Peters suddenly stopped repeating after newspaper announcements of Obama's birth were located, clearly showing a home street address and not a hotel.

One continually popular Obama rumor, which is old enough to actually predate the Birthers themselves, is the claim that President Obama is 6.25 percent black and 43.75 percent Arabic. These figures first appeared on February 14, 2008, on the blog of Kenneth Lamb, a commentator and local radio host. In his blog post, Lamb claimed that Obama had one great-great-grandparent who was black and that the other relatives on his father's side were "ethnically Arabic."[9] Lamb provided no evidence to support this, apart from referencing the one unnamed ancestor. He did not state how he came by this information, and he cited no sources. He simply referred readers to "research the Kenyan records for yourself."[10]

Of course, no evidence to support Lamb's claim ever appeared. To simply look at pictures of Obama's father is to recognize that he was plainly not a man who was 87.5 percent Arabic. Lamb has since shied away from repeating his numerical claim, but he's never explained where it originated from. The obvious answer is too shameful: he simply made it up. Yet the "Obama is an Arab" rumor still surfaces with some regularity in online attacks on the president, despite being completely unsourced, thoroughly debunked, and just patently wrong. Those things, unfortunately, are still not enough to kill a rumor, not even a manufactured one.

Misinterpretation, misremembering, and manufacturing are the three main avenues for generating false claims, and combating those rumors can be greatly aided by identifying which of these courses the rumor took. A house of lies that can't be destroyed directly can sometimes be taken down by the simple observation that it was built on a faulty or nonexistent foundation.

One should always be on the alert for reliable sources. If presented with a novel fact, demand a source. Don't settle for validation just anywhere online; the Internet is filled with other people who unskeptically repeat and regurgitate false information. If it's a newsworthy story, demand a news source. If it's a quotation, demand the source material. If it's a filmed event, demand to see the video. If you have your doubts, don't just trust someone when they say they remember seeing a news story or hearing a quote or seeing a video. Memories can be unreliable. If they claim that a video exists, but they cannot produce a copy of it or even a credible report of its existence, then that should call the credibility of that recollection into doubt.

In particular, always be skeptical of information lacking in significant details, like when and where a supposed event happened. For instance, the rumor that Obama's half brother and half sister claim that Obama was born in Kenya never states the names of the brother or sister. Or when they made these supposed claims. Or to whom. Or where the claims were published. Any and every detail that could be used to verify or debunk the rumor is conveniently absent. This kind of universally missing information should set off skeptical warning alarms.

CHAPTER 5
QUOTATIONS

O n May 2, 2011, after a decade-long manhunt, Osama bin Laden, the mastermind behind the September 11 attacks on the World Trade Center, was finally located and killed by US Navy SEALS. It was an event that was celebrated by most Americans, but not all.

Within hours of the announcement by President Obama, a less enthusiastic response to bin Laden's death began being expressed online. Twitter® and Facebook® users across the country posted and reposted the following, which they attributed to Dr. Martin Luther King: "I mourn the loss of thousands of precious lives, but I will not rejoice in the death of one, not even an enemy."

But these were not the words of Martin Luther King. As skeptical readers quickly pointed out, although the pacifistic attitude of the quote seemed somewhat appropriate for King, there was no good explanation for the context in which he could have ever delivered it. Who could be the enemy's death that King could have referred to? It's difficult to imagine King reacting this way to the deaths of Hitler or Mussolini or even Stalin. And what are the thousands of lives that were lost? Some claimed it was a comment on Vietnam, but as *Atlantic* writer Megan McArdle argued, King would have been speaking before the biggest casualties of that war, and there's no good viable candidate for the singular "enemy" individual being referenced.[1] The quote appears to be reacting to Osama's death in a way that's a little too perfect—so perfect that it becomes almost prophetic coming from King's mouth.

Those suspicions not only proved to be correct but were validated with impressive speed. Before the end of May 3, there were stories from CNN, Salon, the *Atlantic*, the *Huffington Post*, the *Washington Post*, and the *Christian Science Monitor*, all exposing the quote as a fake. However, it was not, as some had initially speculated, an intentional fake. Rather, like many a fake quotation, the origins of the MLK quote were accidental, the result of inattentive reading and the all-too-common failure to fact-check. The quote was actually penned by Jessica Dovey, a twenty-four-year-old English teacher in Japan. When she learned of Osama's death on her iPhone®, she found that she didn't feel happy, and after some soul-searching, she posted this to her Facebook page:

> I will mourn the loss of thousands of precious lives, but I will not rejoice in the death of one, not even an enemy. "Returning hate for hate multiplies hate, adding deeper darkness to a night already devoid of stars. Darkness cannot drive out darkness; only light can do that. Hate cannot drive out hate, only love can do that." MLK Jr.

The first sentence is Dovey's, but the last three, as indicated by the quotation marks, are indeed King's, appearing in his 1963 book *Strength to Live* and originating in a 1957 speech of his. Dovey did not misquote King or attribute her words to him. Her only offense, if any, was poor formatting. Only one of her friends shared the quote, and soon it began spreading. Some attributed all four sentences to King; but on Twitter, where posts are limited to 140 characters, the 116-character first sentence quickly took on a life all its own, carrying the King attribution with it. The quote achieved true viral status when it was re-tweeted by magician Penn Jillette (host of, ironically, *Bullshit!* a TV program that skeptically examined popular claims), putting it on the screens of his 1.6 million followers.[2] Within a mere twenty-four hours, a Google® search of the quote produced over nine thousand results.

The avalanche of articles exposing the quote as inauthentic was notable not just for its speed but also for its scope—if not for its mere existence. Quote debunking is a practice usually left to urban-legends websites like Snopes®, political fact-checking websites, or skeptical blogs. Here, the truth made its way onto the pages of several of the web's most popular news sites.

And yet, despite Jillette's prompt retraction and apology, despite the media debunking, despite the true author herself speaking out and screenshots of her original post being available, the fake quote still didn't die. Less than six months later, on October 20, 2011, Libyan rebels tracked down and shot former Libyan dictator Muammar Gaddafi. Dovey's quote was once again relevant. It even found its way into the Twitter feed of yet another celebrity: British actor Simon Pegg. Pegg (who, coincidentally, also had 1.6 million Twitter followers) posted the one-sentence quote on October 21, complete with attribution to Dr. King, and it was promptly re-tweeted by over a hundred others.[3] A week afterward, well over fifty tweets repeated the quote with an accompanying attribution to King; only one, just one, posted the quote with the correct attribution to Dovey.

The Dovey/King story is hardly unique. Its sequence of mistakes is the standard origin story for many phony quotes. Its dual novelties are in its incredibly speedy propagation and in its equally prompt public debunking. But even absolute proof and a CNN exposé within forty-eight hours of its creation couldn't keep it down. Real or fake, when words find resonance with the public, they take on a life of their own. It operates on the same principles as the rumor mill, applied to a specific statement rather than to an idea.

While the Internet's influence impacts all forms of misinformation, its fingerprint may be most noticeable on fake quotations. The Dovey story is dependent on the speed of the Internet. Without Facebook friends who could misconstrue her words and spread them further, Dovey's quote would never have caught the attention of someone like Penn Jillette, who in turn would have an audience of millions. In less than two days, there were thousands of online sources telling us that the words of an American twenty-something in Japan were actually the words of an American civil rights icon. And those sources are still out there, frozen in cyberspace.

That is where our common sense regarding quotations starts to fail us. Some people may take a quote and blindly repeat it as the gospel truth, but others will take a moment to seek some confirmation. In an age of hardbound books, confirmation of a quote could be time-consuming, with trips to the library a necessity. In the age of Google, confirmation is as close as the search box in a web browser. And while the truth may be found in those Google results, the search will also locate every incorrect attribution as well. A Google search six months after bin Laden's death produced over five hundred thousand results connected with King's name, but only 32,000 with Dovey's. Because of the press associated with the debunking, several of the top results are those news stories, but few fake quotations get that kind of publicity. A less careful researcher, who simply notices the hundreds of thousands of hits, might still take the results as a sign that the quote is legitimate.

The same is true of all fake quotations. Their popularity creates the illusion of validity. This was true long before the Internet, when bad quotes were transmitted through newsletters or editorials or speeches. The process was slower, but if a fake quotation can make it into print, then those printed usages become their own supporting evidence. A bad quotation in a book can come to be treated as its own primary source. David Barton is a minister who has positioned himself as a self-proclaimed expert on the religion of America's Founding Fathers and has developed a reputation for mangling quotations in service of his ideological agenda.[4] When attempting to source one of Barton's quotes, it's not uncommon to trace it back to one of Barton's own books, which is treated as authoritative by the citer because it is a published "history" book.

Twitter, in particular, could hardly be better designed to propagate fake quotes. With a limit of 140 characters, quotations must frequently be stripped of source information; often it is only the quote and the author that can fit the allowed space. Twitter then delivers that misquote to the computer screens of hundreds or thousands of other readers, who can then re-tweet it to their own readers with the click of a mouse. Cross-platform services allow the quote to quickly spread through Facebook and other social media outlets as well. And thus, within a matter of hours, a misquote can be widespread, creating the potential for hundreds of positive hits.

The explosion of social media helps to explain only the spread of misquotes; it doesn't explain how they originate. The Dovey story illustrates one common way: mistake by proximity. Dovey wrote an original thought, followed immediately by an actual quote by Dr. King with his name at the end. It isn't the clearest way to present her thoughts (particularly since Facebook would have allowed her to put an empty space between the separate quotes), but the punctuation is technically correct and suggests no intent to deceive on Dovey's part.

Still, it was all too easy for others to ignore the punctuation and to wrongly assume that the entire paragraph came from Dr. King. And so others reposted the entire paragraph, attributing it all to Dr. King. Then others began dropping the legitimate King quote, perhaps because it was less on-the-nose than Dovey's contemporary comment, and suddenly Dovey's original sentence was being attributed to Dr. King. When Simon Pegg and his hundred-plus followers tweeted the fake King quote, they tweeted only Dovey's words and none of Dr. King's.

Mistake by proximity is an easy and innocent way for a quote to gain a false attribution. It requires no malice, just poor reading by one person; or poor writing by another; or, as in Dovey's case, perhaps both.

My preacher sends a weekly e-mail to church members, and one such e-mail described a random anecdote that caught my attention:

> When a doctoral student at Princeton asked, "What is there left in the world for original dissertation research?" Albert Einstein replied, "Find out about prayer. Somebody must find out about prayer."

This did not sound like the Albert Einstein I knew. Einstein did deny being an atheist and made some well-known statements that employed religious language ("God doesn't play dice with the world"[5]), but he called himself a pantheist and was not known to believe in a personal God as found in Christianity or his ancestral Judaism. Einstein's open endorsement of the power of personal prayer, to the point of suggesting that it is the most important issue facing modern science, would seem apocryphal.

And it is. The quote has been wrongly attributed to Mr. Einstein for some three decades (it appeared in Ben Patterson's *Waiting: Finding Hope When God Seems Silent*, with a citation to the Winter 1983 issue of *Leadership Journal*).[6] It seems probable, however, that the misattribution began not very long before. In James Humes's 1976 book *Roles Speakers Play*, the quote is included among a long list of quotations but is attributed to "Charles Steinmetz, the great scientist." Immediately above it is another quote attributed to, yes, Albert Einstein.[7]

It's difficult to say with certainty that the Einstein confusion began with this book, but the timing and the proximity of the two quotes on the page would seem to support it. The psychological appeal of the Einstein attribution is plainly obvious; Charles Steinmetz, while a highly respected mathematician, engineer, and inventor, is hardly the household name that Albert Einstein is. But apart from familiarity, there is a stronger appeal to authority inherent in attributing a pro-religion quote to the father of relativity. Just as a quote about the death of one's enemies took on greater persuasive authority by putting it into the mouth of the twentieth century's greatest civil rights leader, so, too, a quote promoting the reality of God and the positive effects of prayer takes on greater heft by coming from the mouth of the twentieth century's greatest scientific mind. As if to add further curiosity, though, it appears that not only did Einstein not say those words, but Steinmetz may not have said them either. In fact, the quote itself is a paraphrase.

At least as early as 1938's *My Vocation*, written by Earl Lockhart, the sentiment was attributed to Steinmetz, but the quote itself was somewhat less pithy:

It was Roger Babson, the statistician, who quoted Charles Steinmetz, the head of the research laboratories of the General Electric Company, when asked the question, "What line of research will see the greatest development during the next fifty years?"—as replying, "I think the greatest discovery will be made along spiritual lines. Here is a force which history clearly teaches has been the greatest power in the development of man and history. [. . .] Then the scientists of the world will turn their laboratories over to the study of God and prayer and the spiritual forces which, as yet, have hardly been scratched."[8]

Consult the actual works of Roger Babson, however, and you'll find that in 1920 he wrote, "The greatest development in years to come will be along spiritual lines,"[9] and in 1933 he wrote, "Some day the master minds of a future generation will turn to a study of the intangibles and as great an advance will follow along spiritual lines as the past fifty years have witnessed along electrical lines."[10] Strangely, although Babson seems to be speaking his own thoughts in 1920 and 1933, in the late 1920s he wrote that the words came from Mr. Steinmetz, as spoken to Babson.[11]

Proximity may explain a misattribution that was unintentional; it's similarly possible that a misattribution may be the result of an intentional act, to help or harm someone's reputation. Or it could be to help the reputation of the quotation itself. Misattribution is also only one way in which a quotation can be spurious. It could also be the case that the quotation itself is flawed, having been mangled over time, changing more and more, like a sentence spoken in a game of Telephone. Or it could be that the quote is completely fallacious and was created either to further some agenda or because someone fell victim to their own faulty memory.

In December 2004, an article by journalist Bill Moyers made some controversial allegations about Christian fundamentalists, arguing that conservative attitudes toward environmentalism were due to an active desire to destroy the earth's environment in the hopes of speeding the Second Coming of Jesus Christ. To support his claim, Moyers quoted a very high-ranking Republican official whose very job concerned the American environment: "Remember James Watt, President Reagan's first Secretary of the Interior? My favorite online environmental journal, the ever engaging Grist, reminded us recently of how James Watt told the U.S. Congress that protecting natural resources was unimportant in light of the imminent return of Jesus Christ. In public testimony he said, 'after the last tree is felled, Christ will come back.'"[12]

Over the next few weeks, the quote spread not just over the Internet but through published media as well, even making it into the *Washington Post.* The *Post* ran a correction shortly thereafter, saying there was no record of the quote. Online magazine *Grist,* which in October 2004 had said the quote was made to Congress in 1981, issued a similar retraction and apology in February 2005.[13] *Grist* also stated its own source for the quote: a 1990 book titled *Setting the Captives Free* by former minister Austin Miles. It was around this time that I discovered this online debate and attempted to investigate the Watt quote. Others had already searched the congressional record and found no such quote from Watt, and in Miles's book, he had in fact not identified the quote as being from either 1981 or from congressional testimony. Since the book cited no source whatsoever, I contacted Miles myself and asked him for the source of the quote.

Miles's response was that he had heard Watt say it on an episode of *The PTL Club,* a Christian talk show hosted by evangelists Jim and Tammy Bakker, which had run from 1974 to 1989. He did not, however, recall a date, nor could he point to any other published source prior to his 1990 book. Other bloggers located contemporaneous quotes from Watt that expressed an opposite opinion from the supposed quote; and while one might expect that a radically anti-environment statement from the interior secretary would be newsworthy, I was unable to find any news coverage of the quote from the 1980s. Watt himself issued a public statement directly denying that he had ever said such a thing. By the end of February 2005, the quote had been widely dismissed as inauthentic. No one had proven that Watt did *not* say it, but there was zero evidence apart from Miles's book that he ever had.

And yet, Miles stood by the quote as authentic, even though he had nothing more than his personal memory to support it. Whether intentionally or not, he had picked a source that could not easily be checked; it's not as if an archive of *PTL Club* episodes exists for reference purposes. Still, I found Miles to be more or less sincere in his belief; it seemed he trusted his memory over the record.

Some years later, I found that many Birthers were willing to put the same level of trust in a false memory. A rumor began circulating that, in a 2004 debate with Alan Keyes, Barack Obama had avoided answering a question about his presidential eligibility. But all the videos and transcripts of the Keyes/Obama debates were available online through C-SPAN, and none of them included such an exchange. (Although a vaguely similar statement was made by Obama, who said that he wasn't "running to be minister of Illinois"[14]—a likely inspiration for the fake quote.) One of Keyes's own campaign managers repeatedly said that the exchange never took place. But even that wasn't enough to dissuade the faithful; they fell back on allegations of conspiracy and cover-up, saying that the tapes had been edited and the transcripts scrubbed. More than one person claimed to have witnessed the exchange on television, fully committing to the false memory.

Finally, it could be the case that the quotation is entirely real and the attribution is completely correct but that the quote is simply taken out of context. And having been stripped of that context, it creates a false impression. A particularly funny variation on this scenario is the claim that while running for president in 2008, Barack Obama said, "There are a lot of people in the world to whom the American flag is a symbol of oppression. And the anthem itself conveys a warlike message. You know, the bombs bursting in air and all. It should be swapped for something less parochial and less bellicose. I like the song 'I'd Like to Teach the World to Sing.' If that were our anthem, then I might salute it."

That quote did, in fact, appear in a column by John Semmens in the *Arizona Conservative*.[15] The catch is that Semmens's column is a *satire* column; the story immediately above the Obama anecdote described how New York mayor Michael Bloomberg was going to hire obese food inspectors to order high-calorie meals at city restaurants and then fine the establishments that didn't encourage the customers to change their minds. But stripped of the satirical context, the quote went viral as an illustration of Obama's anti-American attitudes.

What made the story behind this quote even more bizarre was that I personally encountered multiple people online who swore that they had personally witnessed the interview in which Obama made this completely imaginary statement—that they could remember watching it live and being shocked in the moment. Even when confronted with the Semmens article proving that the quote was a fictional creation, they insisted that their memories were correct and the quote was real. The power of false memory was just that strong for them, as it was for those who swore they witnessed the Keyes/Obama exchange that never happened.

In the case of the Semmens column, the context of the quote was satirical, but miscontextualization can happen in other ways. For example, someone could make a comment as a joke and have it taken seriously. In a humorous 2008 speech, Obama joked that his secret middle name was "Steve." Later, some Birthers began seriously suggesting that he had used the name "Steve Dunham" in the past.

Or a person's statements can be edited in such a way as to change their meaning. A favorite quote used to attack President Bill Clinton was his statement "We can't be so fixated on our desire to preserve the rights of ordinary Americans. . . ." It sounds flatly anti-American. But the presence of ellipses should always remind the reader that a cut has been made, and in this case, the cut was significant. Clinton's full sentence was that the public shouldn't "be so fixated on a desire to preserve the rights of ordinary Americans to legitimately own handguns and rifles." Whether or not one agrees with such a stance on firearm ownership (and for the record, I don't agree), cutting those six words change Clinton's quote from a comment on gun control into a prayer for fascism.

A speaker could also make a statement for purposes of illustrating a point, saying something that they're expressing disagreement with. To take that out of context would make it appear as if the speaker was espousing the exact opposite of his intended point.

When I was in law school, the University of Georgia student newspaper ran a surprisingly anti-Semitic column by a freshman who cited a bogus Ariel Sharon quote and referenced this "fact": "The TBS Journal notes that the 'three largest American newspapers—The New York Times, The Washington Post and The Wall Street Journal—and the three national U.S. networks—ABC, CBS and NBC—are owned by Jews.'"[16] The *TBS Journal* is a fairly respectable publication, devoted to covering media in the Arab world and co-sponsored by Oxford University. That it would promote such a classic anti-Semitic myth as "Jews own the media" was striking.

I had little trouble tracking down the original report. What did the *TBS Journal* actually say?

> Alloush added that the three largest American newspapers—the New York Times, Washington Post, and Wall Street Journal—and the three national U.S. networks—ABC, CBS, and NBC—are owned by Jews. "Is that a coincidence?" Alloush pressed.

> Although U.S. administrations have demonstrated time and again undivided support for the state of Israel based on strategic interests, Alloush's remark remains part of a pervasive, though tragically misinformed, conspiracy theory in the Arab world. This misguided theory purports that there is a Jewish and Zionist plot planned by the United States and Israel to weaken Arab states.[17]

The *TBS Journal* never said that Jews owned all the major American media outlets; it simply reported that an Arab correspondent had said so in a television debate, and the *Journal* expressly noted that such a belief was a "tragically misinformed conspiracy theory."[18]

But by taking those words out of context, the anti-Semitic freshman could make it sound like the *Journal* had endorsed this view instead of rejecting it.

As with other rumors and types of misinformation, bad quotes can be created in a variety of ways. Discovering the origins of a misattribution is a matter of research; it could be as simple as checking Wikiquote or Snopes®, but it could be much more involved, possibly even requiring original investigative work. So how does one best spot misattributions or phony quotations in the real world? When one is confronted with a quote, what are the warning signs that it might be spurious?

SPOTTING SPURIOUS QUOTATIONS

Dates

The first thing to look for when verifying a quotation is a date: the year, month, and even day that the quote was first spoken, penned, or published. This is important not only because the presence of a date is strong evidence by itself; even bad quotes have a tendency to attract made-up dates over time. But the absence of a date of origin or of a consistent date ought to be a red flag. If no one can agree on when a suspect quote was made, then its authenticity should be called into question. For the same reason, citation to the original source material is important (more on that below), but the date is the best place to start simply because it's likely to appear more often and in more contexts.

The amount of suspicion that the lack of a date should raise is tied to the level of certainty that ought to exist. Anecdotes and witticisms, like supposed quips made by Mark Twain or Oscar Wilde at social functions, are among the least likely to possess a firm date of origin. (Such quotes are also often unsourced and slightly apocryphal.) Public speeches should be more certain and often rely on news reports covering the event. Personal letters typically bear the dates they were written, books carry the dates they were first published, and newspapers naturally paste a date on at least every other page. As such, there should really be no excuse for not knowing the date of a quote that was supposedly written and shared.

No media, however, should have a greater expectation of carrying a source date than the electronic media. Especially in a world of digital video recorders and online audio archives, there is no excuse for uncertainty as to the date a quote was spoken.

A rather popular illustration of this involves conservative radio host Rush Limbaugh. There's an anecdote well-known among Limbaugh critics that dates back to the days of the Clinton White House. As the tale goes, on his television show, Limbaugh rhetorically asked, "Everyone knows the Clintons have a cat. Socks is the White House cat. But did you know there's a White House dog?" He then flashed a picture of First Daughter Chelsea Clinton. Media Matters, a left-leaning advocacy website that regularly fact-checks conservative claims, has republished this exact story at least a half-dozen times since 2007.

But what is missing from Media Matters' accounts, and from every similar account, is the date that Limbaugh supposedly made the remark about Chelsea Clinton. It is universally agreed that it occurred on his television show, but no one seems to know when. For a program that has published transcripts available, that is an odd omission. (That no one, not even Media Matters, has ever managed to procure a video copy of this television event should also set off some skeptical alarms.) The most specific anyone ever gets to a possible date is "1993."

That's probably because 1993 was the date of a Molly Ivins political column that appears to be the first published telling of the story.[19] Media Matters cited a 1995 Ivins piece in five of its six columns on the topic; the sixth cites to the website of Fairness & Accuracy in Reporting (FAIR), which in turn cites to . . . Molly Ivins.[20] Even Ivins, though, doesn't commit to a date; the closest she gets is saying that it was "early in the Clinton administration."[21] How can it be so difficult to pin down a date for a quote supposedly made on a nationally televised program with published transcripts? Because that quote was never made. Or, rather, it was never made in the way Ivins described. On a November 6, 1992, show, three days after Clinton won the presidential election, Limbaugh referred to a cute kid moving into the White House and a cute dog moving out. An image of George Bush's dog Millie was shown when Limbaugh asked for a photo of Chelsea. The actual event is similar to Ivins's depiction, but it is hardly the same.

And although the transcript of this real incident has long been available online, the false story lives on. Some people claim there were, in fact, two Chelsea/dog incidents on Limbaugh's show; others claim to have witnessed the undated, untaped "second" event. Still, no one is capable of saying when that might have taken place. That lack of specificity ought to be the first sign that the Limbaugh quote is suspect.

Sources

Perhaps even more important than dates, but less often repeated, are the original sources of quotes. Thomas Jefferson's famous words often trace back to his letters; FDR's, to his speeches; Douglas Adams, to his books. Legitimate sources provide not only dates, which hint at legitimacy, but also the necessary tools for independent verification. If a statement was supposedly made by Abraham Lincoln during the Lincoln-Douglas debates, then you know exactly where to start looking for confirmation.

Whereas the reveal of a published source used to be helpful, if potentially time-consuming to check, the Internet has provided an easy remedy. Sites like Amazon or Google Books® permit a reader to text-search a book for specific words or phrases, providing an instant way of knowing whether the quote actually does appear in a particular source.

Sometimes sources don't check out. A quote that became quite infamous online begins "A democracy cannot exist as a permanent form of government. It can only exist until the voters discover that they can vote themselves largesse from the public treasury." This quote is frequently attributed to Scottish historian Alexander Fraser Tytler, supposedly from his book *The Decline and Fall of the Athenian Republic.* Except Tytler never wrote a book by that name or any similar one. The title sounds impressive and authoritative; it is almost certainly inspired by English historian Edward Gibbon's *The History of the Decline and Fall of the Roman Empire.* But what at first glance might seem supportive of the quote suddenly becomes, after a little research, a sign of fakery. If the quote ever appeared in a real book or a real letter by Tytler, there would hardly be reason to manufacture a fictional source.

Thousands of websites and multiple books quote Hillary Clinton as having said, "We must stop thinking of the individual and start thinking about what is best for society." The citation for nearly every such reference is exactly the same: "(Hillary Clinton, 1993)." No source is ever identified, and, for a statement that was supposedly made while Clinton was first lady, that ought to make a reader skeptical. Even the date is vague, never more specific than the year 1993. Radio talk-show host Neal Boortz used to include this Clinton statement among his favorite quotes on his website, and I once wrote him to ask for its source. His response was that it was something she said in a private meeting, thus no record exists. While that could justify the lack of a credible source, the fact that there is still a lack of a credible source means that it's irresponsible to present it as established fact.

A critical thing to remember in researching quotes online is that widespread citation is not a viable substitute for an actual, cited source. Any of the bogus quotes in this chapter could be plugged into Google and produce thousands of hits. Fake quotes appear on lots of sites you may consider trustworthy, sometimes even working their way onto news sites. They may, like a Lincoln quote discussed below, even show up in print. Publication by a trustworthy outlet may be a good sign of authenticity, but it's the original source that needs to be sought, not an intermediate source that just republished the quote.

Language

Discovering the lack of an agreed-on original date or source material for a quote is a sign that it might be unreliable. But what is there about a quote that should inspire such fact-checking in the first place?

The Rush Limbaugh quotation above, for instance, doesn't arouse any particular suspicion by itself. Since Limbaugh has a history both of controversial statements and of rhetorical attacks on the Clintons, it sounds like a plausible, if particularly harsh, thing for him to say (even if it seems slightly more the style of fellow radio personality Howard Stern). And indeed, it does sound like a similar, real event that occurred on Limbaugh's program. It's understandable how a false quote like this could spread without skepticism because, given Limbaugh's reputation when it comes to the Clintons, there's not much to give the reader pause or to cause him or her to ask, "Would Rush *really* say that?"

Similarly, if you're familiar with anti-Semitic tropes like "Jews own the media," then seeing a claim that a professional journal repeated such a sentiment ought to be a red flag. The freshman author of the university article mentioned above included a second fake quote that also rang false, which he attributed to Israeli prime minister Ariel Sharon: "Every time we do something you tell me America will do this and will do that. Don't worry about American pressure on Israel. We, the Jewish people, control America, and the Americans know it."[22]

Most intelligent readers would be hard-pressed to believe that the leader of Israel would say that Jews control the United States, especially in those exact words. Instead, the quote sounds more like something an anti-Semite would *imagine* the Israeli prime minister might say. And, sure enough, that was the origin of the quote, which is now quite widespread, far beyond a student newspaper. Its first appearance was in a 2001 press release from a pro-Hamas organization. The press release, in turn, claimed that the quote was heard on an Israeli radio station, where someone reported that Sharon had made this statement during a meeting with military leaders.[23]

Hearsay, private meetings, and unidentified radio broadcasts do not make for compelling sources. And the only people who seem to have noticed this supposed full confession were anti-Israeli activists. Such self-serving language is highly suspect.

The Tytler quote, on the other hand, does sound like something a historian might say, and the word *largesse* sounds suitably antiquated. But Tytler died in 1813. In what context would Tytler have been writing about democracies before 1813? Revolutionary ideals were still fairly new, and even then, the word *democracy* was used less often than *republic*. And world history had few democracies to base an opinion on. Unless Tytler simply wanted to predict the end of the infant United States, he would seem to have had little reason to make such a statement, especially given the incredibly limited scope of federal authority in those days. There was no public largesse to pay out benefits; Tytler would have to have been a prophet to raise that as an issue.

Another sentence often appended to the Tytler quote credits the historian as also saying, "The average age of the world's greatest civilizations has been 200 years." Apart from the fact that no support is given for this mathematical conclusion, a moment's reflection should call the figure into doubt. The ancient Roman, Greek, Chinese, and Egyptian civilizations all lasted much longer than two hundred years. More modern great civilizations, like the British and Holy Roman Empires, also lasted far longer than two hundred years. One would need a number of short-lived civilizations to bring that average back down, and which of the "world's greatest civilizations" lasted *less* than two hundred years while still being deemed great? As one might expect, then, this quote is not only apocryphal, but the timing of its first appearance is also predictable: its earliest recorded usages were by politicians in the 1960s, in the years leading up to America's bicentennial.

I encountered another suspect quote one afternoon during the 2011 Occupy Wall Street protests, when I visited the Atlanta encampment. One protester had erected a large laminated sign, which read:

> ABRAHAM LINCOLN: As a result of war, corporations have been enthroned and an era of corruption in high places will follow, and the money power of the country will endeavor to prolong its reign by working upon the prejudices of the people until all wealth is aggregated in a few hands and the Republic is destroyed. I feel at this moment more anxiety for the safety of my country than ever before, even in the midst of war. God grant that my suspicions may prove groundless.

As I stood there reading the sign, I snapped a picture of it in order to research it later, because in that moment, something about the quotation didn't seem right. Not only was it just a little too perfect a sound bite to have been spoken by a Republican president, but it didn't strike me as a comment that Lincoln would have made during the Civil War. It seemed odd that Lincoln would be so concerned about corporate power while the country was split in two, and I didn't recall any particular explosion in corporate power or influence during the war. It was during the postwar era, which Lincoln didn't live to see, that America saw something of a corporate revolution. It wasn't until 1873, for instance, that the Slaughter-House Cases—in which the Supreme Court decision first recognized corporate personhood—were decided. One other historical detail that I failed to recall, but was reminded of later, was that prior to his political career, Lincoln was a lawyer for the railroads, some of the most powerful corporations of the day.

Just as I suspected, the quote is completely fake. It is, in fact, one of the most pervasive of fake Lincoln quotes. It was denounced by Lincoln's personal secretary, and Lincoln's son, Robert Todd Lincoln, wrote an insightful article debunking it.[24] Its earliest known appearances were not during Lincoln's lifetime at all, but in the early 1880s—a time by which corporate authority had indeed begun to evolve, thus making the quote sound a lot less anachronistic.

This artificial Lincoln quote also demonstrates the caution that must be taken in researching dates and sources. It is very frequently cited as having originated in a very particular place: a letter from

President Lincoln to one Col. William F. Elkins, dated November 21, 1864. It certainly sounds authoritative in its specificity. After discovering several independent citations to this letter, it wouldn't be unreasonable to tentatively conclude that the quote might be real. But like Tytler's phantom book, the Lincoln letter to Elkins does not actually exist. Elkins was a real person; he, along with Lincoln, was one of nine Whigs elected to the Illinois legislature in 1836, and in 1861, Lincoln appointed Elkins to an Interior Department position in Springfield. No 1864 letter to "Col." Elkins, however, has ever been discovered.

Using language to skeptically parse quotes is a helpful tool, but such a method often depends on one's grasp of history and culture. The anti-Semitic quotes in the student newspaper jumped out at me because I already knew they reflected old anti-Semitic conspiracy theories; the student editors did not know this and thus allowed the quotes to see print. Recognizing the oddities in the Lincoln quote similarly depends on knowing certain facts about Lincoln and nineteenth-century America.

On the other hand, it may be easier to spot a fake quote that has been fabricated or massaged on the basis of some self-serving agenda. When a quote is said to have come from one man's mouth, but the words sound like they were written by his enemies, then that may be reason to doubt the quote's veracity. Ariel Sharon says that Jews run the world? Bill Clinton says that he wants to take away people's rights? Reagan's interior secretary says that he wants to destroy the environment? One need only take a step back to realize that such comments sound more like parodies of what those men might actually say. Sometimes people do say outrageous, insane, uncharacteristic things, but when those things are presented out of context and with no immediate source, that's good reason to investigate.

Personage

There is a second part to the quote attributed to Alexander Tytler that goes as follows: "Great nations rise and fall. The people go from bondage to spiritual truth, to great courage, from courage to liberty, from liberty to abundance, from abundance to selfishness, from selfishness to complacency, from complacency to apathy, from apathy to dependence, from dependence back again to bondage." This quote has appeared alongside the quote about why democracies fail since at least the 1970s. But whereas the true author of the first half is unknown, the author of this "Fatal Sequence" quote is most likely Henning Webb Prentis Jr., the president of the Armstrong Cork Company in the 1940s. Prentis delivered variations on this quote in several speeches, the earliest being in 1943, and gave no indication that he was quoting anyone other than himself. Prentis, unfortunately, was neither a historian nor a household name. And this statement of his is not framed simply as an opinion but as a historical pattern that has been repeated.

In chapter 2, I illustrated the Galileo Gambit with this quotation: "First they ignore you; then they laugh at you; then they fight you; then you win." I did not include an author of that quote because I wanted to return to that issue in this chapter. Virtually every mention of this quote, both published in print and online, claims that it came from Indian social activist Mahatma Gandhi.[25] Citations to Gandhi started appearing in published works at least as early as 1982. But the quotation cannot be found in any of the works or records of Gandhi. Its earliest known appearance—and its appearance in a form remarkably close to its current phrasing—was in a 1918 address by Nicholas Klein to the Amalgamated Clothing Workers of America at their Baltimore Convention:

> And my friends, in this story you have a history of this entire movement. First they ignore you. Then they ridicule you. And then they attack you and want to burn you. And then they build monuments to you.

And that is what is going to happen to the Amalgamated Clothing Workers of America.[26]

While the "sound" of a quotation is not determinative (more on that later), the above quote would seem to sound far more natural coming from a speaker at an American trade union convention than from an activist protesting British colonialism, even if the two have populist motivations in common. But Nicholas Klein, like Henning Webb Prentis Jr., is not a household name. A quotation on the history of democracy means a lot less coming from a cork company president than it does coming from a renowned Scottish historian. And a quotation about fighting authority doesn't strike the same emotional chord coming from a clothing union rep as it does coming from one of the twentieth century's greatest social activists.

This frequently happens when quotes try to convey some kind of social or political message. Even if the words themselves are powerful, an anonymous or unknown author doesn't carry the same weight that a well-known author does. So, union leader Nicholas Klein's words become attributed to Mahatma Gandhi. Roger Babson's comments on religion evolve into Albert Einstein's beliefs on religion. That someone would think prayer is worth investigating is not terribly interesting; that the greatest scientist of the twentieth century would think that turns the quote into a revolutionary idea.

Famous people often do say interesting and noteworthy things. Because of that, they end up being a magnet for claims that they said other interesting or noteworthy things, even if they didn't. Mark Twain and Oscar Wilde did in fact make many witty statements, but even they didn't say all the things that are attributed to them. If a quote sounds polished and perfected, then it may have been the passage of time that did that work.

Despite its open-source nature, a good and easy resource to check a supposed quote of a well-known person is Wikiquote. After locating the person's page, you can check whether the quote is included under the list of legitimate quotes (which are expected to be sourced), or whether it's listed as "disputed" or "misattributed." Inauthentic quotes are often accompanied by commentary explaining why they're questioned or pointing to what the legitimate source is believed to be.

Finally, remember that all these elements involved in spotting fake quotes are just tools of critical thinking. None of them are absolute signs of falsity. This is true of all the types of misinformation covered in this book, but it's particularly important with quotations, because people's words can always surprise us. Sometimes people are wittier or uglier than we expect. What seems anachronistic at first may not be. Sometimes people really do make amazingly prescient or astonishingly stupid remarks.

My favorite unexpectedly true quote comes from John Adams, who said, "The history of our Revolution will be one continued lie from one end to the other. The essence of the whole will be that Dr. Franklin's electrical Rod, smote the Earth and out sprung General Washington. That Franklin electrified him with his rod—and thence forward these two conducted all the Policy, Negotiations, Legislatures and War."[27] It's self-deprecating, prophetic, and surprisingly snarky. His reference to Benjamin Franklin's electrical rod sounds like it ought to come from a twentieth-century schoolchild who just learned about Franklin's scientific experiments. But it's 100 percent authentic, appearing in a letter Adams wrote to Benjamin Rush on April 4, 1790. That can be the flip side to investigating the authenticity of suspect quotes: the wonderful surprise that comes from discovering when they're actually true.

CHAPTER 6
HOAXES

April Fools' Day does not get the credit it deserves.

Where most other holidays are devoted to fellowship or patriotism or various tug-on-the-heartstrings emotions, the essence of April Fools' Day involves actively messing with the minds of others: playing practical jokes, trying to hoax the unsuspecting, and generally exploiting the freedom to simply tell lies on this one day a year. In the abstract, it sounds more like a fictional holiday created for a novel rather than a worldwide holiday with roots going back centuries.

An unfortunate downside of April Fools' Day in modern society is that April Fools' jokes aren't as ephemeral as they used to be. An effective hoax might be circulated around the Internet quickly by more gullible members of its audience, and those reposts are less likely to be as easily identified as well-meaning pranks. Birthers, infamous for their credulity, demonstrate this well. A recurring talking point for years among Birthers has been the claim that President Obama attended his first college while registered as a foreign student, and that he received scholarships reserved for foreign students. The origin of this accusation? A fake Associated Press article circulated around the web and dated "April 1, 2009."[1] Whether the purpose behind the hoax was to incriminate the president or to test the gullibility of Birthers, the claims it made have managed to become core elements of the Birther mythos, still repeated with regularity some three years later.

Not all misinformation is the result of overactive imaginations, poor recollection, or ideological biases. Sometimes false information is created out of whole cloth, consciously and with the express intent to deceive. This may be done in a spirit of good humor, as with April Fools' Day jokes, or it may be done with some more malicious motive. It may even be done inadvertently, where an intentionally fake story is taken seriously by an unsuspecting or credulous reader.

The website Literally Unbelievable is devoted to nothing more than Facebook® comments from people who have taken joke stories from the *Onion* humor website as serious news. Among the top reactions for 2011 was a Facebook user who said that the story "Obama Finishes Deal to Get Every American a Free Parrot" was going to make it difficult for him to defend the president in a campaign year.[2]

Barring those *Onion*-esque exceptions, though, the common thread among hoaxers is simply that they want the reader to believe. There's no misunderstanding at the core of the false claim; there is an active intentionality behind the hoax that has calculated how best to fool its audience. "Good" hoaxers will do a better job of anticipating the weaknesses in their stories than will poor hoaxers. This demonstrates why critical thinking cannot be a rote procedure: behind the hoax is a creative mind that, at its best, can explain away a series of prefabricated inquiries.

To justify this exertion in getting others to believe, there is some sort of benefit that the hoaxer anticipates reaping. It may not be a personal benefit, but, in descending order of the role of or benefit to the author in the hoax, there is attention, profit, and agenda.

ATTENTION

Attention is the simplest motivation, both psychologically and in terms of execution. It's simply a matter of "Look at me" or "Look at this." It's a motivation that necessarily underlies either of the grander motivations, since one can hardly hope to reap money or ideological advantage from a hoax if no one notices it.

The Internet has proven to be ripe for attention-grabbing hoaxes, since there is so little cost involved in creating one. With $10 for a web address and a few hours constructing a fake website, one could quickly produce all the necessary elements for a short-lived online hoax. Such a hoax was perpetrated in December 2011, when a story went viral across social media sites: singer Jon Bon Jovi was dead, having suddenly suffered a cardiac arrest at age forty-nine. Within a matter of hours, reputable news sources were reporting that Bon Jovi was indeed alive. By that evening, Bon Jovi had posted a picture of himself to his Facebook page, poking fun at the hoax with a handheld sign that gave the time and date of the photo.[3] But in the interim, thousands of people had heard and repeated the "news" of his demise via Facebook and Twitter®.

The source of this fake story was a free blog, dailynewbloginter national.wordpress.com, that had been dressed up to look like a legitimate news site. Even I clicked through to the site and failed to notice its less-than-credible URL. The story was heavily cribbed from a 2009 *Los Angeles Times* report on the death of Michael Jackson, making the intent to perpetrate a hoax undeniable.[4] The hoax was widespread but short-lived, and it offered no discernible benefit to the hoaxer apart from whatever personal satisfaction he (or she) gained from seeing his efforts go viral.

PROFIT

On August 15, 2008, Matthew Whitton and Rick Dyer took to a stage in Palo Alto, California, for a press conference, where they announced that they had recovered the corpse of the legendary Bigfoot while hiking in the mountains of north Georgia. They stated that they had kept the body frozen during the two months since its discovery, and that they had also witnessed three live creatures in the woods at the time.

They didn't have the body on display that day in Palo Alto, but they did release a photo of what they said was the corpse stored in a freezer. Along with seasoned Bigfoot hunter Tom Biscardi, they promised the public that further photographic and DNA evidence would be forthcoming. Biscardi stated that tissue samples had already been provided to a University of Minnesota scientist and that he expected to be able to announce the results soon. He said Bigfoot's body would continue to be held at an undisclosed location, but that Russian scientists would be examining the creature and that the autopsy would be filmed and released for the public to see.

Not only were the public and the press skeptical, but other Bigfoot aficionados were as well. Loren Coleman, a prolific cryptozoologist, said that he considered it 99 percent likely that the Georgia Bigfoot was a hoax. And indeed it was. On August 14, Whitton and Dyer had sold the body (frozen solid in a block of ice) to an Indiana buyer for $50,000, and by August 16, the buyer had thawed enough ice to find that he had purchased a $50,000 frozen Bigfoot costume. Online skeptics examining the photo had similarly concluded that the "body" in the freezer was a particular Bigfoot costume, and on August 18, Whitton and Dyer appeared on Atlanta's WSB-TV to admit to perpetrating a hoax. Whitton, an officer with the Clayton County Police Department, was fired the next day. The Indiana buyer filed a criminal complaint in Georgia, and two months later, the costume sold for just over $250,000 on eBay.[5]

Needless to say, Whitton and Dyer were not very effective hoaxers. Their story was met with doubt even before their press conference, and they found themselves so cornered by the flaws in their own story that they were publicly recanting just three days later. They quickly tried to downplay their dishonest behavior, telling CNN on August 21, "All this was a big joke. It got into something way bigger than it was supposed to be."[6]

They certainly went to great lengths for their "joke." Beginning weeks before the California press conference, they had created a website and posted YouTube® videos about the supposed corpse. They held a local press conference on July 23 and appeared on Internet radio shows to talk about their discovery. The two men did not merely freeze a costume in ice; a whole hog had been stuffed into the torso of the costume to give it bulk, and they had added other animal parts, including cow eyeballs and a pig tongue. Their scheme was carried out over several weeks, albeit ineptly.

But why? What had Whitton and Dyer hoped to gain from their stunt? The motivation appears to be simple and straightforward: money. The men owned a website called BigfootTracker.com, from which they sold Bigfoot-expedition packages for $499. As of 2012, Dyer continues to maintain the site and sell these trips, albeit with no mention of his 2008 infamy. Tom Biscardi had also been running his own Bigfoot expeditions under the name of the Great American Bigfoot Field Research Organization; he similarly stood to gain from a heightened public interest in Bigfoot.[7]

And, of course, there was the $50,000 Whitton and Dyer got paid for delivering a party costume in a block of ice.

A far more famous example of a money-driven hoax was the saga of author Clifford Irving and the "autobiography" of Howard Hughes. In 1970, Irving conceived that an in-depth examination of Hughes's life would be a publisher's dream, and that the famous recluse would not choose to call the book's authenticity into question. Irving faked letters and interviews, and got his publisher to pay out $100,000 to himself and $665,000 to "Hughes," with the latter checks actually being cashed by Irving's wife.

It was thus hugely profitable for Irving, and he even succeeded in convincing forensic-document analysts that the handwritten portions were genuine. But the plan fell apart when Hughes reached out to journalists he had known, personally refuted Irving's story, and filed a lawsuit against the publisher. Irving ended up being convicted of fraud and serving seventeen months in federal prison.

In 2009, I played a small role in one of the biggest hoaxes of the Birther movement. It was in late June that an eBay auction appeared offering up the Holy Grail of Birtherism: a Kenyan birth certificate for President Obama. The seller was anonymous, no picture of the document was provided, and the starting bid was $1,000 with a "Buy It Now" price of $1 million.

My role in this was in helping to identify the man behind the auction: a twenty-nine-year-old Iowan who had a history that included a bad-check conviction, criminal charges of forgery, and an attempt to illegally sell a kidney to a dying man. eBay was responsible enough to take down his auction—several times, eventually—and two months later, he finally unveiled his supposed birth certificate in a YouTube video. He went on to become a minor figure in the Birther movement, but his initial attempts to profit off his unseen document resulted in many conspiracy theorists rejecting his very tempting claims as being the profit-driven efforts of a brazen hoaxer.

AGENDA

Some hoaxers aren't primarily interested in direct personal gain. They do hope to benefit from their work, but not on an individual level. They don't want the world to know who they are; to the contrary, they may prefer the security of anonymity. They just have a cause they believe in, and they hope to advance that cause even through overt dishonesty.

During his first run for president in 2000, George W. Bush faced questions about his service in the Texas Air National Guard, and the same accusations reemerged during his 2004 reelection campaign. In the course of pursuing a story on Bush's military service, CBS News was provided six documents by Lt. Col. Bill Burkett, who claimed that they had come from the personal files of the late Lt. Col. Jerry Killian, Bush's commander during his time in the National Guard. Long-time CBS anchor Dan Rather ultimately presented four of those documents during the September 8, 2004, installment of *60 Minutes*, but within days the documents were found to be forgeries. CBS took a credibility hit, and Rather resigned from CBS six months later.

Burkett subsequently claimed that he had been provided the documents by one "Lucy Ramirez." Not only was Ms. Ramirez never located; her existence as a real person was never confirmed. Burkett additionally stated that he no longer possessed the original documents because he inexplicably burned them after faxing copies to CBS. Whether or not Burkett was the original creator of the Killian documents, it seems nonetheless unavoidable that the documents were created by someone who hoped they would damage Bush's campaign.

Finally, there is the motivation that is so sympathetic, it has its own holiday: to hoax out of a sense of fun—although not all fun hoaxes are necessarily as obvious as those with an April 1 date stamp. Being published on April 1 is no guarantee against a hoax taking on a life of its own. In April 2009, an unsourced article began circulating online, claiming that President Obama's transcripts from Occidental College had been released and that they showed that he had received a scholarship from the Fulbright Foundation that was reserved for foreign students. The article claimed to be from the Associated Press, but it was clearly dated "April 1, 2009" at the top, and that date managed to survive intact when the article was reposted across the web.

Beyond the date, there were various clues throughout the article that it was a fake. For example, there was a reference to a nonexistent organization named Americans for Freedom of Information. The date was the obvious giveaway, and yet it wasn't enough to stop the gullible from believing it and repeating it for years thereafter. Over three years later, Birthers are still referring to a story they read about Obama receiving a foreign scholarship. Even those who recognize that the original story was an April Fools' joke at their expense regularly try to wring some hope out of it; instead of saying that Obama's transcripts prove he *was* receiving foreign-student scholarships, they argue that the president's college transcripts should be released to prove he *wasn't* receiving such scholarships. They've flipped the burden of proof, considering that they have no positive evidence of such scholarships, and their motivating reason for such undue skepticism was nothing more than an April Fools' joke.

How, then, does it help to know the motivations behind hoaxes? When confronted with a suspect story, it's not as if we can know the motivations behind it; if we did, then spotting hoaxes would be far easier. But understanding motivations at least helps us to understand *why* hoaxes happen; whereas so much misinformation is the result of logical fallacies and cognitive biases, hoaxes are the product of a direct intent to deceive. Conspiracists, denialists, and pseudo-scholars may be mistaken or even deluded, but more often than not they do believe the things they preach. Hoaxers lack any such sincerity; they want others to believe as true what they fully know to be a lie.

That advance intent adds to the difficulty of spotting hoaxes. Because a hoaxer knows that his story is likely to be fact-checked eventually, he can construct his story in such a way as to avoid detection. He can consciously exploit the average person's cognitive biases or take advantage of what he knows will be the public's blind spots. He can identify the weak spots in his story as he builds it and find ways to work around them or explain them away.

Not all hoaxers are this meticulous. Many attention-grabbing hoaxes, including flash-in-the-pan Internet hoaxes like the Bon Jovi death story, aren't designed to last much longer than a single news cycle. Once the hoax is widespread enough to attract media attention, it will also likely attract the attention of news agencies that will promptly and prominently debunk it.

So while the specific facts of a good hoax are not necessarily immediately recognizable as fake (Jon Bon Jovi *could* have died of cardiac arrest at forty-nine; CBS *could* have procured negative records about Bush's National Guard service; it's even conceivable that someone *could* have bagged a Bigfoot), the machinations of constructing a half-decent hoax instead leave telltale signs that can be easily spotted.

SPOTTING HOAXES

Anonymous or Unavailable Sources

The "Bon Jovi is dead" rumor fell apart immediately because multiple people did the same thing: they called Bon Jovi. Even though he wasn't cited as the source of the story (few people report their own deaths to the media), he and the people close to him were the obvious sources to verify or debunk the report.

Hoaxers can avoid this immediacy problem by putting their claims in the mouths of people who cannot be so easily reached. One option is to cite people who may be difficult to contact, which is what Clifford Irving was hoping for. He was confident that Howard Hughes could not be contacted for verification, and he thought it unlikely that Hughes would speak out on his own.

It's not necessary for a made-up source to be a recluse, either. If the alleged source speaks a different language than the hoaxer, that person will most likely be more difficult to reach for comment. So if an English-speaking American hoaxer wants to promote a fake scientific study, he's better off crediting it to obscure German researchers than to professors at Stanford University.

Still, in the Internet age, even foreign sources can be readily reached by e-mail, so a more creative hoaxer may choose to simply make up fictional people or publications. This was the route taken by Stephen Glass in some of the fake articles he wrote for the *New Republic*. In one, he described visiting the meeting of heads of a company called Jukt Micronics and included interviews with the people. When Glass's story was investigated by another reporter, it was found that Jukt Micronics did not exist, and neither did the people Glass "interviewed."

In 2010, I found several online "news" articles by anonymous right-wing blogger "Ulsterman," who told stories about people who did not appear to exist.[8] Media Matters followed up on one of my findings concerning an article in which Ulsterman reported on a research paper published by "Jan Wendt of Canada's Mount Royal College" in the *Canadian Journal of Naturalism*. When Media Matters contacted the college, what I'd found was confirmed: there was no professor by the name of Jan Wendt. And there is no *Canadian Journal of Naturalism*.[9]

Any of these methods can hinder a skeptic's ability to fact-check a hoaxer's work, but they also leave the door open to completely discrediting the hoaxer. Once the real source is reached, or once the fictional person is exposed as a lie, then there's little that can be done to save the hoaxer's reputation. This is why the final method is popular with hoaxers: citing an "anonymous" source. Say that the source is influential or educated or highly placed, but just don't give a name. Claim that the source wishes to remain anonymous out of fear of retribution or a desire to stay out of the public eye. An anonymous source can be contradicted by others, but it's nigh-impossible to prove that the anonymous source doesn't actually exist.

This is actually the primary shtick of Ulsterman, who made a name for himself with his scandalous reports from his "White House Insider." Purportedly, someone very close to the president's administration decided to regularly divulge wild stories about the private activities at the White House and opted to do so anonymously through another anonymous nobody on the Internet. It's an utterly suspicious set-up, but Ulsterman garnered enough of a following to launch his own website because people trust his anonymous "Insider" who can't be directly impeached. His relative success also resulted in the appearance of two other anonymous informants, a "Wall Street Insider" and a "Military Insider," who regularly provide salacious political gossip and who just happen to sound exactly like the "White House Insider."

Anonymous sources, thus, need to be eyed with caution. If a claim relies on the word of anonymous people, then it becomes all the more necessary to scrutinize the evidence they're putting forward. This is the next hurdle for the hoaxer.

Invisible Evidence

When Matthew Whitton and Rick Dyer announced that they'd found a Bigfoot corpse, there was something conspicuously missing from their press conference: a Bigfoot corpse. And good photos of their Bigfoot corpse. And a scientific report from a researcher who had inspected the body. Whitton and Dyer knew that the weak link in their hoax was that they didn't actually have a Bigfoot corpse. They could create a believable backstory for how they found it. They could enlist the aid of others to further their hoax. They could even buy a Bigfoot costume and fill it with meat to help stage some not-very-clear pictures. But they had to hide the fact that they didn't have the real thing. So they did their best to obscure that fact. They claimed that the body was being kept at a secure location and that it would be studied by scientists. Russian scientists. *Anonymous* Russian scientists. They let a few people see it, but they put the fake in ice to make a hands-on inspection impossible. With no actual evidence, they resorted to excuses and unnecessary complications to delay the production of their prize evidence.

Whenever a hoaxer's claim rests on evidence that ought to be in his possession or at least be accessible to him, it's necessary to manufacture ways to avoid sharing that evidence. He may describe something amazing he's found but say he's holding it for release on some future date. He may try to offer an inferior substitute, like the poor-quality Bigfoot photos. He may fall back on some kind of pro-prietary interest, suggesting that he's only protecting his interests by not being more forthcoming.

Let's say there is a man who wants to sell his cold-fusion inven-tion to rich buyers. He conducts a demonstration, and the machine appears to produce energy. But he won't let anyone inspect the machine. He won't allow anyone to take their own energy measure-ments or verify his figures. He won't even fully disclose how the machine works. In essence, he's conducting a magic trick: creating an illusion for onlookers but refusing to let anyone look behind the curtain. While that makes for great magic, it also makes for poor and rather suspect science.

Sometimes there may be a good reason for holding back evidence, and hoaxers would certainly like the public to believe they have good reasons of their own. But in spotting hoaxes, one needs to recognize when evidence should be expected and when it's being withheld for less-than-adequate reasons.

Nontraditional News Outlets

A successful hoax might eventually make it into the major media, but unless it's the work of a Stephen Glass or a Jayson Blair (former *New York Times* journalist whose plagiaries and fabrications were discovered in 2003), that hoax had to begin somewhere else before it could fool the press. Today, that "somewhere else" could be nothing more than Twitter or Facebook. It could be a blog or an online identity set up for the purpose of promoting the hoax. It could be someone eager for the news to notice him so that he can turn a quick buck.

Major media outlets are hardly perfect. There's a reason newspapers have "correction" boxes. CBS fell for the Killian documents. But an original story on CNN.com can probably be trusted more than, say, an original article on dailynewbloginternational.wordpress.com.

As with any other suspect claim, seeking out an original source is essential to finding the truth. With hoaxes, that original source is, more likely than not, a source you might not otherwise trust.

Conflict of Interest

This brings us back to motivation. If a hoaxer intends for his tale to earn him money or to help promote some agenda, and if the hoaxer himself isn't anonymous, then the relationship between the story being promoted and the benefit received can be conspicuous.

Part of the reason that individuals like Jayson Blair and Stephen Glass are fascinating is because they would seemingly have so little to gain from their fakery. They kept their jobs and earned some accolades, but their accomplishments weren't much different than what they might have achieved through serious journalism.

The money-motivated hoaxer is the easiest to identify. He's the guy auctioning a suspicious document on eBay, or the hunter selling the world's first Bigfoot corpse, or the visionary who wants investors for his cold-fusion machine. Even if it's not obvious at first, sooner or later, that guy wants you to give him money. And if he's anonymous and asking for cash, then that's all the more warning.

The ideological hoaxer may be harder to spot, but the existence of a conflict of interest is just one more factor to look out for. When CBS was contacted by Bill Burkett, the recognition of Burkett's previous history of Bush-related accusations would have justified scrutinizing his evidence a little further. In that case, what eventually happened when Burkett was pressed to produce the original 1970s-era documents he claimed to have procured? He said he'd burned them. Conveniently for his story, the central evidence in his claim was, according to him, completely unavailable for inspection. That, one hopes, would have helped CBS spot just how suspicious his story was.

The Great Moon Hoax

Chronicled in Matthew Goodman's *The Sun and the Moon*, the so-called Great Moon Hoax of 1835 provides a rich example of a hoax that operated on all levels. It's also just a fascinating bit of Americana.

That August, a relatively minor New York City penny tabloid named the *New York Sun* successfully conned much of the city, as well as a number of people and publications outside New York, into believing that life had been discovered on the moon, and that it included birds, unicorns, and, most spectacularly, flying bat-men. The six published reports cited the work of the world-famous astronomer Sir John Herschel, as relayed through one Dr. Andrew Grant in the *Edinburgh Journal of Science*. The stories were printed and reprinted, and they made the *Sun* a small fortune within a matter of days. For a brief moment, this tawdry New York tabloid sold more daily papers than the *London Times.*

The man behind the Great Moon Hoax, Richard Adams Locke, was no fool. His hoax featured many of the typical methods described above. Sir John Herschel was the preeminent astronomer of the day and was an impeccable source to whom to credit the moon discoveries. He also resided in South Africa and was thus unavailable for comment. "Dr. Andrew Grant" did not exist at all. The *Edinburgh Journal of Science* was a real publication, but it had closed three years earlier. Ultimately, the story collapsed when it was determined that none of these sources existed, but they sufficed in the short term.

The hoax was, of course, a huge financial boon to the *Sun,* but Locke's motive behind the hoax was more complex than making a quick buck. He was fascinated by science, and various religious astronomers of his day were promoting pseudoscience that he found objectionable. They predicted that the moon not only had life but that it was a religious paradise. And so Locke used his position at the *Sun* to offer up an exaggerated version of the fantastical lunar landscape they envisioned. As Goodman writes, "Great Astronomical Discoveries had not been intended as a hoax at all; it had been intended as satire."[10]

Locke thus had an ideological agenda behind his journalistic stunt; the *Sun* found that there were massive profits to be made from running Locke's stories; and in the nineteenth-century heyday of newspaper competition, anything that could bring attention to one's own paper was a welcome marketing tool.

The widespread attention brought with it considerable scrutiny from both scientists and other news agencies, and by September, the stories were widely recognized as the hoax they were. Looking back on it now, the Great Moon Hoax seems like a quaint joke that unexpectedly caught the public imagination, a viral phenomenon before viruses were even discovered. It was debunked fairly quickly, but the stories' impact lived on. Herschel would later write about how he continued to be pestered with questions by people asking about the hoax. It's impossible to say with certainty how many people ever took the stories as honest truth, but some percentage of the population surely continued to carry the wholly unscientific belief that the moon was inhabited by exotic creatures. It's fun to hoax others, and it's often fun to be the victim of a well-planned and good-spirited hoax. But when the belief in the hoax is not dispelled, when it continues to contaminate a person's thinking and interpretation of the world around him, then the hoax has done a serious disservice.

CHAPTER 7

PSEUDOSCIENCE

Therapeutic touch is a pseudoscience that rivals homeopathy or remote healing for improbability. The alternative medicine of therapeutic touch involves a practitioner's hands being waved over a patient's body to manipulate the patient's energy field. The practice is somewhat similar to the religious laying on of hands, except that there is often no laying. Therapeutic touch, ironically, does not require any actual touching to take place. Practitioners say they can sense the patient's energy field by moving their hands on or near the body and thus work to heal it.

The April 1998 issue of the *Journal of the American Medical Association* ran a piece titled "A Close Look at Therapeutic Touch," which handily refuted the claims of therapeutic touch. Several practitioners of therapeutic touch were enlisted for a study wherein they were asked to put both hands through a screen and, having been blinded to the person on the other side of the screen who was holding up only one palm, were asked which of their hands sensed an energy field. The practitioners performed with 50 percent accuracy—no better than chance. The experiment was both simple and elegant, and yet it provided strong evidence that therapeutic-touch practitioners could not actually detect energy fields around a person's body.[1]

The mind behind this experiment, and the coauthor of the journal article, was Emily Rosa. Ms. Rosa was all of nine years old when she conducted the experiment, and just eleven when her article was published, making her the youngest person to publish original research in a peer-reviewed journal. Amazingly, although Ms. Rosa held that record for a decade, she appears to have been bested by a class of British schoolchildren. In the November 2010 issue of the journal *Biology Letters*, an article titled "Blackawton Bees" described the relationship between bumblebees' vision and their choice of flowers to pollinate. The principal finding of the study, as expressed in the paper's abstract, was this: "We discovered that bumble-bees can use a combination of colour and spatial relationships in deciding which colour of flower to forage from. We also discovered that science is cool and fun because you get to do stuff that no one has ever done before."[2] The budding scientists who conducted this study—and who illustrated the published paper with crayons—were a group of twenty-five eight- to ten-year-olds from Blackawton Primary School in southern England.

Pseudoscience is a massive topic, possibly the broadest topic covered in this book apart from conspiracy theories. Entire books have been written on pseudoscience and on individual pseudosciences. Filling a chapter on pseudoscience is not a problem; deciding what samplings of its variety to include is. So why begin a chapter on pseudoscience with the stories of published papers by elementary school students? Granted, Ms. Rosa's experiment involved a pseudoscience, but the Blackawton study was a straightforward animal test. These studies are important to include because scientists and the field of science itself are often attacked for being "elitist." This allegation is particularly common among pseudoscientists themselves in their attempts to explain their outsider status. Scientists, they say, are afraid of change. Not willing to question their previous conclusions. Deaf to the arguments of the nonelite common public whose arguments scientists would surely find compelling if they'd only have an open mind. But Emily Rosa and the Blackawton students serve to disprove these stereotypes. Science, in the long run, is not swayed by status; it is swayed by evidence. If the evidence is compelling, it doesn't matter if it comes from a nine-year-old child. And if it's not compelling, it doesn't matter if it comes from a former Nobel Prize laureate.

Emily Rosa and the Blackawton class were published because their research was good. An insular group of "elitists" would never allow schoolchildren to be treated as their peers in print, but that's what happened. It didn't matter that the kids weren't professional scientists; what mattered was that they conducted science, and they conducted it well. Pseudoscientists don't. They shirk the scientific method. They confuse correlation with causation. They don't use adequate controls or blinding of their test subjects. Their claims aren't reliably predictive. Their results aren't reproducible. They cherry-pick data to suit their predetermined conclusions. They may even falsify data outright. They're not branded pseudoscientists because they disagree with the establishment or because they challenge accepted views or because they don't have fancy credentials. They're branded as pseudoscientists because their work product is substandard and their hypotheses don't stand up under testing and scrutiny.

Science is frequently broken down into branches and fields. The two major categories of science are the natural sciences and the social sciences. Grouped under the natural sciences are the physical sciences (physics, chemistry, astronomy, and so on) and the life sciences (biology, genetics, environmental science). The social sciences include fields like anthropology, archaeology, economics, and sociology. Some science-based fields of study, like engineering and medicine, are interdisciplinary and don't fit neatly into one category.

Pseudosciences can be categorized as well, and not just as the mirror image of the real sciences they dispute—pseudo-biology and pseudo-sociology and so on; they can also be broadly grouped based on the common mistakes they share in approaching the study of the real world.

ANCIENT WISDOM

Science as we know it is just a few hundred years old. Before that, our history was not completely devoid of scientific thought, but our successes were far fewer. We understood some general physical principles; we had discovered some folk medicine; we had developed some decent farming and engineering capabilities; and we had astronomy, perhaps the most ancient of the physical sciences. But even in our successes we were lacking. We didn't understand what constituted matter, and we believed the world was made of a handful of elements. Our good medicine was equaled or outweighed by our superstitious and often harmful attempts at healing. And even though we'd mapped the sky and measured the movements of the heavenly bodies, we still believed the earth to be a flat surface at the center of the universe. In short, we had learned a few facts, but we were committed to a lot more fictions.

And then, with the Enlightenment and the development of the scientific method, we began to change that. We discovered the building blocks of matter and constructed the periodic table to organize them. We built microscopes to peer into molecules, and telescopes to explore the universe. We made people live longer and healthier. In less than two hundred years, we went from building the first working steamship to putting a man on the moon.

Meanwhile, as we were developing and mastering new aspects of science, we were evaluating our old habits with our new sets of skills. Some traditional medicines were found to have active ingredients that facilitated healing, and sciences like ethnobotany became concerned with isolating which plants might have actual medicinal value and why. The old beliefs that stood up to tests and experiments were simply incorporated into modern science.

But plenty of ancient and traditional beliefs didn't hold up under scientific scrutiny. Their origins instead lay in anecdotes, myths, primitive rationalizations, and confirmation biases. They seemed compelling as stories and practices, but new discoveries and the scientific method have shown them to just be myths themselves.

But just because a belief has been proven false doesn't mean people stop believing it. Various claims of ancient wisdom have survived as pseudosciences, forever denying that they have been debunked or dispelled.

Antique Cosmology

Just as astronomy may be the oldest of the sciences, astrology may be the oldest of the pseudosciences. Astronomers studied the sky and documented how the stars and the planets moved through it, and astrologers attempted to ascribe meaning to those movements and say that every individual's life was intimately affected by the extraterrestrial bodies.

Astrology was mysticism, assuredly borne out of a pattern-seeking impulse to tie human behavior to the behavior of the heavens, and then generations of confirmation bias cemented those beliefs. Astrology offered no functional mechanism to explain how the stars could affect a person's entire future. Its predictions about people were ambiguous and weak, making it easier to count the hits and overlook the misses. And astrology's predictions about the heavens were even worse. Astrologers failed to predict the existence of Uranus, Neptune, and Pluto. They failed to predict the presence of the dozens of planetary moons in our solar system and the ever-increasing number of extrasolar planets elsewhere in our galaxy. Despite their insistence that a human life is influenced by alignment of the stars and planets at the time of its birth, they never realized that they were operating with a terribly incomplete map of the universe.

Even if its primary presence in modern society is seen mainly in newspaper columns and bar pick-up lines, astrology still has some cultural cache, with many people having a casual interest or belief in their "sign." Faring far less well in contemporary times is a fellow shard of ancient astronomy: the theory of the flat earth.

It's understandable from the point of view of an early human why one would assume the earth is flat. There's no detectable curve to the ground, and there's no noticeable movement through the air. The ground looks flat, the environment behaves like it's flat, and earth's size is so huge that an early human would have difficulty processing it. At the same time, we flatter ourselves if we think that humankind continued to insist on a flat-earth model until the time of Christopher

Columbus—as if America was somehow responsible for correcting a worldwide misconception of planetary geography. In fact, the ancient Greeks had settled on a model of a spherical earth as early as the fourth century BCE, when it was advocated for by Aristotle. Eratosthenes made an impressively accurate estimate of the earth's circumference in the third century BCE. And while Magellan didn't circumnavigate the planet before Columbus, he did so less than thirty years later.

Nonetheless, there remains a tiny number of persons committed to believing that the earth is flat. Or, rather, there are people who *claim* to be so committed; it is difficult to determine with certainty whether they are sincere in their publicly stated positions, or whether they are engaged in an elaborate ruse for their own amusement. The Flat Earth Society's membership peaked at two thousand but was down to merely two hundred by 1980. The society ceased to exist entirely in 2001, then it was resurrected in 2004. Its website today boasts a membership list of over three hundred members. One might wonder, however, how many joined (for free) simply as a novelty?

Whether sincere or not, the arguments presented by flat-earthers demonstrate wonderful pseudoscience. All the photos and videos of a spherical earth taken from orbit or from the moon? Flat-earthers claim those are faked. The fact that one can board a plane and fly around the world? They insist that the plane is not circumnavigating a globe; it is traversing a circle on the surface of a large disc. How to explain all the forgery and deception? As the head of the Flat Earth Society himself put it, "The space agencies of the world are involved in an international conspiracy to dupe the public for vast profit."[3] All discrepancies are thus erased with the invocation of *conspiracy*—a conspiracy that includes not just the world's space agencies but a surprising number of airline pilots and flight attendants as well.

Other pseudosciences are often treated with a polite smile and a nod, dismissed as harmless nonsense or fun. *Astrologer* or *ghost hunter* aren't common insults, but the pejorative *flat-earther* has become shorthand for a person of inexcusable ignorance, an achievement that's rivaled only by those who deny the Apollo moon landing.

(*Holocaust denier* may be a harsher indictment, but it carries a political aspect, whereas *flat-earther* is simply synonymous with *stupidity*.)

Unlike the belief in astrology, the flat-earth model did not gradually dwindle over the centuries as the science of geography steadily improved. According to Christine Garwood, author of *Flat Earth: The History of an Infamous Idea*, the globe had been widely accepted since antiquity, and it was only in nineteenth-century England that belief in a flat earth experienced a sudden resurgence.[4] The revival was largely the brainchild of Samuel Birley Rowbotham, who published, among other writings, an 1851 leaflet titled *The Inconsistency of Modern Astronomy and Its Opposition to the Scriptures!!* and an 1864 book succinctly titled *Earth Not a Globe*. Rowbotham argued that the earth was a disc with the North Pole at its center, and that the sun and moon were some three thousand miles away (less than the distance from New York to London).[5] He attracted a number of followers, one of whom, Lady Elizabeth Blount, founded the Universal Zetetic Society after his death in 1884. The society published a magazine, *The Earth Not a Globe Review* and, from 1901 to 1904, even published its own journal devoted to the "science" of the flat earth.

Naturally, the "evidence" in favor of the flat-earth hypothesis is flimsy even by pseudoscientific standards. Much of it involves constructing a hypothetical flat world that could, in flat-earthers' estimation, operate in a similar fashion to what is observed on earth. Then it would be necessary to build a conspiracy narrative to explain away the fact that every objective measurement and observation says they're wrong. In 1885, flat-earth advocate William Carpenter penned *One Hundred Proofs That the Earth Is Not a Globe*, which contains such "proofs" as the fact that still water appears level, that rivers do not flow uphill, and that moonlight is not warm.[6] At the midpoint of Carpenter's one-hundred-item list, he cites what he says provides "a store from which to take all the proofs we need": the Bible.[7] Carpenter quotes biblical passages such as one describing the earth as being "stretched out" and declares them to be proof that the earth cannot be a globe.

Carpenter's religious arguments for a flat-earth model were not anomalous; they were frequently the standard. Note again the title of Rowbotham's tract: *The Inconsistency of Modern Astronomy and Its Opposition to the Scriptures!!* The foundation for the modern flat-earth movement is firmly based in the most literal of biblical literalism, where even poetic turns of phrase are taken to be factual representations of astronomical principles.

Flat-earthers are not the only modern pseudoscientists to rely on the Bible for their cosmological models. Closely related, but with slightly more followers, is geocentrism, the belief that the sun revolves around a stationary earth. Geocentrism was disproven far more recently than the flat-earth model, and various thinkers had proposed a heliocentric model of the solar system over the centuries, but it was only after the sixteenth-century work of Nicolaus Copernicus and the seventeenth-century research of Johannes Kepler and Galileo Galilei that it became widely accepted that the sun, not the earth, was at the center of the solar system.

And yet, four hundred years later, this fact still encounters resistance. Flat-earthers may only measure in the hundreds, but studies have shown that one in five Americans still believe the sun revolves around the earth.[8] In a 2011 study, nearly one-third of Russians believed the earth was the center of the solar system.[9] Even a BBC production of a twenty-first-century Sherlock Holmes included a joke about the famed detective not understanding that the earth revolved around the sun.

Scientific ignorance, however, is not the same as pseudoscience, even though it definitely contributes to its popularity. Twenty percent of Americans are not committed to a belief in the geocentric model; that's simply their default, and it doesn't mean they've rejected modern astronomy in the same way flat-earthers dismiss photos taken from the Hubble Telescope.

Truly committed geocentrists are far fewer in number, and, like their flat-earth counterparts, they are inevitably biblical literalists. Their "evidence" has the initial appearance of being better, since their disagreement is over how best to model bodies in motion rather than the plain form of the earth, and so their literature is littered with diagrams and mathematical calculations. In the end, however, their work product is interested first and foremost with proving what they believe to be the biblical model of the solar system.

A modern geocentric organization held an actual conference in 2010: "Galileo Was Wrong: The Church Was Right: First Annual Catholic Conference on Geocentrism." (There does not appear to have been a second annual conference.) The handful of lectures included such topics as "The Biblical Firmament: Outer Space Is Not Empty," "Galileo and the Church: What Really Happened?" and "The Fathers and Exegesis of Scripture on Geocentrism."[10] The book at the center of the conference, also titled *Galileo Was Wrong, the Church Was Right*, was authored by Robert A. Sungenis, PhD. The nature of his doctorate? It was in theology and religious studies and was issued by Calamus International University, an unaccredited correspondence college.

To be fair, as Phil Plait, the "Bad Astronomer" points out, geocentrism is not technically *wrong* as a model. Astronomers regularly map the sky using measurements of latitude and longitude. Establishing what is at the "center" of an astronomical arrangement is simply a matter of what frame of reference to work from, although to say this is "simply" done is disingenuous. A geocentric model of the solar system can be constructed, but it would be horribly complicated once you start working with the solar system as, well, a system. One could construct a model of the solar system with Pluto's moon of Charon at the center, but why? The math works far better if the sun is put at the center.[11]

Indeed, once you expand your scope beyond our immediate solar system and out to the larger Milky Way, the heliocentric model becomes similarly impractical, and astronomers adopt a still different frame of reference. One of the lessons of Einstein's theory of relativity is that there is no one "true" frame of reference. And the problem with geocentrism is that it claims there *is* one true frame of reference, that it has the earth in the center, and that all other frames are wrong. This is not unlike holding a globe upside down with Australia at the top and insisting that any other orientation is incorrect. Unlike geocentrism, an inverted universe works equally as well as the more common model, but it would be foolish to argue that it should be the *only* acceptable model.

The final lecture at the "Galileo Was Wrong" conference would seem to have no relevance to geocentrism at all: "Carbon 14 & Radiometric Dating Show Young Earth." Another geocentric website at fixedearth.com calls itself the Non-Moving Earth and Anti-Evolution Web Page, and states: "Today's cosmology fulfills an anti-Bible *religious* plan disguised as 'science.' The whole scheme from Copernicanism to Big Bangism is a factless lie."[12]

And so we come to the greatest and most pervasive of the pseudosciences grounded in ancient wisdom: creation science and the young-earth hypothesis. For much of written history, the earth was assumed to be only several thousand years old; an age, not accidentally, that more or less coincided with the length of what might pass for civilization. Perhaps unsurprisingly, some of the earlier great civilizations also have some of the earliest recorded dates of creation in their mythologies.

In China, the historian Xu Zheng calculated the creation as being around 39,000 BCE when a cosmic egg was formed out of the chaos. That egg gave birth to Pangu, who then separated the Yin (earth) from the Yang (sky) and spent eighteen thousand years pushing the sky away from the earth.

In Egypt, the chronologies varied from the earth being created as late as 18,000 BCE, to as early as 49,000 BCE; the differing estimates were the result of calculating the lengths of the reigns of Egypt's mythical kings. Egypt similarly had a diverse set of creation myths owing to its distinct cultures and its polytheistic beliefs. In the Heliopolis version of the creation myth, there was originally only a body of chaos of bubbling water called Nu, out of which Ra, the sun god, emerged. The next day, Ra created a fellow god in Shu, the god of air, and Shu's wife, Tefnut, the goddess of moisture. On the third day, Shu and Tefnut gave birth to the earth god Geb and the sky goddess Nut, thus creating the physical universe as we know it.

Ancient Sumeria similarly had a chronology of legendary kings, each of whom were claimed to have ruled for eighteen thousand years or more before the time of a great flood. None of these antediluvian rulers have been archaeologically validated, but their combined tenure would push the Sumerian creation date back to 244,000 BCE. The Babylonians also had creation dates as early as 400,000 BCE, but it is questioned by modern scholars whether these cultures actually believed in these dates, whether the dates have been miscalculated, or whether the Babylonians and Sumerians themselves did not take such claims of antiquity seriously.

The Mayan calendar put the date of creation at August 11, 3114 BCE. In their mythology, the two creator gods attempted to make man in their image, first failing with mud, then failing with wood, before finally forming man out of maize.

The Arabian creation was just before 6000 BCE, not far removed from the creation dates of the other Judeo-Christian religions, and their creation is very much like the one presented in the book of Genesis.

The Genesis account is undoubtedly the most well-known creation story and is the subject of some of the modern world's most dedicated pseudoscience. The two branches of this pseudoscience, distinct but overlapping in principle, are creationism and the young-earth hypothesis. Genesis, the first book of the Bible, begins familiarly enough:

> In the beginning God created the heavens and the earth. Now the earth was formless and empty, darkness was over the surface of the deep, and the Spirit of God was hovering over the waters.

> And God said, "Let there be light," and there was light. God saw that the light was good, and he separated the light from the darkness. God called the light "day," and the darkness he called "night." And there was evening, and there was morning—the first day.

And God said, "Let there be an expanse between the waters to separate water from water." So God made the expanse and separated
the water under the expanse from the water above it. And it was so.
God called the expanse "sky." And there was evening, and there was
morning—the second day.

And God said, "Let the water under the sky be gathered to one
place, and let dry ground appear." And it was so. God called the dry
ground "land," and the gathered waters he called "seas." And God
saw that it was good.[13]

And so on through the creation of the sun and moon on the
fourth day, animals on the fifth day, man on the sixth day, and God
resting on the seventh. The second chapter tells the story of Adam
and Eve, the first humans:

the Lord God formed the man from the dust of the ground and
breathed into his nostrils the breath of life, and the man became a
living being.

Now the Lord God had planted a garden in the east, in Eden; and
there he put the man he had formed. . . .

But for Adam no suitable helper was found. So the Lord God
caused the man to fall into a deep sleep; and while he was sleeping,
he took one of the man's ribs and closed up the place with flesh.
Then the Lord God made a woman from the rib he had taken out
of the man, and he brought her to the man.[14]

According to the Jewish calendar, the creation occurred in 3761
BCE. Early Christians dated the creation of the world to around
5500 BCE, but beginning around the turn of the first millennium, it
became more common to pin the earth's beginning at roughly 4000
BCE. The most famous calculation of creation came from Church
of Ireland archbishop James Ussher, who in the seventeenth century
calculated not only the year of the Genesis account but also the

specific day of the first day of creation: Sunday, October 23, 4004 BCE. The popularity of Ussher's chronology is largely attributable to its being cited in copies of the King James translation of the Bible starting from the earliest years of the eighteenth century.

In the eighteenth and nineteenth centuries, scientists began pushing that date back, with new discoveries in paleontology and geology as their support. When paleontologists began closely studying the fossil record, they also found that their discoveries were far more consistent with a changing earth that was tens of millions of years old, if not older. The several millennia permitted by Genesis were simply not sufficient to accommodate the vast changes that were seen in the paleontological record.

In 1778, French naturalist and cosmologist Georges-Louis Leclerc, Comte de Buffon published *Les Époques de la nature*, in which he discussed his theories for how the solar system was created. In the book, Leclerc postulated that the earth was actually seventy-five thousand years old based on measurements he had taken of cooling iron; he included his estimates as to how long it would have taken for the earth to cool to its present temperature. A few years earlier, the Russian polymath Mikhail Lomonosov (whose achievements include the discovery that Venus has an atmosphere) proposed that the earth was actually hundreds of thousands of years old. But few of the two men's contemporaries followed their thinking.

In the 1860s, Leclerc's idea of using planetary cooling as a marker was borrowed by physicist William Thomson, who later became Lord Kelvin and whose discovery of absolute zero led to the creation of the Kelvin temperature scale. Believing (correctly) that the earth had once been much hotter and that it still had a molten core, Thomson concluded that the planet was between twenty million and four hundred million years old. He subsequently brought the upper limit of the earth's age down to just forty million years, a far less accurate number, as later research would demonstrate. By the turn of the century, though, an estimate of a hundred million years was a standard belief in the field of geology.

With geologists among the pioneers of an old-earth model, scientists in other fields soon followed. In defending his theory of evolution and natural selection, Darwin argued that Thomson's refined estimate was too low, and that more than forty million years must have passed for modern life to have evolved. Simon Newcomb, perhaps America's first great astronomer, calculated that the sun was one hundred million years old, and that same result was independently found by German physicist Hermann von Helmholtz. Others, including Darwin himself, began theorizing about the moon's origin and dating it as over fifty million years old.

Through the discovery of radioactivity around the turn of the twentieth century and the study of radioactive elements and their half-lives, physicists found that the earth was at least one billion years old. In the 1920s, astrophysicists determined that the Andromeda Galaxy was not merely a local nebula but was instead an estimated 2.5 million light-years away; the very light that ancient astronomers studied was older than a mere few thousand years. And it is astronomers and astrophysicists who have estimated the age of the universe as approximately 13.7 billion years old.

What this truncated history shows is that the rejection of a six-thousand-year-old earth is not the product of a single line of science; it is independently rejected by multiple fields of science. Paleontologists could not rectify a young earth with the fossil record. Biologists could not rectify a young earth with the emergence of complex organisms. Geologists' calculations about natural processes produced results of tens or hundreds of millions of years. Physicists studying radioactive elements discovered the earth was at least a billion years old, and today they believe it is approximately 4.5 billion years old. Astronomers pegged the time of the universe's creation as nearly fourteen billion years ago. As French naturalist Jean-Baptiste Lamarck put it: "Oh how very ancient the earth is! And how ridiculously small the ideas of those who consider the earth's age to be 6000 odd years."[15]

Yet what Lamarck thought was ridiculous in 1802 is still believed by many people over two hundred years later. According to a 2011 survey, 46 percent of American Protestant pastors still believe the earth is only about six thousand years old, in spite of all the scientific evidence discussed above.[16] Meanwhile, a 2010 poll found that only 40 percent of Americans believe God created humankind within the last ten thousand years, which therefore means that even fewer than 40 percent believe that the planet is only six thousand years old.[17] Just as was seen among believers in geocentrism and a flat earth, a proven scientific fact about our planet finds itself at odds with a belief related to religion, and religion appears to play a role in how that conflict is resolved.

As is the case with geocentrism and the flat-earth model, the evidence against a young earth is overwhelming, and yet even larger numbers of people are willing to dispute that evidence. And that is where the denialism begins to appear, as those people attempt to rationalize why the geologists, the paleontologists, the physicists, and the astronomers cannot be trusted. One early but not terribly popular attempt at an explanation was provided by Philip Henry Gosse in his 1857 book *Omphalos: An Attempt to Untie the Geological Knot.* Gosse explained away the geological evidence by simply arguing that the world had been born old and had been created with the appearance of millions of years of age, complete with geologic features and fossilized remains of life that never lived.[18]

Gosse's idea is elegant in some ways. It cannot be disproved, since its central postulate is that all physical evidence is unreliable. That means, however, that it is also completely untestable and is thus not very scientific. It failed to garner a lasting following, in part because it required God to act as a universal deceiver, having manufactured a fake history for the world. Similar approaches do, however, crop up in modern creationism, which sometimes explains away the light from distant stars and galaxies by suggesting that the universe was created with that light already midway to earth.

With science unable to vouch for the chronology of the Bible, some found the solution in the Bible itself. Genesis states that Noah's Great Flood covered the earth for a full year, and such a deluge would leave evidence of itself behind. Fossilized remains had been known for centuries, and some early Christians believed that they came from animals killed by the Flood. Around the world there are unusual geological sites, such as inexplicable boulders, which we now know were deposited during the ice ages but which others believed had been moved by the Flood.

Flood geology gained prominence in the nineteenth century in response to mainstream geology's ever-older estimates of the earth's age. Geologists say that the earth's strata demonstrate millions of years of erosion and change? Modern-day flood geologists propose that the Flood did it. Geologists say that the Grand Canyon was formed gradually over the course of millennia? Again, flood geologists say the Flood is responsible. Meanwhile, the fact that geologists cannot find hard evidence of a massive, worldwide flood that covered the globe for a year, or the fact that such an event is scientifically implausible, if not outright impossible? Not a problem. A similar approach is taken with other lines of evidence. Carbon dating shows that living things were in existence some sixty thousand years ago? Not reliable, the flood geologists say. Radioactive decay shows that elements have been in existence for millions or even billions of years? Also not reliable. The level of consistency in test results across the board is simply glossed over.

Distinct from, but very closely related to, the question about the earth's age is the question about how long life, and humankind in particular, has inhabited it. Even as the age of the earth was pushed back into the millions and billions of years, there was resistance to perform a similar recalculation for humanity. Leclerc, one of the first scientists to suggest that the earth was older than a few thousand years, still believed that humankind had inhabited the earth for only six thousand years. Lord Kelvin, while advocating for an earth that was tens of millions of years old at the least, was unconvinced by Darwin's arguments for natural evolution; just as Darwin believed that Kelvin's timeline was wrong because it was too restrictive to allow for evolution, Kelvin was skeptical of evolution because it could not transpire within the time he'd calculated.

By the turn of the twentieth century, with geologists convinced of an earth that was one hundred million years old, and with physicists about to find that it was at least ten times that old, the difficulty of believing in the literal six-day creation account of Genesis was becoming untenable. Those interested in preserving the historicity of the events of Genesis, chapter 1 began exploring theories of old-earth creationism that would keep the events intact without denying the overwhelming evidence that the earth was far, far older than several thousand years. Gap creationism attempted to reconcile the two competing ideas by simply inserting a pause of sorts between the first and second verses of the first chapter of Genesis. In other words, God created the heavens and the earth in one day, then millions of years passed, and then God began creating light and life, and he completed the rest of creation on five successive, twenty-four-hour days. This theory, sometimes called the ruin-reconstruction view, was first described by Scottish theologian Thomas Chalmers in 1814 and gained in popularity later in the century, before being eclipsed by other creationist theories.

One of those theories was that of day-age creationism, which stretched out the six-day chronology not by interrupting the days but by redefining the word *day*. Since the New Testament states that to God, a thousand years is like a day, day-age creationism proposes that each "day" of creation is actually an epoch unto itself. Thus the events of Genesis, chapter 1 are allowed to play out over millions or even billions of years, rather than over a single week. This approach is used by progressive creationists, who believe that God created all species but did so on multiple occasions throughout history. Theistic evolutionists also subscribe to this view, believing in the historicity of evolution but arguing that God was the guiding hand behind the course it took.

Today there are various creationist organizations that advocate for these competing theories. Answers found in Genesis support young-earth creationism, as evidenced by the exhibits of humans living alongside dinosaurs at the Creation Museum in Petersburg, Kentucky. Both the Institute for Creation Research and the Creation Studies Institute similarly support a young-earth view. Websites Reasons to Believe (http://www.reasons.org) and Old Earth Ministries (http://www.old earth.org) reject the young-earth hypothesis in favor of the science supporting an old earth and believe instead in progressive creation. The Discovery Institute may be the most famous creationist organization, promoting intelligent design as an alternate to the theory of evolution but not taking a firm stance on the age of the earth.

What all these organizations have in common is their rejection of evolution as the explanation for life on earth and the disbelief in common descent. They believe that all species were independently created, more or less in their current state, by a supernatural power—namely, God. Some species have suffered extinction, such as the dinosaurs, but radically new species did not evolve from other species. Members of these organizations maintain that there were no common ancestors between humans and primates, or between birds and reptiles, or between elephants and manatees, and so on. Still, even the most committed creationist does not deny that natural selection exists at all. Minor evolutionary changes, commonly dubbed *microevolution* in contrast to the *macroevolution* of common descent, are widely accepted. That is because the existence of microevolution is as plainly obvious as the fact that the earth is round; its effects can be directly observed, even within a single human lifetime.

Microevolution is most easily observed on the bacterial level, where generational growth can be measured in minutes instead of decades. The problem of antibiotic resistance, whereby harmful bacteria become increasingly resilient to antibiotic treatments, and thus disease becomes harder to treat, is a prime example of microevolution through selective pressure. The bacteria with no resistance to antibiotics are killed, while the bacteria with resistance survive and pass on that resistance to a new generation.

The peppered moth is perhaps the most well-known example of microevolution through natural selection in the animal kingdom. Prior to the Industrial Revolution, the vast majority of these British insects had a light, speckled coloration, which allowed them to blend in with the bark of local trees. Only a tiny percentage, less than 1 percent, was dark gray. When the Industrial Revolution arrived and parts of Britain were blanketed in black soot, that light coloration proved to be far less beneficial than a solid, dark coloration, as the moths could more easily be spotted by predators. Dark-colored moths now had the advantage of camouflage, and within a matter of decades, the dark variants constituted 98 percent of the moth population.

A century later, a similarly impressive illustration of natural selection was documented in America, this time with no involvement from human actors. The deer mice of the Sand Hills of Nebraska are light-colored, allowing them to blend in with the sand dunes that were created by the glaciers of the last ice age. Their dark-colored relatives that live on browner soils nearby are similarly well suited for their environment. Harvard University scientists who studied the genes of the mice found that not only did a single gene control the mouse's coloration, but this shift in coloration occurred approximately eight thousand years ago, roughly the time the Sand Hills were formed. Although this change was not directly observed, as it was in the case of the peppered moth, because of the single genetic trigger and the minimal nature of the change, the deer mice, like the moth, represent another straightforward example of microevolution.[19]

An example that's even closer to home is domesticated dogs, whereby all breeds, despite their radically different appearances, are the result of selective breeding over thousands of years, with certain traits being favored over others.

But microevolution differs from macroevolution only in degree, not in type. The theory of evolution does not posit that within a matter of a few generations, selective pressures can turn a wolf into a poodle, much less a primitive hominid into a man. Rather, it states that those gradual evolutions can be drawn out over millions of years, with those subtle microevolutions punctuating the process along the way. Macroevolution is nothing more than a zoomed-out view of many, many years of microevolutionary changes. An animal's color gets a little darker. Its legs get a little longer. Its beak or its teeth get a little more specialized. It gets a little more or a little less hairy. String enough of those little changes together over a few million years, and the animal at the end won't much resemble its original ancestor.

Instead of focusing on the strong consensus across multiple scientific fields, both young-earth and old-earth creationists act as denialists and zero in on the unanswered questions and perceived anomalies in the evidence. They try to rebut the scientific consensus with their own arguments, typically dressing up their rebuttals with a sheen of scientific language and presentation. But underneath that gloss is nothing more than pseudoscience. As with most modern denialists, they recognize the power and persuasiveness of scientific thought and thus hope to appropriate that image for themselves. Organizations like the Discovery Institute exist for the express purpose of justifying the "science" in "creation science" by retaining supposed experts and publishing literature and taking the dissenting side in public-policy arguments over the teaching of evolution in schools.

Their lack of scientific rigor is demonstrated in their research supporting their hypotheses, in that there is little to no such research. The Discovery Institute website proudly lists fifty "scientific publications supporting the theory of intelligent design."[20] A review of the papers themselves, however, shows that they don't *support* a theory of intelligent design so much as they object to the theory of Darwinian evolution. They ask questions, they try to poke holes, and on occasion they may actually conduct an experiment.

But as "science," it's a failure. They have a hypothesis, but their efforts are less concerned with bolstering that hypothesis than with trying to tear down a competing one. If one assumes upfront that there are two, and only two, possible explanations for life as we know it, then that could be a partially valid approach. But such an assumption is unmerited. Demonstrating that there are unexplained aspects to evolution doesn't prove that evolution is factually incorrect, and it certainly doesn't prove that intelligent design is correct.

Feng Shui

Not all "ancient wisdom" pseudoscience plays out on a cosmic scale, nor do all types rely on passages from the Bible. Other pseudosciences have their origins in ancient Eastern mysticism, and some are even still viewed favorably by portions of the scientific establishment in that part of the world.

One such example is feng shui, which translates as "wind-water." It is an ancient Chinese philosophy that promotes living in harmony with one's environment and surrounding oneself with positive influences rather than negative ones. And that's all fine; it's well recognized that colors can affect people differently, and, depending on the interior design, a room can feel welcoming or distancing. But traditional feng shui also teaches that locations have a mystical energy called qi that can be detected and manipulated by persons skilled in feng shui. By positioning furniture in special arrangements, by designing a building to face a particular direction, or by having doors in certain places, feng shui "experts" work alongside architects in China, informing them how buildings should be constructed.

To assist in their work, feng shui practitioners use a "bagua," a chart that attempts to break down one's life into eight areas: wealth, fame, relationships, family, career, and so on. Apart from the basic psychological aspects of design, though, there is no proven legitimacy of the "energies" that feng shui claims to massage and manipulate. Mystical energies are notoriously hard to detect scientifically, and believers often have excuses for why that's so. So proving or disproving the existence of qi in this context is impossible; the most that can be said is that no objective instruments have yet been able to detect qi.

At the same time, however, a practice like feng shui can be tested fairly easily. Feng shui does not depict itself like the art of advertising, where different minds may have different but equally persuasive ways of promoting a product. Feng shui says that there is an optimal way to design a building or room, and that the invisible energies provide the necessary information for finding that optimal arrangement. So even if the existence of these energies cannot be tested independently, the practice of feng shui can still be tested through comparison. Multiple feng shui practitioners could be asked separately to analyze a particular location, and their respective explanations could be compared to see if they agree.

There is a possibly apocryphal account of a study of speaking in tongues along these lines. As recounted, a person who could supposedly speak in tongues was recorded, and the tape was played to several people who could reportedly translate such speech. The translations varied radically. Such an experiment would seem to be small and imperfect, but such a study design could be utilized to examine a supposedly spiritual power. While there do not appear to have been any similar formal studies performed on feng shui, the TV show *Bullshit!* featuring Penn & Teller conducted a casual test of feng shui with three experts. The results were unsurprising: the three practitioners not only disagreed but also contradicted each other. Such a small and uncontrolled test is far from conclusive, and the failure of the test participants is not the same as proof that no one can sense the qi energies. But with no scientific evidence that such energies can be sensed or that qi even exists, the burden should be on the practitioners to prove that what they're doing is real and is not just good design advice wrapped in a veil of mysticism.

Traditional Medicine

Another category of "ancient wisdom" pseudoscience is traditional, or folk, medicine. It's important to note upfront that not all traditional medicine is ineffective, much less pseudoscientific. Much traditional medicine was the product of generations of trial and error, of testing treatments and remedies to see which ones worked and which ones didn't. In some cases, these treatments gained a cultural foothold because they were actually medically effective. They may have had an active ingredient that was medicinally valuable but that was unknown to the primitive treatment provider.

On the other hand, there are traditional treatments that were retained despite having no proven benefit. Perhaps there was a spiritual or ritual element that encouraged the use of a particular medicine, like the philosophies that underlie acupuncture. Perhaps a treatment produced effects that were confused with healing in a prehistoric variation on "treating the symptom."

More than anything else, however, there is the high risk of confirmation bias. When people in prescientific societies fell ill for various reasons, they received similar treatments, and some would recover and some would not. The difference between the two could be as simple as an infected wound, an obvious distinction to modern medicine but unrecognizable before the germ theory of disease. Those who received the medicine and recovered were remembered as testimonials to the effectiveness of the treatment; those who received the medicine but died were overlooked. That's confirmation bias in action: remember the hits, forget the misses.

Modern medicine had to distinguish between those traditional medicines that legitimately worked and those that had merely gained an undeserved reputation for working. And over the past century or more, such experiments have been conducted and continue to be performed. Even when the traditional medicine may not be particularly potent, it can still lead to the discovery of an active ingredient that, when concentrated, can offer new forms of relief. But it's through such testing that the modern world determines the efficacy of traditional medicine, not through the word of mouth of prior generations. If the medicine works, it ought to be able to demonstrate its efficacy in controlled studies. And if it fails, and fails repeatedly, then it's all too likely that it never worked in the first place and that the folk legends about its medicinal effectiveness were no more reliable than folk legends about the origins of the universe.

That's true across the board when it comes to "ancient wisdom" pseudoscience. Earlier generations may have had valid and lasting insights on philosophy or ethics or even politics. But when it comes to science, there's little reason to trust their beliefs over modern discoveries.

MYSTERIOUS CREATURES

Another branch of pseudoscience includes claims that may be inspired by ancient beliefs but that are much more concerned with contemporary events and firsthand investigations. These are the Bigfoot hunters, the ghost hunters, the alien investigators, and the like.

Their work isn't suitable for the lab, and they fancy themselves to be explorers rather than scientists. Unlike their peers, who advocate for things like creationism or alternative medicine, these types of believers typically feel that science isn't wrong on any particular subject so much as it is incomplete. They aren't dismissive of the scientific method; they often behave as if they're trying to respect it.

On the flip side, this branch of pseudoscience is also the most difficult to declare as "wrong." Medicinal treatments and paranormal abilities can be evaluated in controlled studies, and although they cannot be declared impossible, their repeated failure in the lab serves to discredit their effect. Alternate theories of astronomy or physics or chemistry can be tested against observations of the physical universe, and a researcher can determine whether they're capable of making accurate predictions. But when it comes to ghosts or aliens, often the most that can be said is that there's no positive evidence to support their existence. It's impossible to prove that there aren't spirits who survive beyond death, or that there aren't extraterrestrials capable of visiting earth, or that there aren't unphotographed "monsters" hiding from our eyes. Singular claims and events can be explained away, but the underlying belief is not so easily impeachable. Nonetheless, it is the continued belief and commitment in spite of the lack of positive evidence that earns these fields the pseudoscience label.

Cryptozoology

Cryptozoology might well be the most scientific of the pseudosciences. Bernard Heuvelmans, who coined the term *cryptozoology* in the 1950s, held a doctorate in zoology. His first book, *On the Track of Unknown Animals*, is one of the central texts of cryptozoology, and Heuvelmans helped establish at least three major cryptozoological organizations during his lifetime.

"The science of hidden animals" was Heuvelmans's definition of cryptozoology. His first book addressed such mythic monsters as the Mokele-mbembe, the Yeti, and the Loch Ness Monster, and a second book, *In the Wake of the Sea Serpents*, examined its title subject in detail. These and other undiscovered animals are the focus of cryptozoological research. The common term for these "hidden animals" is *cryptids*: species, of plants or animals, that are rumored to exist but have not yet been confirmed with physical evidence and that are not generally accepted by scientific consensus. The supporting evidence for a cryptid's existence is typically anecdotal witness accounts, although there is also occasional circumstantial evidence, such as the supposed hair or footprints of a Bigfoot.

On the more realistic end of the cryptozoological spectrum, where it meets serious scientific zoology, are recently extinct animals that some argue may still be alive, like the ivory-billed woodpecker or the Tasmanian tiger. These animals definitively did exist in the very recent past, but there's not yet any firm confirmation that any are alive today. Some ornithologists have reported seeing the presumed-extinct ivory-billed woodpecker within the last decade, but subsequent searches have failed to find proof that the species still lives. It's not pseudoscientific to keep an open mind about such surviving populations or to studiously investigate credible sightings, as it is certainly possible that the woodpeckers might still live, but the evidence has yet to support their continued existence. If one were to insist on their survival, in spite of that lack of evidence, that is where pseudoscientific traits start to emerge.

Considerably less probable, and more representative of the pseudoscience of cryptozoology, are claims of surviving enclaves of long-extinct animals, like plesiosaurs in Loch Ness or dinosaurs in the Congo. Less probable still are unknown species like Bigfoot or sea serpents, which are biological in nature but are unlike any known species. At the most speculative end are paranormal and supernatural creatures like Mothman, the Jersey Devil, or werewolves, where cryptids take on magical traits and abilities.

The potential for merit in cryptozoology is that new species of animals, even large animals, are still being discovered by science from time to time. Western scientists did not confirm the existence of the gorilla until 1847, and the mountain gorilla wasn't discovered until 1902. The giant panda was discovered in 1869, but it wasn't until 1936 that one was actually captured alive. Europeans had heard stories of the African unicorn, but the okapi, a relative of the giraffe that looks like an antelope/zebra hybrid, was recognized as an actual species only in 1901, after a carcass specimen was brought to London. (The okapi is the mascot of Heuvelmans's International Society of Cryptozoology.) The Komodo dragon wasn't discovered until 1912. The coelacanth, a lobe-finned fish thought to have been extinct since the Cretaceous period, was famously discovered alive in 1938 off the South African coast. Similar discoveries continue to be made today, although the new animals are rarely as singularly unique as the gorilla, panda, or okapi. A new species of giant peccary was located in Brazil in the 2000s, and the dwarf manatee was discovered in the Amazon in 2007.

Cryptozoologists point to these animals as proof that their claims are not baseless and that hidden creatures do exist. That fact does lend some credence to the mission of cryptozoology, but there are critical differences between the real science of these new discoveries and the pseudoscience of cryptozoology.

While some of these animals were rumored to exist prior to confirmation, it was, in every case, the discovery of an actual body that cemented their status as a real species. Not local legends, not distant sightings, not a set of curious footprints. It was a corpse, a live specimen, or a reasonably intimate and credible firsthand encounter. Cryptids, by contrast, are consistently supported only by anecdotal evidence, and anecdotal evidence is notoriously unreliable. "Anecdotes do not make a science," says sociologist Frank J. Sulloway.[21] Anecdotes can be a good starting point for more serious research, but when investigations fail to turn up any better evidence, particularly when such investigations are as intensive as searches for Bigfoot or the Loch Ness Monster, that continued failing serves to undermine the credibility of those anecdotes.

On the other hand, if those anecdotes eventually lead to a real breakthrough, then science is accomplished. The giant squid was a subject of sea lore for centuries, but it was not until the mid-1800s that actual specimens were recovered. In an instant, the giant squid went from sailor's myth to recognized reality. This may be the closest example of the discovery of a truly mythic creature, even though it predated the creation of cryptozoology by nearly a century. One major reason the giant squid went undiscovered for so long was because it was difficult to locate specimens. Corpses of giant squids would sink to the ocean floor, leaving little physical evidence that could be obtained or preserved. It was only when corpses began washing up on shores that the squid was confirmed to be real.

Many cryptids should not be so difficult to find, or the circumstances of their existence may be highly improbable. A species of Bigfoot would require a sustainable population size, adequate food sources, and some form of habitat. In other words, the bodies of dead Bigfoots ought to be discoverable; this should be true in areas of the United States that are reasonably well populated and well traveled.

The Yeti of the Himalayan Mountains has a better excuse for evading direct observation because of the harsh weather and limited possible observers, but those same conditions also raise significant questions about the Yeti's food source. How could bands of giant ape-men survive in a region so bereft of nutrition?

Scotland's Loch Ness supposedly is home to a giant sea creature, one that in modern times is often depicted as a plesiosaur.

Coelacanths surviving in the oceans lend support to the idea that prehistoric monsters could be living in other waters, but, while reasonably large, Loch Ness is no ocean. There is limited space to hold a sustainable population of plesiosaurs, a population that also manages to avoid leaving any concrete evidence.

These are the sorts of problems that cryptozoologists tend to explain away but that science cannot ignore. Animals need food, they make tracks, they have habitats, and they die and leave corpses. When there is no credible and compelling evidence of any of these activities, there is a problem with the hypothesis that an unknown creature exists. There is nothing wrong with continuing to search for the unknown, but resources expended on any one endeavor are resources that can't be spent on another. There are assuredly more valuable things to be discovered in the Amazon rain forest, and an expedition there is far more likely to bear fruit than the umpteenth submarine dive into Loch Ness.

There are unproven animals that continue to divide scientists and are still waiting to be officially confirmed. Two photos taken in the jungles of Borneo in 2003 appear to show a small dark-red mammal with a long tail, dubbed a "cat-fox."[22] Some scientists believed it was a new species, while others saw in the photos nothing more than a civet or a giant squirrel. Without a body or remains to test, the truth about the animal is uncertain, but the pictures are solid evidence that can justify further investigation. This is how real, new species are discovered. Stories inspire searches, which turn up trace evidence, which leads to hard evidence, which ultimately results in locating a new animal. And if the evidence trail falls apart, then the initial hypothesis of "Creature X exists" either gets modified or abandoned.

Cryptozoology isn't fond of declaring its hypotheses to be wrong. The modern mythology of the Loch Ness Monster began in the 1930s, and there have since been almost eighty years of unproductive research, producing no bones, no living specimens, and no clear photographs or video. Eventually, the decades of fruitless searches support the conclusion that there is no monster.

UFOlogy

Cryptozoology maintains its near-scientific status not only because it approximates some of the methods of scientific inquiry, but also because its subject matter is at least conceivable, if not plausible. If you're hunting for a Bigfoot, you have a pretty good idea of what you're looking for: a physical mammal bearing some resemblance to real mammals that ought to leave behind evidence of its existence. And the sorts of evidence can be readily anticipated: physical remains, hair samples, footprints, habitats, and so on. In other words, the sorts of evidence scientists look for in hunting other animals.

This is why UFOlogists and alien hunters rank below cryptozoologists when it comes to the "mysterious creatures" variety of pseudoscience. The biggest factor in their favor is that it is quite possible, if not likely, that extraterrestrial beings could exist elsewhere in the galaxy. The likelihood that there is an alien population somewhere in the universe is arguably higher than the likelihood that there is a population of prehistoric monsters living in a particular Scottish lake. But just because aliens may exist somewhere else does not mean that they are interacting with humans, are visiting earth, or have ever visited earth. And yet it's precisely that kind of contact that alien hunters are concerned with.

Because extraterrestrials are obviously not terrestrial, the kind of evidence they would leave behind is more ambiguous than what would be expected of a simple secret species. They may not have skeletons. Their bodies or their bodies' by-products may not be recognizable as such. And if they are intelligent enough to travel the galaxy, they may be at least as good as a Boy Scout troop at cleaning up after themselves.

On the other hand, if aliens have in fact traversed the galaxy to visit the earth, it's curious that they have not been more conspicuous. They certainly haven't made any overt and public attempts at contact, such as landing a ship in a populated city. Some people, of course, claim that they *have* been conspicuous, as evidenced by the number of supposed abductions; then again, as Carl Sagan noted based on the number of alleged abductions, aliens ought to be visiting earth so frequently that "it's surprising more of the neighbors haven't noticed."[23]

In particular, people who promote theories of alien contact necessarily demand a greater evidentiary burden than do cryptozoologists. When the claim is that aliens are interacting or communicating with humans, or that they've done so in the past, it follows that they should leave concrete evidence of that interaction. And yet, the "evidence" that is trotted out in support of extraterrestrial interaction is even more pitiful than Yeti footprints or blurry photos of lake monsters. Supposed alien abductees will sometimes offer up tiny "implants" that they claim were placed in their bodies by their abductors. But none of these implants have stood up to any level of scrutiny. Not a single one has ever been shown to be the highly advanced piece of technology an alien-tracking device would have to be. Instead, if anything is offered up for inspection, it inevitably turns out to be mundane; an ordinary shard of metal, not an unexplainable technological marvel.

Just as no one has produced a Bigfoot corpse, no one has yet produced an alien corpse—or any part thereof. The lack of this particular form of evidence is not especially damning, except in the context of abductions. If aliens were actually intruding into people's homes on a regular basis and experimenting on them, one might imagine that they would eventually visit someone who strongly believes in his Second Amendment rights. But abduction stories never end with the alien being shot or bleeding as it flees; there is inevitably the special pleading of how the aliens prevented retaliation, usually by rendering their victim incapable of moving.

As Carl Sagan discussed at length in *The Demon-Haunted World*, such incapacitation of nighttime victims for the purposes of exploitation is not a new phenomenon.[24] Rather, it has a long history in multiple cultures, usually taking the form of a witch or demon who sits on a person's chest in the night and prevents him from moving.

Modern reports of alien abductions closely mirror these ancient myths, only with a science fiction twist. But the underlying cause is neither mystical nor extraterrestrial; the symptoms are the consequence of sleep paralysis, a condition in which a person's mind regains a degree of consciousness while the body remains paralyzed in its natural dream state. Hallucinations can also accompany this mismatch in body signals, and if a person has been culturally primed to believe in demons or witches or aliens, that can influence his internal experience.

Much like blurry monster photos, there is no alien evidence more prevalent than that of UFO photos or videos. Many of these can be explained upon review, but some manage to retain their "unidentified" label and are touted as being strong evidence of alien visitors. Being unidentified, however, is not at all the same thing as being shown to be not of this earth. If something is unidentified, it simply means we can't conclusively determine *what* it is. This is especially understandable when the footage shows nothing more than a dark spot in the distance or a glowing light in the nighttime sky.

Photos of UFOs are an excellent example of recognizing and appreciating the larger context of evidence for a suspect claim. First, consider what is implied by a photograph or video of a UFO. It says that the UFO can be captured on film, obviously. In most cases (except those where the image was captured accidentally), it also means that the UFO is visible to the naked eye. It used to be argued that the poor photographs were simply an unfortunate result of people being unable to adequately record the supposedly much more convincing things they witnessed.

Today, however, cameras are omnipresent, such that nearly every person with a cell phone is capable of recording high-resolution images at a moment's notice. Where, then, are the high-resolution pictures and videos of alien spacecraft? The improvement in technology should have resulted in improved pictures of UFOs, of YouTube® being flooded with convincing footage of flying saucers; if anything, such advances have led to a loss of interest.

The alien hunter's explanation for failing to provide proof is usually an exercise in special pleading: the UFOs don't stay in sight long enough, they have cloaking devices, or they've simply stopped visiting. The same sort of special pleading is similarly essential in explaining why human eyewitnesses can spot flying saucers, but thousands of orbiting satellites cannot.

Ghost Hunting and Angels

World cultures are replete with supernatural and mystical creatures, beings that transcend the natural order in a way that ordinary cryptozoological creatures don't: dragons, fairies, werewolves, succubi, and so on. Modern fiction may love vampires, but it's rare to find an educated person who believes they're real.

Some legends live on due to their cultural cache more than anything. In Iceland, for instance, enough people still believe in the elf-esque Huldufólk that an aluminum company reportedly had to have a government expert inspect their property and certify that it was elf-free.[25] Meanwhile, most paranormal creatures don't command literal belief anymore, since the contemporary public is more inclined to believe in science fiction aliens than in mystical monsters. Two significant exceptions remain, however. The first are angels, particularly those of the "guardian angel" variety that interact directly with worldly affairs. But the very nature of angelic beings doesn't lend itself to testing or investigation; they don't leave physical evidence. There are no "angel hunters," and the only proof offered of their present-day existence is faith and personal anecdotes. Such anecdotes can be scrutinized in the same way as other anecdotes of mysterious encounters, but there's little more to do than that in evaluating angel stories. And without phony investigations, there's not really any angel pseudoscience to speak of.

On the other hand, ghosts have managed to retain their popularity to the point that there are numerous televisions shows like *Ghost Hunters* devoted to folks who engage in the pseudoscientific pursuit of ethereal spirits.

Communicating and interacting with the dead are ancient activities that have evolved over time. For centuries, the techniques employed were mystical and spiritual, reaching out to the dead through séances and other rituals. In more modern times, such efforts at necromancy have become more associated with morally neutral psychic powers than with sinister mysticism. And attempts to prove the existence of ghosts have turned to technology to build a pseudoscientific foundation.

Whereas mythical creatures and aliens are at least corporeal and fit within a naturalistic worldview, ghosts are a different creature altogether. The hypothesis that the disembodied spirits of the deceased continue to observe and interact with the world proposes something that is well outside anything established to be true. However, so long as the hypothesis is that these spirits do, in fact, interact with the physical world or with people in it, then that provides an opportunity for that hypothesis to be tested.

What is the expected evidence in support of such a hypothesis? In the case of straightforward communication, strong evidence might be the relaying of information that only a deceased person would know. If it's alleged that the ghost can physically interact with the world, then tests can be constructed. Ghost hunters, however, don't conduct this sort of science. They like to carry equipment that measures heat signatures or electromagnetic fields, and they like to broadcast when they've found some anomalous reading that they suggest is evidence of a specter. But such "investigations" skip over an incredibly important scientific question: are ghosts associated with heat signatures or electromagnetic fields? Ghost hunters take that as a given, but it's an unmerited assumption, such as when a creationist assumes there are only two opposing explanations for life. Even if it can be proved beyond a reasonable doubt that there is no known source for an electromagnetic pattern, there is still absolutely no evidence that the *actual* source is the disembodied spirit of a deceased person.

Beyond onsite investigations, spectral pseudoscience is also heavily reliant on anecdotal evidence, such as first-person accounts of encounters with ghostly presences that, like compelling-looking flying saucers, never manage to be captured on tape. Eyewitness accounts are already unreliable and subject to all manner of biasing factors, and those are compounded in the context of a ghost story. The witness may be frightened, confused, or tired, and the location is liable to be dark or unfamiliar. Pareidolia can turn slight sounds and shadows into spirits. And ghosts are an area where hoaxers and charlatans have a long and rich history.

Ultimately, all claims of mysterious creatures are subject to the same sort of null hypothesis: until good evidence is presented demonstrating that they *do* exist, it is presumed that they do not. The burden is always on the person making the novel claim, and that burden is not met by merely asking questions or creating doubt. It is the cryptozoologist's responsibility to show that discovered hair fibers belong to a human-like primate; it is not the skeptic's responsibility to determine what animal those fibers actually belong to. It is the UFOlogist's burden to produce a clear photograph of a spaceship; it is not the skeptic's burden to explain what normal phenomena the blurry picture depicts. It is the ghost hunter who must demonstrate a proven causal relationship between ghosts and heat signatures; it is not the skeptic who must point to an alternate heat source.

PARANORMAL POWERS

In the 1984 comedy *Ghostbusters*, Bill Murray plays a character named Peter Venkman, who claims to hold doctorates in psychology and parapsychology. In one of the film's first scenes, Dr. Venkman is seen testing the psychic abilities of two college students, holding up flashcards and asking them to identify what is depicted on the side facing away from them. If an incorrect guess is made, Venkman will administer an electric shock. The scene is played for laughs (particularly because Venkman flirts with the cute female student by telling her that all her guesses are correct), but parapsychological research has a long, rich, and not terribly illustrious history.

While the scientific revolution was under way in the nineteenth and early twentieth centuries, and innovations were being made into discovering the origins of life and the operations of the physical world, some researchers turned their attention toward the study of psychic abilities: telepathy, hypnosis, telekinesis, extrasensory perception, and so on.

At the time, this was not as absurd a mission as it may seem. People had long made claims of such paranormal abilities, and the newly refined methods of scientific investigation allowed for such claims to be studied and scrutinized. Independent societies were created to study parapsychological abilities, and universities as prestigious as Stanford and Duke conducted research into ESP and psychokinesis. Over time, however, the results that came back proved to be disappointingly consistent: claims of such paranormal powers did not stand up to scientific scrutiny. In blinded and controlled studies, test subjects were unable to demonstrate any measurable psychic skills. Parapsychology research largely folded under these findings, much as Dr. Venkman's department was shuttered at the beginning of *Ghostbusters*.

That demonstration of good science, though, gave way over time to pseudoscience, as some researchers refused to accept negative results. They believed more strongly in the supposed powers than in the experimental results that showed no evidence for such powers. And so pseudoscientists pressed on, determined to find justification for their beliefs.

Just as there can be a strong emotional appeal to the existence of aliens or ghosts, so, too, is there an understandable appeal to the reality of innate superpowers. Telekinesis, the ability to move things with one's mind, is only a step away from the ability to fly like Superman. The discovery of such untapped potential would be a true scientific breakthrough, the sort of revolutionary work that could quite literally change the world.

That sort of new paradigm is what the US government was hoping for as it continued to conduct psychic research even into the 1970s. As famously (if humorously) documented in Jon Ronson's 2004 book *The Men Who Stare at Goats*, the US military conducted experiments in psychokinesis and remote viewing, hoping that if such powers could be proven and field-tested, they could then be used in the context of battle. Remote viewing would allow a spy to watch the enemy up close with no risk of being observed. And if a soldier could mentally stop the heart of a goat, why not the heart of an enemy soldier? Needless to say, the military's efforts to weaponize psychic powers failed, and the government expended time and resources to discover the same thing research scientists had concluded decades earlier.

The reason that research into claims of paranormal powers was so popular a century ago is that they are eminently testable. Just as Peter Venkman could use flashcards to gauge a subject's psychic powers, so, too, can experiments be devised to test for telepathy, psychokinesis, or ESP. Unlike the need to observe an alien or a chupacabra in the wild, paranormal abilities can be evaluated in the laboratory. It requires only a willing subject and a solid test protocol.

Unfortunately, most such experiments often lack the subject and/or the test protocol. The James Randi Educational Foundation (JREF) has long offered a $1 million prize to the applicant who can demonstrate a paranormal ability under controlled circumstances. The applicant is entitled to participate in the designing of the test protocol, not to make it less neutral but so that the test is fair and achievable. It is also agreed upon beforehand what will constitute a successful demonstration; correctly guessing the suit of a random playing card 55 percent of the time is above the natural odds, but it is hardly compelling evidence of psychic abilities. These JREF tests are also designed with an eye toward preventing trickery or sleight of hand. To date, no one has even made it past the first round.

While the JREF has the necessary test protocols, its offered reward is somehow insufficient to attract the interest of the world's most popular psychic and paranormal practitioners. They claim their powers are real, but they hesitate to submit themselves to a controlled evaluation. Sometimes the excuses are the same sorts of special pleadings that failed applicants fall back on: their powers can't be tested, their powers don't work around skeptics, the demonstration of their powers requires that certain test controls not be employed. Others use external excuses, claiming they don't need the money or that they don't trust the JREF to be fair.

So as skeptics have experiments in need of more participants, pseudoscientific researchers have the opposite problem: they don't lack for test subjects, but the tests they employ are inevitably flawed. The sorts of mistakes they make are commonly repeated, and recognizing those types of errors is a huge benefit in spotting bad tests in all sorts of pseudoscience. In one way or another, they fail to rigorously control for variables that can bias the study.

One basic error is the failure to have a control group to compare against. If the results can be influenced by anything other than pure, random chance, then a test subject's performance must be compared against some baseline. And because it cannot always be determined in advance whether as-yet-unidentified factors will influence an outcome, the importance of a control is all the more important.

Another basic error is the failure to fully blind the test subject. "Psychics" employ a technique called cold reading, whereby they claim to see a person's past, future, or even present. There are all manner of visual "tells" that a person gives off about his life simply by interacting with the psychic—his age, his manner of dress, his accent. Does he have a wedding ring? Does he have scars or tattoos? How do his shoes look? These details are the sorts of things that a fictional detective like Sherlock Holmes would study to draw conclusions about a person; the psychic uses them the same way but attributes those conclusions to mystic powers.

But cold reading doesn't stop with appearances. Questions can be posed to elicit information from the visitor. When John Edward hosted his psychic show on the Sci-Fi Channel, it was a daily demonstration of this sort of cold reading. With an audience of potential "hits," he could claim to be hearing from someone's relative who died of, say, stomach cancer, and at least one audience member would likely think he was referring to them personally. He would continue with non-distinct references: names that began with certain letters or references to generic life events. He knew he could rely on confirmation bias to ensure that the audience would remember when he was almost right and to ignore the times he was totally wrong. (And the miracle of television editing helped to cut down on the latter for home audiences.)

Those sorts of tricks of the trade have to be ensured against in a test of such supposed powers. And all too often in pro-pseudoscience tests, they're not.

Less obvious, but equally disastrous for the test, is the failure to adequately blind the other participants. Cold reading depends not just on evaluating the person but also on gauging his or her responses. And even if a person doesn't respond verbally, facial expressions or changes in posture can be enough to provide clues to someone skilled in reading body language. Reactions of surprise or disappointment can subtly hint at what someone is thinking.

Tests of paranormal powers also need to account for a variable that other scientific tests often don't have to: the potential for fraud. Demonstrations of psychokinesis in particular are ripe for trickery, even under close observation. Magic tricks, after all, manage to create the illusion of improbable events through misdirection and sleight of hand. When talk show host Johnny Carson had psychic Uri Geller on the *Tonight Show,* he provided Geller with a prepared tray of items to test him. Geller had achieved fame by claiming to bend spoons with his mind, but when provided with spoons by Carson, he declared that he wasn't feeling "strong" that night and so was unable to perform the same miraculous demonstrations he was known for. Much like a magician, when he hadn't provided his own props, he couldn't perform his tricks.

When all these factors are accounted for, and a thorough test is constructed, demonstrations of paranormal abilities inevitably fail.

ALTERNATIVE MEDICINE

Medicine, as we know it, was largely invented in the last few centuries, with such revolutions as the germ theory of disease, the invention of vaccines, and the development of antibiotics and pharmacological drugs. And while policymakers debate the ethics of the medical industry or the availability of medical services, one thing cannot be denied: modern medicine is effective. It's not perfect, and it's always improving, but it is immeasurably better than what passed for medical treatment for our ancestors.

Some dissenters, however, see modern medicine not as a branch of science interested in discovery but as an elite club that wishes to exclude "alternative" treatments for illnesses and maladies. They may promote the use of "traditional" medicines, as discussed earlier in this chapter. Or they may favor treatment methods that have been proposed only recently. But modern medicine does incorporate new treatments all the time . . . if they work. One of the central tenets of modern medicine is that it is evidence-based; medicines and treatments are adopted for use if they can objectively demonstrate their effectiveness in studies.

"Alternative" medicines run the gamut from ancient therapies to modern supplements, but the thing they have in common, the thing that puts them all under the "alternative" umbrella, is that they *don't* demonstrate any effectiveness when studied.

Occasionally a new study finds some benefit to an alternative treatment; acupuncture is a common subject for such claims. Headlines may even state that acupuncture was shown to provide some sort of relief. However, what study after study has shown with regard to acupuncture is that while the insertion of needles can provide some subjective relief (reducing complaints of pain, increasing relaxation), it performs no better than a placebo.

Understanding placebos is essential to understanding the fallacies behind alternative medicines. It is well recognized in medicine that a person given even a completely ineffectual drug or treatment can still report improvement. The mere act of taking a drug that is said to be medicinal, or receiving a therapy that is said to be helpful, can provide perceived or even actual benefits. For instance, a person who takes a sugar pill but who is told that it will slow or increase her blood pressure can experience an actual change in blood pressure because her brain is telling her body to expect that.

The mechanisms of the placebo effect are less important here than what the effect itself means: if the mere act of taking a drug can create a medicinal effect, then a truly functional and effective drug has to perform better in testing than a fake and useless drug. And so all tests of medical treatments involve control groups who are told that they are getting something that works, in order to provide a baseline for comparison. If a new blood pressure drug is no better at reducing blood pressure than a sugar pill is, then it's an ineffective drug.

With a lot of alternative medicines, creating a control is not as easy as handing out fake pills. For example, anyone performing acupuncture has to create the illusion of having needles inserted. In a 2009 study on acupuncture, it was found that subjects received some relief for pain in their lower backs but no more relief than control patients who were gently poked with toothpicks. The toothpick patients had the personal time with a treatment provider, the relaxing time on the table, and the physical sensation of pinpricks, and that was enough to equal the "alternative medicine" of acupuncture.

To some people who read the study, that may have sounded like a successful result for acupuncture; people felt somewhat better after being pricked. But the medicinal theory is not just about the insertion of needles; it also claims that the needles must be inserted in special places on the body, unique acupuncture points that are located along meridians where the body's qi, or energy, flows.

Tests of acupuncture have also been conducted to evaluate whether the designated acupuncture points truly are special, if they provide a benefit that isn't produced if the needles are inserted in other places on the body. The result is negative. It doesn't matter where the needles are placed; whether along the "meridians" or not, the same minimal effect is found. Thus, not only is the medicinal value of acupuncture called into question, but the underlying belief in special energy points is similarly undermined.

Like acupuncture and its qi, many alternative medicines are premised on questionable claims about how the body works on a basic level. Chiropractic claims that the entire body can be treated through the manipulation of the spine. Reflexology makes a similar claim but substitutes other parts of the body, like the feet or hands. Naturopathy is built around the notion of vague bodily "energies," not entirely unlike the Chinese qi, which it claims can be affected through various practices. Reiki takes that notion further and is little more than faith healing and hand waving, purporting to massage qi through the direct manipulation of a person's aura.

Alternative medicines also make unproven claims about how science itself works. Homeopathy is the most notorious for this, with its premise that maladies can be treated with diluted samples of the same element that causes the illness itself. Moreover, homeopathy says that the treatment becomes more powerful the more the element is diluted; homeopathic "medicines" sold in stores are in fact so diluted that they don't contain even a single molecule of their supposed active ingredient. But homeopathic proponents claim that water has a "memory" that magically retains the properties of the ingredients that are no longer in it.

So while alternative medicines are disputed on their effectiveness, many of them are also questionable because of the premises they're built on. When one is evaluating the merits of an alternative-medicine claim, asking whether it works is only one possible question. It's also important to ask whether its theory of healing is feasible or even realistic. Evidence-based medicine is built on a foundation of biological and chemical interactions in the body, which can be isolated and measured. Alternative medicine, all too often, is built on foundations of meridians and qi and other quasi-magical properties of the body that have never been shown to exist at all.

Admittedly, it's not essential to know what the precise mechanism of healing is in order for a treatment to be proven effective. If a blinded and controlled study shows that a treatment produces a measurable benefit, then further research can be conducted into *how* that benefit is produced. The problem with so many alternative medicines isn't that their mechanisms aren't proven; it's that they run completely counter to our understanding of biology and anatomy. Shy of a sudden revolution in those fields, alternative treatments are incredibly unlikely to work for the reasons they claim to work. Some, like Reiki, involve such little actual activity that if the mechanism (for example, manipulating the aura) is groundless, then there's hardly an actual treatment being rendered, apart from the amount of one-on-one time spent in a room with the Reiki provider.

While many alternative medicines rely on arguments that our ancient ancestors understood the human body better than do modern scientists, another common error underlying their treatments is the naturalistic fallacy. This is the notion that a given medicine, treatment, or even food is healthy simply because it's natural, and that the less natural something is, the less likely it is to be good for one's health. This is the argument used for everything from promoting herbal medicine to rejecting vaccinations. Nature does indeed provide many avenues for nutrition and health, but it's false to equate "natural" with "good." Natural things can be objectively bad or dangerous, like arsenic or hemlock. More often, though, alternative medicines are simply neutral and ineffective for the purposes claimed. Eating a diet rich in fruits and vegetables and low in fat and cholesterol is undeniably healthy, but it's not going to cure cancer, and it's risky and dangerous to forego serious cancer treatments in favor of just improving one's diet.

Vaccine denialism, on the other hand, is increasingly one of society's bigger health problems, and it includes several kinds of naturalistic arguments. Denialists complain about certain ingredients in vaccines, such as trace amounts of mercury used as preservatives. The science says that such amounts are not dangerous, and studies have borne out that conclusion as correct. But to the denialist, the impulse is that mercury is bad, and so vaccines must be bad.

There are also vaccine protesters who claim that diseases are good because they're "natural." In 2011, a self-published children's book titled *Melanie's Marvelous Measles* took "children aged 4–10 years on a journey of discovering about the ineffectiveness of vaccinations, while teaching them to embrace childhood disease, heal if they get a disease, and build their immune systems naturally."[26]

Vaccines, however, have been one of the greatest successes of modern medicine. Smallpox has been completely eradicated for over three decades. I'm in my midthirties, and I've never personally known anyone who had polio, measles, or mumps. Millions of people have been spared suffering or have had their lives saved because of vaccination.

The drastic decrease in vaccinated diseases is the sort of objective result that alternative medicine cannot produce. Nor does alternative medicine have good evidence to support it; again, if there is compelling science to support a medicine or a treatment, then it can be fairly grouped with evidence-based medicine. Alternative medicine, in the end, earns its title because it is alternative to medicine based on actual evidence.

Lacking scientific evidence to support their beliefs, alternative-medicine supporters rely on pseudoscience. This reliance can take the form of something as simple as the use of logical fallacies, like the above-mentioned naturalistic fallacy; or as something more complex, like ancient wisdom and custom, as is the case with acupuncture. Such reliance is frequently denialist, rejecting the efficacy of modern medicine, like vaccinations. It's even conspiracist, commonly claiming that Big Pharma is hiding valuable cures from the public because it *wants* the public to be sick so that companies can profit off them.

More insidious still is the alternative-medicine industry itself, which creates a mirror image of evidence-based medicine to promote "alternative" remedies and treatments. The pseudoscientific studies discussed above, with their inadequate controls and frequent lack of blind testing, are just the beginning. Whole organizations are devoted to the active promotion of alternative medicine. Schools are created to teach the practice of such medicine, handing out degrees like "doctor of naturopathy." Self-help and advice books, like Kevin Trudeau's conspiracist-friendly *Natural Cures 'They' Don't Want You to Know About*, peddle poor advice. Useless homeopathic drugs line the shelves at real pharmacies; the CVS chain even has a section of its website devoted to promoting homeopathy.[27] For all its conspiracist fears of Big Pharma and Big Medicine, alternative medicine is a hugely profitable industry. It's estimated that Americans spend some $35 billion annually on alternative medicine.

Because of this widespread interest, the federal government created the National Center for Complementary and Alternative Medicine (NCCAM) in 1991 to study the efficacy of alternative-medical treatments and to determine whether they had any merit. In 2011, the agency's budget was over $127 million, and it has spent over $1.4 billion since its founding on evaluating various alternative treatments. Some of these studies have been attacked for being implausible from the start and a waste of taxpayer money. For instance, $666,000 was spent on a study to determine whether AIDS could be healed through distant prayer.[28] But even assuming that more plausible treatments ought to be scientifically evaluated before being dismissed, the findings of NCCAM have not caused any upendings of modern medicine. Studies carried out by the NCCAM have found that massages make sick people feel better. That yoga may improve fatigue. That Echinacea does *not* help the common cold. And that many alternative treatments perform no better than do placebos when tested. So many NCCAM studies found that the tested remedies performed the same as placebos that in 2011 the agency resorted to running a "Research Spotlight" on the medical benefits of placebos themselves.[29]

Admittedly, there is some merit in proving that these remedies *don't* work, particularly if NCCAM's published findings lead to people abandoning worthless medicine. But the federal government has a budget, and there are finite resources that are committed to scientific research. Money that is spent on studying distant prayer or coffee enemas or acupuncture is money that isn't being spent on finding a cure for Alzheimer's or a vaccine for HIV or on better detection methods for pancreatic cancer.

SPOTTING PSEUDOSCIENCE

There's a reason this is the longest chapter in this book. Pseudoscience is incredibly varied, potentially complex, and more sophisticated than your average Internet conspiracy theory. It's why whole books, magazines, and podcasts are devoted to the skeptical response to pseudoscience.

It's one thing to be able to recognize the biggest cranks, those deluded individuals who believe they have made a wild discovery that overturns conventional wisdom. Whether it's Gene Ray's Time Cube;[30] Neal Adams's Expanding Earth;[31] or Erik Andrulis's theory of how the world is composed of "gyres" that support his "incommensurable, trans-disciplinary, neologistical, axiomatic theory of life from quantum gravity to the living cell"[32]; the worst (or best) crank science quite simply *looks* like nonsense.

But beyond that, spotting pseudoscience depends on one's own familiarity with current scientific knowledge or at least on a knowledge of the scientific method and an active curiosity in self-education. Pseudoscience is not always easily distinguishable from real science at first glance; in some cases, like cryptozoology, it may even have a lot in common with real science.

The first thing to look for when evaluating a questionable scientific claim is, of course, the source. Perhaps the biggest sources of help are multiple peer-reviewed journals dedicated to sifting the scientific wheat from the pseudoscientific chaff. Claims supported by published studies can be granted a greater degree of trust than those made by someone posting to an alt-med website or self-publishing a book. This is not always a guarantee, as even nonsense like Andrulis's theory of gyres made it into a published journal (albeit a very young one, and a board member resigned in response), but even Andrulis was a respected biology professor.

The next item to consider is expertise in the given field. Long gone are the days when a person could be informed in all areas of science, and even then education in one field does not necessarily correlate with being reliable in another. Isaac Newton was the father of modern physics and one of the most influential scientists in history, but he was also obsessed with alchemy, and he tried to calculate the date of the end of the world from supposed clues in the Bible.

The status that accompanies the Nobel Prize makes it tempting to deem a prize winner to be thoroughly credible, but even Nobel laureates can exhibit pseudoscientific leanings in other fields. Brian Josephson won the Nobel Prize in Physics in 1973 but has since become a proponent of telepathy and parapsychology. Kary Mullis won the Nobel Prize in Chemistry in 1993, yet he avidly believes in astrology and denies that HIV causes AIDS. Linus Pauling is one of only four people to win two Nobel Prizes, but in his later years, he took to claiming that high doses of vitamin C could cure cancer, despite studies that said there was no benefit. There is no doubt that these men were incredibly smart in their respective fields of expertise, but that scientific expertise does not always translate into expertise, or even adequate skeptical thinking, in other fields.

Of course, many pseudoscience advocates have credentials much less respectable than a Nobel Prize. The stereotypical crank is someone with a background in accounting or art who suddenly discovers that he understands the way the world *actually* works. But there are many more subtle distinctions that can confuse the unsuspecting: doctors who get sucked into alt-med remedies or architects who promote 9/11-conspiracy theories about controlled demolition. And even if an outlying individual believes in a pseudoscientific argument, like a molecular biologist promoting creationism, that does little to undermine the overwhelming scientific consensus in the opposite direction.

Finally, attempting to apply the scientific method to a questionable claim can sometimes help in spotting pseudoscientific arguments. Has the claim been tested, and how credible were the tests? Is it even testable at all? What's the weight of the evidence for and against the claim? Is it consistent with other accepted scientific facts?

Does the claim come from a credible source, and does it have the support of legitimate scientists? Does it attempt to invoke conspiracies and cover-ups to explain why it doesn't? Scientists don't deal in conspiracies, but pseudoscientists often do. If there are no legitimate scientists willing to vouch for a claim, why not? Serious, compelling research, regardless of the source, can find support in academia. Even if it comes from a nine-year-old child.

CHAPTER 8

PSEUDOHISTORY

The History Channel began broadcasting on basic cable in 1995. Throughout the 1990s, it earned the pejorative of the "Hitler Channel" as a result of its omnipresent coverage of World War II. Although it was perhaps narrow in its subject matter, the channel was nonetheless an outlet for legitimate programming on world history.

This began to change in the 2000s, as the History Channel became increasingly less about actual history. The network expanded its scope to include such programming as *Nostradamus Effect*, *Haunted Histories*, *UFO Files*, *UFO Hunters*, and the apocalyptic prophecy–centered *Decoding the Past*. But nothing to date better demonstrates the mission drift of the History Channel than *Ancient Aliens*, the 2010 series that took the network beyond the historical equivalent of campfire stories and well into the realm of insane historical speculation. Not content with discussing anecdotal UFO sightings in modern times, *Ancient Aliens* posits that extraterrestrials have been visiting the earth for thousands of years and have been influential in historical progress, involved in everything from the construction of the pyramids to the success of the Apollo space program to the start of the Black Death.

Ancient Aliens succeeded in being widely criticized by scholars and yet popular enough with the viewing public to earn four seasons thus far. And with its production, the History Channel left no doubt that its new mission statement firmly embraced unabashed pseudohistory.

Just as pseudoscience encompasses ideas and conclusions that have been rejected by modern scientific consensus, pseudohistory similarly makes claims that fall outside legitimate historical scholarship. Few, if any, respectable historians would entertain specific claims of alien influence in world history, or that Nostradamus's writings have proven to be reliable predictors of future events, or that African or Chinese explorers traveled to the New World before Columbus.

But pseudohistory is necessarily less firmly definable than pseudoscience, and even the pseudoscience label has its vagaries. The scientific method provides science with a system of hypotheses and testing by which to judge the validity of novel ideas. Proposals that continue to be promoted, despite repeatedly failing to meet the rigorous standards of the scientific method, readily earn the moniker of pseudoscience. Other pseudosciences may simply make unsupported propositions that are designed to be outside the scope of scientific testing entirely.

The study of history does not have boundaries that are quite so well delineated. Historical consensus is not reached through the use of testing and controls but through the collection and analysis of historical data. Some of this evidence is physical, with artifacts that can be examined firsthand. Other evidence, particularly regarding human history, comprises the written accounts of earlier civilizations, which may carry biases or even inaccuracies but which still provide valuable insight into the past. Also valuable but even less reliable are oral histories passed down to the present day. And just as rumors and spin are regularly created today, our ability to fabricate and misrepresent events is nothing new, and so such accounts from the past must be viewed critically.

At the intersection of science and history are, naturally, the historical sciences. Anthropology, archaeology, and paleontology rely heavily on collected evidence rather than on laboratory testing, and the scientific conclusions they reach are constructed based on the best and most current evidence available. New discoveries can and do make significant changes to earlier conclusions in these fields in ways that don't happen in the hard sciences of physics or chemistry. The current scientific consensus favors the notion that the earliest

American settlers arrived around 12,000 BCE, but a minority believes that the migration may have begun as early as 55,000 BCE. While this is currently a matter of contentious debate, the discovery of earlier tools or settlements could radically change the consensus view.

In the same vein, it's possible that tomorrow archaeologists could unearth a 150,000-year-old spaceship that proves that aliens from the Twelve Colonies landed on earth in prehistoric times and interbred with early humans. Such an artifact wouldn't be merely suggestive; it would be all but conclusive. But in the absence of any such compelling evidence, there is no justification for believing that extraterrestrials have been interacting with humans for millennia.

Most types of pseudohistory fall into one of two categories, with the distinction between the two roughly the difference between denialism and conspiracism. Historical revisionism involves the rejection of orthodox beliefs about history in favor of a more novel theory. Of the two types of pseudohistory, this view is closer to legitimate scholarship, and in fact the general concept of revisionism is not pseudo-scholarship at all. Whenever new evidence is uncovered that conflicts with existing evidence and theories, previous conclusions must be reevaluated and perhaps even rejected in favor of new conclusions. When Frank Calvert and then Heinrich Schliemann began excavating the fabled city of Troy in the 1800s, their discoveries ultimately led to the revision of scholarly beliefs about the factual historicity of Troy itself. Troy was long believed to have been a fictional metropolis, no more real than Atlantis or Shambhala, and its status among historians was completely reversed because the archaeological evidence compelled it.

In December 2011, a novel pseudohistorical claim went viral; I first encountered it on Facebook® during the writing of this book. According to the story, Mayan ruins had been discovered in the mountains of northern Georgia, and the fabled Mayan city of Yupaha— for which Spanish explorer Hernando de Soto had unsuccessfully searched in 1540—may have been located near Brasstown Bald, the tallest mountain in the state. The article promptly exploded across social networking sites and the web at large.[1] Fortunately, most main-stream outlets were less rash when it came to reporting on the story. When news agencies like ABC covered the story, it was treated as the highly unlikely flight of fancy that it was.

As was pointed out by the blog *Boing Boing* just two days after the story's initial publication, there were immediate reasons to question the legitimacy of this "discovery," even before reaching the supposed evidence itself. The public reaction to the story reflected the significance of its claims: the actual discovery of Mayan ruins in the Appalachian Mountains would be an explosive discovery, the kind that calls for textbooks to be literally rewritten.[2]

It is natural to expect that a discovery of such huge import would come from a reliable outlet, most likely as a paper published in a reputable historical journal or perhaps as a press release or public announcement from a recognized institution. But the Mayan ruins story first appeared as original content on the website Examiner .com, a "news" site that consists of user-submitted material with little to no editorial oversight. Imagine *Wikipedia* reinvented as a newspaper, with less quality control.

What about the author? Even if the news outlet itself is less than reliable, perhaps the story originated from someone with legitimate credentials in the field and would thus be worth considering. But that was not the case. Richard Thornton, the man responsible for the story, described himself in his Examiner profile as an "architect and city planner." Although Thornton expressed a long-time interest in pre-Columbian civilizations, there was no indication that he had any education or professional experience in the field. A look at his credentials turned up a bachelor's degree in architecture and a master's in city planning, but there was no record of higher education in anthropology, archaeology, or history. Any background in history appeared to be entirely self-taught and independent, and Thornton's area of expertise, as given by the website, was "architecture and design examiner."[3]

Thus a reader would be justified in taking a highly critical view of Thornton's claims even before reaching the specifics of the claims themselves. Here was an architect making an incredible claim of historical revisionism on a website that published user-submitted material with minimal discretion.

The central focus of the critical response to Thornton's article was quickly personified in University of Georgia archaeologist Mark Williams, whom Thornton had cited in his Examiner article. Just a day after the article's publication, Williams posted in the comments section, saying, "This is total and complete bunk. There is no evidence of Maya in Georgia." When pressed by fellow posters for further comment, Williams provided a succinct description of pseudohistory itself and how it contrasts with the legitimate study of history: "Science is not performed by wild discussions on Facebook or 'the Examiner.' The idea by the author is interesting—just like the one that the mounds were made by Martians. There simply is no evidence in the ground that supports the idea, however, of anything in the Southeast being actually associated with the Maya. Period. Do you think the Mayas invented moving dirt? If you are more interested now in Georgia archaeology, great. The information we do know is fascinating without having to resort to pseudo science."[4]

Many of the other comments were supportive of Williams and skeptical of Thornton's claims, but a vocal few came to the defense of Thornton and attacked the scholarly establishment:

> So the idea that "there's no evidence" is itself bunk. There's plenty of evidence . . . just none that modern mainstream academics accept as evidence.

> Mark Williams seems to me to be representative of that worst kind of academic—the kind that can't accept anything that goes against their world view so they dismiss it as bunk but offer no logical argument in return. It's all about protecting their little fiefdom.

> Based on Dr. Williams [sic] attitudes expressed in full view of the public on this website, it seems clear we need fresh, new blood in

Georgia. Archaeology [*sic*] who aren't so committed to established theories.

Mark Williams, thanks for being the prime example for why the masses reach out for answers in articles like this. You so-called "professionals" are so pompous and dismissive that you feel you have the right to make definitive statements and just expect people to believe you because you are who you are. Academia is a JOKE and there's no reason I would ever believe someone like you over the author of this article.[5]

Where legitimate historical revisionism differs from its pseudo-historical counterpart is where it crosses the line into denialism. The revisionist still challenges the orthodox beliefs and attitudes but does so without putting forth new evidence and without adequately justifying why the orthodox beliefs should be rejected.

Holocaust denialism is the most prominent and infamous form of this type of pseudohistory. The existence of the concentration camps, the postwar investigations and trials, the firsthand accounts of survivors themselves, and more all firmly support that the Holocaust happened and that some six million Jews were murdered. Holocaust deniers rarely deny that the Nazis did engage in mass murder, just as they don't deny that Germany invaded Poland or bombed England. Attempts at total denial are rare in the West, but they are prevalent in the Arab world, where Holocaust denial starts to bleed into claims of outright conspiracy by the Jews to fabricate a fictional genocide. That level of denial depends heavily on not only a mindset predisposed to believing such a conspiracy was possible but also on a lack of access to or trust in orthodox research. Even the most adamant deniers in the West have difficulty denying that hundreds of thousands of Jews at least died in camps, even if they argue that those deaths were the result of neglect and abuse rather than of a specific genocidal intent.

The relatively more common Holocaust denialism and revisionism typically occurs in the details and the specifics. Revisionists deny that Jews were specifically targeted for genocide. They deny that the number of Jews killed was as high as six million, claiming the number was "only" in the hundreds of thousands. They deny that the gas chambers were used for human murder. They deny that the orders for the murders came from the German high command, instead saying they were the product of malicious Nazi middle management.

This last claim hearkens back to what is likely responsible for the earliest pseudohistorical scholarship advocating Holocaust denial: the desire to defend the German state. As was discussed in chapter 2, Harry Elmer Barnes, Paul Rassinier, and other early deniers believed that Germany was the victim of unjustified aggression, and they saw the Holocaust as just one attempt to defame the country. It also cannot be overlooked that Holocaust deniers heavily trend toward anti-Semitism, and their personal beliefs about Jews undoubtedly help drive the historical conclusions they draw about the Jewish genocide.

Another widely recognized form of historical revisionism is found among the so-called anti-Stratfordians, who dispute William Shakespeare's authorship of the works that bear his name. Shakespeare (of the British town of Stratford-upon-Avon, hence the denier label of "anti-Stratfordian") penned some 38 plays in the late 1500s and early 1600s, along with 154 sonnets and a number of other poems. Shakespeare was relatively well respected in his time, and his reputation steadily rose over the subsequent centuries. By the nineteenth century, he was seen as a literary genius.

It was also during the nineteenth century that the first doubts were expressed about the authorship of Shakespeare's plays. Shakespeare, it was argued, did not have the education, experience, or culture that were implied by his plays. This is not entirely unjustified as an avenue of study, but it tends to display an attitude of cultural elitism. It's argued that William Shakespeare was too much of a commoner and that works of such genius must have been the product of someone formally educated in the classics and personally fluent in high culture. Some have also complained that there is insufficient documentation of his authorship and that his death was not more widely mourned.

The known facts certainly support Shakespeare's authorship. He was recognized as the author in his own day, and he continued to be credited without question for another two hundred years after his death. There is contemporary documentation of his authorship, and he was acknowledged by other writers and actors during his lifetime. In all, Shakespeare was credited as the author of the works bearing his name at least twenty-three times during his life.

Whereas Holocaust revisionism is built around the claim that supposed events did not, in fact, happen, Shakespeare revisionism is forever plagued with the problem that if William Shakespeare did not write his thirty-eight plays, someone else must have. More than seventy alternate authors have been proposed, including Francis Bacon, Christopher Marlowe, and Edward de Vere. One of the more bizarre candidates was King James I, the English monarch responsible for the King James translation of the Bible, who was first posited as the true author by human rights activist Malcolm X.[6]

The weakness of Shakespeare revisionism is displayed in its failure to settle on a single preferred candidate. The evidence against Shakespeare deals heavily in perceived anomalies or a lack of certainty, and so the proposed alternate authors are not chosen based on any particular positive evidence. And with no positive evidence to build a case for any one candidate, the revisionists split into irreconcilable camps. It's similar to the pattern seen with JFK-assassination revisionists, who argue that Lee Harvey Oswald was not the true assassin—but even after a half-century, they cannot agree on a single preferred culprit.

Researchers at the University of Massachusetts–Amherst conducted a computational stylistics analysis of Shakespeare's plays and found that they all bear the same "literary fingerprint," which is strong evidence of a common author.[7] Since anti-Stratfordians may deny that William Shakespeare wrote any of his own plays, such an analysis cannot rule out the fact that some unidentified person may have penned all the works. But to date, the analysis has not supported authorship by any of the other proposed candidates whose known works can be compared to Shakespeare's.

A modern variation on anti-Stratfordianism has played out with President Barack Obama and his memoir *Dreams from My Father.* Jack Cashill, a columnist for the pro-Birther website WorldNetDaily and a fierce proponent of conspiracy theories about TWA Flight 800, first argued in 2008 that Obama was not the author of his own autobiography, and he expanded on this claim in his 2011 book *Deconstructing Obama: The Life, Loves, and Letters of America's First Postmodern President.* Cashill argued that the true author of *Dreams from My Father* was William Ayers, a former left-wing terrorist, current educator, and friend of Obama. In its broad strokes, Cashill's case against Obama is similar to the anti-Stratfordian case against Shakespeare. He argues that Obama was not a good enough writer to produce *Dreams* (even as he simultaneously argues that *Dreams* is not very good). He says that Obama lacked the life experience to write various passages in the book and that he sees similarities between the 1994 *Dreams* and Ayers's 2001 autobiography *Fugitive Days.*

Cashill's hypothesis was devastated when a supporter asked Peter Millican, a professor at Oxford University, to perform a computational analysis of Obama's memoir—an analysis not unlike the one performed on Shakespeare's works. Millican's finding? "I have found no evidence for Cashill's ghostwriting hypothesis, and rather strong (albeit limited) evidence against." And, as he further noted, this rejection of Cashill's hypothesis was largely based on the excerpts that Cashill himself had singled out as the strongest evidence of his claim.[8]

Cashill's "Ayers-as-ghostwriter" theory garnered some press during the 2008 presidential campaign, but after Millican's statements, it largely disappeared from the public consciousness, except for among the fringe that was already prone to spreading stories about Obama being a Muslim or being born in Kenya. Even the failure of this theory demonstrates one man's attempts to create a pseudohistorical narrative, whereas similar claims about Shakespeare have managed to thrive. Cashill's theory had the disadvantage of pertaining to a living subject, as well as the fact that he was perceived as engaging in an intentional partisan smear campaign. And whereas the alternate authors for Shakespeare's plays are unavailable for comment, Cashill was forced to resort to claims of a cover-up when his proposed ghostwriter, Ayers, publicly rejected the allegation.

Assassinations are a consistent target of pseudohistorical revisionism, as they represent a nexus of factors that attract such theories. They are highly public events, carrying a great deal of emotional weight. The more people who know about them, and the more people who have strong emotional responses, the greater the opportunity for amateur theories.

Because assassinations necessarily involve high-profile people and political figures in particular, they can readily be seen as affecting the flow of history. Or, at least, one can theorize how an assassin could have hoped to influence events through murder. How did the assassinations of Martin Luther King and Malcolm X affect the civil rights movement? How might JFK's presidency have been different from Lyndon Johnson's? Because of the high-profile and influential nature of assassinations, they are a breeding ground for conspiracy theories for the reasons discussed in chapter 3. We desire to see the world as orderly and fair; this view does not accommodate important historical figures being randomly murdered by unknown nobodies. If a president or a king or a political revolutionary is killed, it seems only fair that it must have been for an equally significant reason, and that it must have been carried out by an equally significant enemy, not by an angry and manic kid.

All these factors combine to encourage historical revisionism with regard to assassinations. The assassination of JFK is the pinnacle of this phenomenon, with multiple, conflicting theories about who the "real" assassin was. According to a 2003 survey, only a third of Americans believed that Lee Harvey Oswald acted alone in killing President Kennedy.[9]

The conspiracism that met Kennedy's death was seen in response to other political assassinations of the 1960s. The 1965 shooting of

Malcolm X engendered conspiracy allegations within a matter of days. Relatives of Dr. Martin Luther King continue to allege that his assassination in 1968 was the result of a conspiracy. Theories of conspiracy have even been leveled regarding the assassination of Senator Robert Kennedy, even though assassin Sirhan Sirhan was detained on the spot as he continued to fire his gun, and he'd written in his diary about the need to kill Kennedy. (One of Malcolm X's three assassins was similarly stopped by the attendant crowd.)

Kennedy's assassin was a twenty-four-year-old former marine and communist sympathizer. The primary gunman involved in Malcolm X's assassination was a twenty-four-year-old militant Nation of Islam member who felt that X had betrayed the group's leader. Martin Luther King's assassin was a forty-year-old petty burglar who'd never graduated high school. And Robert Kennedy's killer was a twenty-four-year-old Christian immigrant.

These four men could have easily been demeaned as "losers" if not for the high-profile murders they committed; that they were able to take down some of America's most important and powerful men with a handful of bullets is unsettling. This phenomenon wasn't new in the 1960s, either; Leon Czolgosz, the assassin of President William McKinley, was a twenty-eight-year-old unemployed anarchist who, until shortly before he murdered the president, was still living with his parents. History, we like to think, is created by great leaders and influential powers, not by angry twenty-something nobodies with shotguns and mental health issues. One of King's friends put it in almost exactly those words: "There is no way a ten-cent white boy could develop a plan to kill a million-dollar black man."[10]

And so, consciously or not, the revisionist seeks a more emotionally satisfying villain. The assassination, he says, was not the act of an angry young man acting alone; it was part of a covert government operation, spearheaded by the FBI or the CIA. Or it might have been a criminal conspiracy engineered by the Mafia. Or it could have been perpetrated by one of America's enemies, like Cuba or the USSR, seeking to throw the nation into social and political panic.

Any number of possible culprits can be fingered for any assassination by first asking one of conspiracism's favorite questions: *Cui bono,* or "Who benefits?" When a political leader dies, *someone* can be construed as benefiting. For instance, Lyndon B. Johnson ascended to the presidency following John F. Kennedy's death, and racist Southern Democrats were probably not distraught over the murders of civil rights leaders. Once a person or group is identified as gaining some benefit from a leader's death, then a narrative can be built around blaming them for being behind the assassination.

Of course, plenty of evidence exists to support the guilt of the accepted assassin. The Warren Commission concluded that Lee Harvey Oswald was the only gunman in Dallas. Sirhan Sirhan was arrested on the scene for killing Robert Kennedy. James Earl Ray was witnessed fleeing the scene of King's murder, and his rifle and binoculars were discovered bearing his fingerprints. To argue that any of these men were framed or that there were additional unknown gunmen requires some degree of denial of incriminating evidence.

Because these exercises in revisionism so readily invoke claims of high-level conspiracy, the requisite denialism is made all the easier. Any given piece of incriminating evidence can simply be dismissed as having been created by the conspiracy itself as part of its frame job. The photo of Lee Harvey Oswald holding a rifle and newspaper? Faked. James Earl Ray's fingerprint-laden gun and binoculars? Planted. Sirhan Sirhan's diary entry reading "My determination to eliminate RFK is becoming more and more of an unshakable obsession. RFK must die. RFK must be killed. Robert F. Kennedy must be assassinated"?[11] Forged.

With the incriminating evidence thus brushed off, the revisionist then pulls out the standard bag of tricks to build a case against his preferred villain. Anomalies are singled out and elevated to the utmost importance. What were the sounds that bystanders in Dallas reported hearing when JFK was shot? Who were the unidentified men in a photo taken at the hotel where Robert Kennedy was killed? Details are then interpreted to be consistent with the conspiracy theory. It's argued that Oswald could not have fired the necessary bullets and that the mysterious people on the grassy knoll are to blame.

In a rather embarrassing exercise in jurisprudence, the family of Martin Luther King initiated a wrongful-death civil suit against Loyd Jowers in 1998, claiming that the Memphis restaurant owner was part of a government conspiracy to kill Dr. King. When the US Department of Justice investigated Jowers, his story lacked credibility. However, the civil trial resulted in a win for the King family, as the jury concluded that a government conspiracy had existed.

The King family is quite proud of this result; transcripts of the case are available on the website of the nonprofit King Center.[12] But as is so often the case with conspiracist evidence, this victory for the conspiracist interpretation is far less than it seems. The entire hearing was pretty much all for show, an exercise in which both sides agreed to play a certain part. The King family's attorney argued that Mr. Jowers had played a major role in a government conspiracy to kill Dr. King; Jowers's attorney (who had a history with the Kings), by contrast, argued that Jowers had played only a *minor* role in a government conspiracy to kill Dr. King. The jurors heard no arguments from either side dispelling the notion of a government conspiracy; however, they did hear a considerable amount of hearsay evidence, including statements made by unsworn and unidentified trial witnesses.

It shouldn't be surprising that, after days of hearing conspiracy mongering—with the two sides disagreeing only about the scope of the supposed conspiracy—the members of the jury were willing to say they believed there was a conspiracy. The King family reveled in this result; King's son was quoted as saying, "We don't care what the Justice Department does. . . . We believe that this case is over. . . . We know what happened. This is the period at the end of the sentence."[13] But it wasn't. Despite the King family's hopes, the Jowers trial is all but forgotten outside of conspiracist circles, having been recognized as a sham put on by self-interested historical revisionists.

The Jowers trial illustrates the flexibility of assassination conspiracists in their theories. Just as both attorneys agreed on the existence of a conspiracy but disagreed over its extent, assassination theorists are typically more committed to the notion that a conspiracy was behind a given assassination, rather than believing in an individual culprit. This is common among historical revisionists, as it was with anti-Stratfordians; they're not wedded to a specific alternative theory so much as they're opposed to the accepted one. Anti-Stratfordians have a laundry list of suspects, and they're willing to entertain any number of them. JFK-conspiracy theorists aren't willing to commit to a particular gunman, but they'll happily rule out Oswald. This is true even when the "evidence" supporting their various theories is inconsistent or even contradictory. To listen to a JFK theorist is to hear a grab bag of complaints about Oswald's guilt and pieces of evidence they say point to a conspiracy, but their evidence rarely adds up to a single, coherent conspiracy. Again, their denialism shines through if one can only step back and take in their "evidence" as a whole.

SECRET HISTORY

Whereas historical revisionism argues that historical events as we know them happened differently than we're told, the secret-history branch of pseudohistorical scholarship claims that there are sweeping aspects of history that we don't know about at all. It's revisionism on a much grander scale, proposing that significant events have been completely erased from the public consciousness, covered up by some interested party. In this way, it is the conspiracist approach to history, contrasted with the more denialist attitudes of other pseudohistorians.

The most famous example of secret history is the legend of the lost city of Atlantis. An island that supposedly existed over nine thousand years ago, Atlantis was first mentioned in Plato's dialogues *Timaeus* and *Critias*, written in the fourth century BCE. Plato tells an epic myth about this ancient island of Atlantis, which was described as being larger than Libya and Asia Minor combined. Following a war with Athens, a great earthquake hit Atlantis, and the entire island disappeared into the sea.

In the context of Plato's dialogue, there is little reason to see Atlantis as anything more than a literary device to illustrate a point. Some writers during the subsequent millennia would express belief in a historical Atlantis, but the general consensus remained that it was fictional. Those who did believe did not embellish much on Plato's account; when Atlantis was referenced as a literal location, it was treated simply as an ancient island civilization that sank—a historical curiosity, albeit one with mythic trappings.

That belief changed drastically in 1882, with the publication of Ignatius Donnelly's *Atlantis: The Antediluvian World*. Donnelly, an eccentric US congressman from Minnesota, was not content with simply arguing that Atlantis was a real place. He contended that Atlantis, which he placed in the Atlantic Ocean, was the cradle of all civilization. Atlantean immigrants moved across the world, spreading culture, religion, and innovations that began on the island continent. Members of Atlantean royalty were the true inspiration for other ancient religions. Atlanteans invented the alphabet and Bronze Age tools, and they were the first forgers of iron.[14] By establishing Atlantis as not just an ancient civilization but as *the* ancient civilization, Donnelly was inspiration for much of the Atlantis myth as it is known today. Popular culture's vision of Atlantis, from Aquaman comics to Disney cartoons, is more the product of Donnelly's Atlantis than it is of Plato's.

Atlantis wasn't the only area of pseudohistory that Donnelly dabbled in. He was an advocate of Shakespeare authorship revisionism, believing that Sir Francis Bacon was the true author of the works attributed to Shakespeare. And with his follow-up book to *Atlantis*, titled *Ragnarok: The Age of Fire and Gravel*, he became one of the earliest proponents of catastrophism.

Catastrophism, which blurs the lines a bit between pseudohistory and pseudoscience, proposes that geologic events that science says were slow and gradual were instead brought about suddenly by catastrophic events. In *Ragnarok*, Donnelly suggests that Atlantis was destroyed by a comet that impacted earth thousands of years ago, and that the same comet was potentially responsible for the Great Flood described in the Book of Genesis and for the extinction of Ice Age mammals like the woolly mammoth. The book relies heavily on Donnelly's amateur scientific views and incorporates a considerable amount of biblical and mythic literature to support his conclusions.[15]

Donnelly's writings helped inspire the work of psychiatrist Immanuel Velikovsky, who brought prominence to catastrophism with his 1950 bestseller *Worlds in Collision*. Velikovsky published several books on the subject and produced a wealth of theories, including that the Great Flood was caused by Saturn; that Mercury was involved in the destruction of the Tower of Babel; and that the planet Venus, which he said used to be a comet, was responsible for events in the Book of Exodus and for the incident in the Book of Joshua describing how the sun stood still.[16]

The pseudoscientific trappings of the above claims, and the lack of overt conspiracy theories, distinguish them from other types of secret histories. Ancient-astronaut theories, much more in the secret cover-up vein, don't claim that extraterrestrial *bodies* are affecting history, as in astrology, but that extraterrestrial *beings* are doing so. These claims began appearing in the last century or so, seemingly inspired by science fiction. To be fair, there are respected scholars and scientists who believe that earthly life may have extraterrestrial origins, even if only on a molecular level. Proponents of ancient-astronaut theories go much further than that. They claim that the earth has a long history of visitation by alien species who not only came to earth but who interacted with our primitive ancestors and left behind hints of their presence. Not surprisingly, this notion was not seriously proposed until the early twentieth century.

One of the leading proponents of ancient-astronaut claims is Erich von Däniken, who has been writing about them since the 1960s. Where earlier generations had myths of Olympian gods or magic beings that may have interacted with humans in the past, the development of modern science opened the door for aliens to fill that niche—much in the way alien-abduction stories in the twentieth century filled the void left by succubi stories featuring nighttime attacks by evil spirits.

Däniken and others believe that aliens have been involved in such ancient achievements as the construction of the pyramids in Egypt, of the giant stone heads of Easter Island, and of the Nazca Lines of Peru. This theory drastically underestimates the ingenuity of earlier generations. There is a cultural and temporal bias in assuming that ancient civilizations couldn't have accomplished such feats on their own. Furthermore, historians and scientists have been able to successfully determine how these accomplishments were carried out. Granted, they weren't *easy*, but they didn't necessitate the aid of alien architects.

These claims also underestimate the capabilities of the supposed aliens. If extraterrestrials were visiting earth, that means they had already mastered interstellar travel and were far more advanced technologically than humanity is today. If a cadre of human visitors traveled back to 2000 BCE and provided technological aid to their own ancestors, the evidence of that would be far more conspicuous than stone carvings. There would be sudden quantum leaps in technological ability, if not preserved examples of inexplicable technology itself. The tombs in the pyramids were sealed for centuries; when they were cracked open, they were found to be filled with ancient treasures, not with MP3 players and battery-powered devices.

In the absence of such concrete evidence of visitation, ancient-astronaut proponents fall back on things they perceive to support their hypothesis. They point to cave paintings in Italy that supposedly show helmeted astronauts in 10,000 BCE or other artwork that seems to show aircraft or persons in flying ships. But much like cave paintings that supposedly show humans painting dinosaurs (a favorite of young-earth creationists), these are examples of confirmation bias. Artists are inherently creative, and nothing in any of the proffered examples is convincingly alien. If a person has been primed to see an astronaut suit or a UFO, then pareidolia might kick in and an image might stand out. Otherwise, what some claim is a space helmet could instead be interpreted as emanating beams of light.

As Carl Sagan wrote of the claims made by Däniken and others, it's impossible to definitively say that the earth was *not* visited by aliens in the past, and indeed it's possible that such visits took place.[17] But the scientific approach demands evidence, and there is no compelling evidence of such visitation. Consequently, it's premature at best and fallacious at worst to declare that such visits did happen. This way of thinking applies to all secret-history types of pseudohistory. Proponents make fantastic claims, and, as the old adage says, extraordinary claims demand extraordinary evidence. A four-century-old MP3 player would be incredibly compelling; vaguely ambiguous cave paintings are not. Unfortunately for secret-history proponents, their claims are inherently without evidence; if any persuasive evidence existed, the "truth" wouldn't be secret.

Now that we've looked at pseudohistory in practice, what are the common elements that can be used to spot it?

SPOTTING PSEUDOHISTORY

Myths, Anecdotes, and Ancient Knowledge

Just as ancient cultures are not reliable sources for scientific knowledge, neither are they the most reliable sources for historical knowledge. As seen in the last chapter, ancient cultures believed a variety of strange and incompatible things about how the world was created. A number of them had societal histories that listed kings who reigned for centuries at a time. In prescientific and preliterate times, cultures passed down mythologies that embellished or even fictionalized the past.

Immanuel Velikovsky's historical allegations on catastrophism revolve heavily around biblical events. Similarly, Ignatius Donnelly's *Ragnarok* relies on biblical sources; in a chapter called "Genesis Read by the Light of the Comet," Donnelly implicates his comet not just in the Great Flood and the destruction of Sodom and Gomorrah but also in Adam and Eve's choice of clothing after they leave the garden. The story of Atlantis is rooted in the nonhistorical writings of Plato, who suggested that the island had perished millennia earlier. And even then, only the broad strokes of the Atlantean saga were included in Plato's account; the island's mythology was fleshed out by later writers who themselves had no better resources than Plato had.

That's not to say that ancient historical beliefs are useless to modern scholarship. For centuries, the Trojan War depicted in the works of Homer—and the city of Troy itself—was thought to be fictional mythology, even though the ancient Greeks believed it was historical fact. And in the nineteenth century, when the city of Troy was excavated in modern Turkey, it turned out that the ancient Greeks had not been so wrong. The accuracy of the Greek account should not be overstated, however. Homer's *Iliad* and *Odyssey* recount stories filled with larger-than-life characters and active involvement by magical deities. While the city and the conflict may be real, Homer's accounting of those events is hardly reliable as history.

And so there may be merit in myth as a starting point for research, for providing a hypothesis for further study. What separates science from pseudoscience is not just distinguishing which starting points are worthy of investigation but also recognizing when the collected evidence fails to support that hypothesis. Spotting pseudohistory involves not only noticing that research has been fruitless, but, more importantly, also taking into account the pseudohistorian's confidence and certainty in his belief in spite of his lack of evidence.

Fake Experts and Amateur Publications

Pseudohistorical "experts" are generally possessed of no more expertise than their pseudoscientific counterparts. They typically have no specialized education in history, archaeology, or anthropology, and their experience is more akin to a personal hobby than to a professional career.

Ignatius Donnelly was a lawyer and politician. Immanuel Velikovsky was a psychiatrist. Jack Cashill is a writer and columnist. Richard Thornton is an architect. As detailed in chapter 2, the members of the deceptively named Institute for Historical Review included only one person with legitimate historical credentials, and his career experience consisted entirely of working with anti-Semitic causes.

An author's expertise is one of the best places to start when critically examining a novel claim and then determining whether that claim might be pseudo-scholarship. Other considerations come into play once you have the opportunity to review the evidence presented, but the claimant's credentials can be given a cursory evaluation simply by checking out the author's background. Regarding the "Mayans in Georgia" claim, your skeptical radar should have pinged at the first eight words of the bio at the bottom of the article: "Richard Thornton is an architect and city planner."[18] Once you realize that this stunning archaeological discovery was made by an architect, it's good reason to be cautious about believing it too quickly.

And just as Thornton published his amazing discovery on a website devoted to user-submitted content, pseudohistorians rarely get published in recognized, respectable outlets. Peer-reviewed historical journals will screen out claims that have been debunked or that have little to no evidence backing them up. Self-publication or publication through a vanity press can also be warning signs of crankery.

Unfortunately, major houses are willing to publish books advancing pseudohistorical claims. Gavin Menzies's book *1421: The Year China Discovered the World* was roundly dismissed as pseudohistory, but its hardcover edition was published by a HarperCollins division in 2002, and the paperback was published in 2004 by a subsidiary of Random House. Menzies's self-explanatory follow-up, *1434: The Year a Magnificent Chinese Fleet Sailed to Italy and Ignited the Renaissance*, was also published by the same division of HarperCollins, as was

Menzies's third book: *The Lost Empire of Atlantis: History's Greatest Mystery Revealed*, which ought to settle any doubt as to Menzies's pseudohistorical leanings.

The fact that HarperCollins would publish such "drivel" (as one professor called it[19]) is disappointing, but it's a cautionary warning about putting too much faith in the discretion of publishers. Jack Cashill's book *Deconstructing Obama* was published by an imprint of Simon & Schuster despite being derided as conspiracy mongering. The failure of a historical theory to get published is a good sign that it's crankery, but the success of such a theory in finding a publisher is hardly proof that it's not.

Agenda-Driven

"History is written by the winners." It's a well-known sentiment, spoken appropriately by George Orwell, and there is a grain of truth to it.[20] The winners and losers throughout history can influence how the narrative of history is framed. Support for or against a cause can also color the image that is painted. Leaders of a successful rebellion are revolutionaries; leaders of an unsuccessful one are insurrectionists.

Among an international community of scholars, however, there is room for competing interpretations of events and people. Some people revere Che Guevara; some dislike Mother Teresa. Where pseudohistorians go wrong with Orwell's quote is in using it as justification for pretending that the *facts* of history are determined by the winners. History may not be a "hard" science, but it does not make up facts as it sees fit. Evidence is still gathered, hypotheses are still advanced and refuted, and the scholarly environment ensures that findings will be checked and validated, not created out of whole cloth to justify an agenda.

Perhaps because they view serious history as a product of bias and agendas, pseudohistorians are often unafraid to develop theories as the means of promoting specific agendas of their own. And they can be surprisingly naked in displaying that agenda.

The agenda may be religious. As seen above, catastrophism is heavily motivated by a desire to explain and justify significant biblical events, particularly ones that may be lacking in support from mainstream historians (for example, the Great Flood). Some conservative writers, particularly David Barton, have depicted Thomas Jefferson and James Madison as being far more Christian than they really were in order to argue that the Founding Fathers specifically intended the United States to be a Christian nation first and foremost. An agenda can also be antireligious, as seen in the inherently anti-Semitic conspiracies underlying the *Protocols of the Learned Elders of Zion.*

Agendas can also be political. Jack Cashill opposed Barack Obama in the 2008 election, and so he developed a ghostwriter theory that conveniently doubled as a political smear against Obama.[21] Early Holocaust denialism was born as result of efforts to defend the reputation of Germany. In the years after the Civil War, disgraced Confederates found themselves living in a world where slavery was illegal, and where the secession they instigated led to the deaths of over six hundred thousand Americans. Acknowledging that the South had been primarily interested in preserving the institution of slavery did not do any favors for the South's reputation or self-esteem. And so the South's motivations began to be rewritten retrospectively by Southern apologists, downplaying slavery in favor of the more legalistic doctrine of "state's rights."

There may also be cultural agendas. There seems to be a strain of elitism in the Shakespeare authorship theory: Shakespeare is dismissed as being too much of a commoner, and the leading alternate authors are mostly prominent and well-connected Britons. Anti-Semitism feeds Holocaust denialism and belief in the Zionist conspiracy of the *Protocols.* When people say that aliens must have been involved in constructing the Egyptian pyramids, they're suggesting that the Egyptians couldn't have done it themselves.

Selectivity, Credulity, and Conspiracy

The same cognitive biases that underlie conspiracism in general are frequently present in pseudohistory. Unlike science, history is not easily tested and has to rely on whatever evidence can be found. Additionally, unlike science, history is heavily dependent on human actors and actions; the study of prehuman history is more of a science than a social science.

Because history is dependent on understanding human actors, it can be mangled by misunderstanding those human actors. Such misunderstanding may take the form of questioning their motives, doubting their skills, disputing their statements, impugning their characters, or making any number of allegations. History does have objective truths, but historians endeavor to determine what those truths are. Although there is less opportunity for experimentation, historians still gather evidence and use that evidence to draw their conclusions, like scientists do. With enough evidence, a consensus can be reached. The existence of a broad consensus without an active controversy among experts, then, suggests that there is evidence to support it.

The study of history deals not only with documenting the known events of history but also with uncovering the forgotten facts. A professional historian could easily establish his notoriety by discovering some previously unknown facet of history. But in evaluating any new proposal, it is the null hypothesis that must first be overcome, as is the case with science. In history, the null hypothesis would be that the proposed event didn't happen as proposed—that aliens didn't build the pyramids or that Atlantis didn't exist. Overcoming the null hypothesis simply requires the production of credible and persuasive evidence.

Pseudohistorians reject the consensus view of history, and in order to do so, they also have to reject the evidence that gave rise to that consensus and rely instead on whatever they can construe to be evidence in their own favor. This approach necessitates that they adopt many of the habits of conspiracists and that they resort to conspiracism themselves. For starters, they have to be especially selective in the evidence they choose to recognize or dismiss. Since sufficient evidence exists to create a consensus view, that means there is a lot of evidence that historical revisionists must be willing to dismiss. Holocaust deniers have to find ways to argue that the overwhelming evidence of Jewish genocide is not overwhelming at all but is instead entirely unconvincing. This is a standard exercise in denialism: focusing on anomalies in the evidence, dwelling on minor points rather than on the full weight of the evidence, arguing that a single mistake justifies rejecting a whole swath of evidence.

Secret historians' selectivity is more subtle, since the evidence they're rejecting is negative evidence. It's not as if there is an artifact or ancient text that one can point to as evidence that Atlantis did *not* exist or that the Mayans did *not* settle in Georgia; there simply is no evidence to support that they did. Responsible historians interpret that lack of evidence as reason to not support those hypotheses, even though they would welcome such revolutionary discoveries if there was adequate proof to support them. But secret historians can easily gloss over that lack of evidence, as easily as believers in ancient astronauts can ignore the lack of inexplicable technology or sudden revolutions in knowledge.

With the evidence of the consensus dismissed through selectivity, pseudohistorians then bolster their own arguments with questionable evidence that mainstream historians have rejected and deemed unconvincing: the opinions of fake experts; creative interpretations of art or texts; individuals' anecdotes that run counter to better evidence; myths and legends; fake documents; or just wild speculation. They use this less-than-credible evidence to pretend that the null hypothesis has been overcome. They may find the evidence persuasive, but taken on its own merits, it's invariably insufficient to justify their belief.

The pseudohistorian then finds himself in the position of arguing that the consensus evidence, while widely accepted, is faulty, while *his* evidence, which is widely rejected, is more persuasive. And once this line of logic is followed, he has to explain why the educated community would find consensus on the wrong side, and why they would label his own theories as pseudohistory. Thus he is prone to fall back on conspiracism. He may allege that there is an academic conspiracy in which scholars refuse to recognize the pseudohistorian's claims because they're afraid of looking foolish or because they're afraid of the social implications of his findings. This is a favorite of Holocaust deniers who say that historians and politicians don't want to admit that Hitler's greatest crime was fictionalized. Or he may point to a historical conspiracy and propose that past historians or the actual historical figures themselves are to blame for obscuring the truth. This, too, is common among revisionists, who can create motivations that are then assigned to explain why such a cover-up would have been worth pursuing. Virtually any assassination theory posits that the responsible party itself tried to cover its tracks. Finally, the pseudohistorian might presuppose a conspiracy by some interested third party whose agenda is advanced by obfuscating the truth about the past. Here he can apply the conspiracist question of *Cui bono* and then presuppose that the beneficiary played some role in the cover-up. He can even blame third parties that may not exist or that are the subject of pseudohistorical claims themselves. Most any systemic conspiracy, and certainly any super-conspiracy, is broad enough to encompass a simple historical cover-up as part of its agenda.

While historical conspiracies do exist, such as the one behind Lincoln's assassination, serious historians don't rest their arguments on claims of conspiracies and cover-ups. Either the available evidence supports their view or it doesn't. When someone claims that the evidence that would validate one's theory is being suppressed, or that there are powerful interests that have hidden the truth from the public, that's a good sign that the claim being made is a pseudohistorical one.

CHAPTER 9
PSEUDOLAW

Pseudolaw is the least well-known of the three major pseudo-scholarships. There is a considerable amount of research and reporting of pseudoscience, both in support of its claims and in terms of more evidence-based scientific responses. Disappointingly high percentages of Americans believe in pseudoscientific claims. Most pseudohistory is somewhat less pervasive than pseudoscience, both among scholarly and public circles, but its influence is nonetheless widespread in our culture. Pseudolaw, by contrast, is on the fringe to the extent that, as of this writing, it doesn't even have its own entry on *Wikipedia*. RationalWiki—a site devoted to debunking pseudoscience—does give pseudolaw a respectable entry, defining it as "any legal theory developed or action taken that relies heavily on frivolous arguments trumped up in legal language."[1] A list of examples is provided, as well as warning signs that a legal argument may be pseudolaw.

Pseudolaw shares some features with the other two pseudo-scholarships, but in many ways it's a very different creature. Pseudoscience and pseudohistory both deal with external truths and our ability to identify them. To that end, science provides its system of hypotheses and testing to separate accurate models of our world from inaccurate models. The historical sciences are less friendly to controlled testing, but they still depend on the discovery of supporting or discrediting evidence. Historical conclusions can be and are modified when new findings are made; just as the findings of earlier and earlier pre-Clovis artifacts compel historians to push back the date of the earliest American inhabitants, the unearthing of an actual UFO in Egypt would instantly lend credence to the currently unsupported notion that aliens helped build the pyramids. (Not to mention all the other consequences of discovering evidence of extraterrestrial life.)

But pseudolaw is less black-and-white than pseudoscience. There are no tests to run. There are no discoveries to be made. There are no null hypotheses to test against. There are no external truths of reality to point to and say, "That proves your legal argument is wrong." Pseudolaw is wrong simply because other law says it is.

It's not just that proponents of pseudolaw hold a minority view, however. There are minority views among science and history as well—typically in disputed areas of study, but the law is built on a foundation of clashing views. And just as scientific and historical knowledge is driven by novel ideas and new discoveries, the law is continually built by new arguments. When the Supreme Court issues a ruling on the scope of the First or Second or Fourth Amendment, that decision is not expected to be unanimous. Rather, such legal conclusions are often made with three or four justices expressing their own educated disagreement. If four of the country's most prestigious judges can believe in a minority view on a legal question, then pseudolaw must be something more than merely having a dissenting opinion.

That "something more" is what happens when a dissenting opinion has no legitimate support among serious legal scholars. When it has repeatedly been brought before the courts and has repeatedly and universally been rejected as incorrect. When its arguments can't be found in legal texts because the issue is considered unequivocally settled. When its most prominent supporters aren't formally trained in the law at all but are instead armchair attorneys and self-taught "constitutional scholars."

In short, pseudolaw is fringe law. Not "fringe" in the sense of being novel and cutting edge, but in the sense of being antiquated and abandoned by better-informed students of the law. Pseudolegal arguments are, in the legal parlance, frivolous. On the occasions they make their way into court, it is typically at the hands of eccentric attorneys and pro se litigants.

Consequently, there are relatively few beliefs that can fairly be labeled as pseudolaw, compared to the rich diversity of pseudoscientific and pseudohistorical beliefs. Not all areas of the law are equally vulnerable. Most fringe legal arguments are pointedly antigovernment and thus focus on criminal law, tax law, or constitutional law. General civil law, such as tort law, family law, or estate law, is rarely targeted. A common theme among pseudolegal claims is that they assert themselves to be representative of the "true" law, which proponents allege has been misinterpreted, ignored, or suppressed.

Suppression then demands the existence of agents to carry it out—agents with the motive to hide the "true" law and to replace it with illegitimate law, in service of some underlying agenda. Such agents have the influence to not only enact these changes but also to cause the courts, the legal scholars, and the practicing members of the bar to play along. And so the pseudolawyer begins to display the characteristics of the classic conspiracy theorist. Conspiracism is so integral to pseudolaw that it very nearly demands that the believer be conspiracy-prone; indeed the "true" believer is more likely than not to also subscribe to notions of organized assassinations, government mind control, and FEMA internment camps. Further, while there is nothing inherently conservative or liberal about most pseudolegal beliefs, they're often held by individuals who would place themselves on the right side of the political spectrum (or who, at least, have vocal objections to those on the left side).

In much the same way that the JFK assassination takes center stage among conspiracy theorists, the sovereign citizen movement is the nexus of pseudolaw in the United States. It is the primary public advocate for most major pseudolegal arguments, and a person who identifies with the sovereign citizen movement is assuredly a believer in one or more pseudolegal claims. The sovereign citizen movement is not a single organized entity but rather is made up of loosely knit groups and persons with strong antigovernment beliefs, bordering on anarchism. According to the Anti-Defamation League, the sovereign citizen movement has its origins in the Posse Comitatus organizations of the 1970s, the first of which, the Sheriff's Posse Comitatus, was founded by Henry Beach in Portland, Oregon, in 1969. Beach's idea spread, and by the mid-1970s, there were some eighty branches of Posse Comitatus nationwide.[2]

The rejection of state and federal authority was perhaps the central tenet of these Posse groups. They believed that the county was the highest legitimate level of government and that the local sheriff was the highest authority, to whom all other government officers must answer. *Posse comitatus* is, in fact, Latin for "power of the county." Members of these groups questioned the legitimacy of the Federal Reserve and insisted that gold was the only real currency. They further pioneered new forms of pseudolegal activism, inventing false liens and engaging in "paper terrorism" to harass their enemies through frivolous litigation, burdening the courts in the process.

Conspiracism was also present from the beginning and was itself a core element of the groups' philosophy. The Posse's own handbook set forth the argument that America had a "hidden history" that had been somehow rewritten: "The rule for the Judiciary, both State and Federal, has been subtle subversion of the Constitution of these United States. The subversion and contempt for the Constitution by the Judiciary is joined by the Executive and Legislative branches of government. It is apparent that the Judiciary has attempted to alter our form of Government. By unlawful administrative acts and procedures, they have attempted to establish a Dictatorship of the Courts over the citizens of this Republic. The legal profession has, with few exceptions, conspired with the Judiciary for this purpose."[3]

By the mid-1980s, the Posse groups were dwindling, but the ideas they espoused continued to be promoted by former leaders. This proved to be the beginnings of the modern sovereign citizen movement, with its rejection of various governmental authorities and its advocacy for a multitude of pseudolegal arguments. Several of these are worth detailing.

TAX PROTESTERS

Possibly the most well-known pseudolegal arguments are those made by tax protesters. In 1789, Benjamin Franklin famously said that "in this world nothing can be said to be certain, except death and taxes,"[4] and tax protesters preach that the latter isn't nearly so certain.

The appeal of tax protester arguments is far easier to understand than virtually any other form of pseudolaw: people don't like paying taxes. Theories of jurisdiction or of levels of citizenship are niche by nature, but the idea that paying taxes is optional, or is somehow not mandatory, has a built-in audience. And the bogus theories of income tax denialists are as numerous as the pages of the tax code they reject.

It was the Sixteenth Amendment to the Constitution, ratified in 1913, that formally gave the federal government the power to tax individuals' incomes. It read, simply, "The Congress shall have power to lay and collect taxes on incomes, from whatever source derived, without apportionment among the several States, and without regard to any census or enumeration."[5]

It is not surprising then that the Sixteenth Amendment is the target of more than one tax protester argument. One argument is that the amendment was never properly ratified by a sufficient number of states, and without adequate ratification, the federal government never gained the power to tax. Like the "missing" Thirteenth Amendment, which will be discussed later, this argument is an attempt to use historical events to justify a legal conclusion.

By 1913, there were forty-eight states in the Union. Thirty-six states (three-quarters of the total) were needed to ratify the Thirteenth Amendment. In February 1913, Delaware became the thirty-sixth state to do so, and by March of that same year, a total of forty-two states had ratified the amendment. More than enough, right? But it has been argued that some states had "irregularities" in approving the bill, that the wrong person signed the legislation, or that the states somehow violated their own state law by ratifying the amendment. One argument claimed that there were minor textual errors in the bills passed by several states; for example, "income" instead of "incomes" or "states" instead of "States." This argument was brought to the attention of the US secretary of state in 1913. After determining that the claims were inconsequential, the secretary declared the amendment adopted.

William J. Benson, a vocal tax protester, presented these same arguments in his 1985 book *The Law That Never Was: The Fraud of the 16th Amendment and Personal Income Tax.* In 2007, a federal court ruled that his arguments were fraudulent, and he was prohibited from selling his "Reliance Defense Package" to the public.

Pennsylvania attorney Daniel Evans maintains an incredibly thorough Tax Protester FAQ, which documents dozens of such tax arguments.[6] The IRS itself lists a similar collection on their website under the heading "Frivolous Tax Arguments in General."[7] There are various constitutional arguments, such as that the income tax applies only on federal lands or that the Sixteenth Amendment illegally conflicts with other constitutional provisions. Some tax protesters argue that income tax is a violation of the Thirteenth Amendment's prohibition against slavery.

Then there are arguments based in the misunderstanding of tax law itself: that the Internal Revenue Code isn't a law, that "income" isn't defined, or that the code doesn't actually require payment of taxes. There are also claims of technical loopholes in the procedure of tax collection that allow a person to revoke his duty to pay taxes or avoid tax liability by filing special documents.

One of the favored arguments of tax protesters is that persons who have challenged US tax law have won, but, like all their arguments, this is hardly true. Some protesters have avoided criminal punishment for their actions, usually by asserting that their disobedience wasn't "willful"; that is, they didn't know any better. But even a criminal acquittal doesn't spare a person from civil liability or from the potential for tax garnishments or penalties.

And the truth is that tax protester arguments have been made before judges for decades, and protesters have consistently lost.

FLAG FRINGE

Far less well-known among the general public, but a popular object of ridicule among skeptics, are the arguments over the legal significance of gold fringe on courtroom flags. The bane of public solicitors nationwide, the flag fringe argument is the standard-bearer of silliness for pseudolaw. It is, appropriately, a fringe belief about fringe itself.

The website of the American Patriot Friends Network has a page with the exclamatory title "GET THAT GOLD FRINGE OFF MY FLAG!" Why the capital-letter concern? As the page explains:

> What Does The Gold-Fringed Flag Signify?
>
> It is commonplace to see a gold-fringed United States flag standing in the present-day courtrooms. Is the gold fringe there for decoration only, or does it signify a certain jurisdiction? Make no mistake about it—the American People have been put on notice that the normal constitutional functions of government have been suspended and that their Land has been placed under martial law.[8]

Yes, according to the APFN and other believers, the simple presence of gold tassels trimming the edge of a flag in a courtroom is sufficient reason to remove that courtroom, and all persons who submit to its jurisdiction, from the constitutional law of the United States. They argue that the fringe somehow puts that court under admiralty law or martial law.

The basis for this belief is grounded in army regulations that required various military flags, including those in military courtrooms, to be "trimmed on three sides with golden yellow fringe."[9] Meanwhile, the law does not require such gold fringe to be present on other American flags. As the "logic" goes, if a military courtroom is required to have a gold-trimmed flag, then the presence of a gold-trimmed flag *must* signify a military courtroom. And if the courtroom does not otherwise appear to be a military courtroom (for example, if it happens to be a local municipality's traffic court), then it has been put under military authority through the power of the fringe.

The supporting rationale for this conclusion is sparse, even by pseudolegal standards. A 1994 article by J. Krim Bohren states decisively that a gold-fringed flag "signifies a military jurisdictional presence" but provides no evidence apart from quoting the Flag Resolution of 1777, which describes the stripes and field of stars.[10] The APFN website is far more comprehensive but nearly as uninformative. It devotes considerable space to quoting military regulations and to citing case law that is entirely unrelated to flags. It is obvious, perhaps, that one is not reading a paper written by a real legal scholar when one of the highlighted cases on the issue of the US flag is an obscure 1869 Kentucky Supreme Court case. The only attempt at evidence the APFN provides is located, conveniently, at the top of the page:

> Martial Law Flag "Pursuant to 4 U.S.C. chapter 1, §§1, 2, & 3; Executive Order 10834, August 21, 1959; 24 F.R.6865; a military flag is a flag that resembles the regular flag of the United States, except that it has a YELLOW FRINGE border on three sides. The President of the United States designates this deviation from the regular flag, by executive order, and in his capacity as Commander-in-Chief of the military. The placing of a fringe on the national flag, the dimensions of the flag and the arrangement of the stars in the union are matters of detail not controlled by statute, but are within the discretion of the President as Commander in Chief of the Army and Navy." 34 Ops. Atty. Gen. 83.

> President, Dwight David Eisenhower, by Executive Order No.10834, signed on August 21, 1959 and printed in the Federal Register at 24 F.R. 6865, pursuant to law, stated that: "A military flag is a flag that resembles the regular flag of the United States, except that it has a yellow fringe border on three sides."[11]

With this, the APFN crosses the line from being merely irrationally conspiratorial to being consciously disingenuous. Why?

Because further down on the page is a link to President Eisenhower's Executive Order Number 10834 . . . which does not contain the above quotation. Nor is the quote given in the cited attorney general's opinion. Both quotes appear to be entirely fabricated.

In fact, the attorney general's opinion could not be more devastating to the fringers' argument. In the 1925 advisory opinion (the actual citation for which is 34 Op. Atty. Gen *483*), US Attorney General John Sargent wrote: "The fringe does not appear to be regarded as an integral part of the flag, and its presence can not be said to constitute an unauthorized addition to the design prescribed by statute. An external fringe is to be distinguished from letters, words, emblematic designs printed or superimposed upon the body of the flag itself. Under the law such additions might be open to objection as unauthorized; but the same is not necessarily true of the fringe."[12]

As a judge put it in a 1997 flag case, "Jurisdiction is a matter of law, statute, and constitution, not a child's game wherein one's power is magnified or diminished by the display of some magic talisman."[13] Such mystical or "magic" powers of words and symbols are an incredibly common theme in pseudolaw and are one of the features that help to distinguish legitimate law from frivolous arguments.

FOURTEENTH AMENDMENT CITIZENSHIP

The sovereign citizen movement, in addition to its other faults, has an uncomfortably high amount of crossover with racists and bigots.[14] The Posse Comitatus groups that gave birth to the movement were commonly anti-Semitic, and early adherents often held that only whites could be sovereign citizens. This association has become less pronounced over time; few modern sovereign citizen beliefs are overtly racist. The biggest exception is their claim of a distinct species of Fourteenth Amendment citizens.

Any person born today on US soil is born a citizen of the United States (with limited exceptions, such as the children of foreign ambassadors). However, this was not always the case. In the notorious 1857 case of *Dred Scott v. Sandford,* the Supreme Court held that no one descended from a slave was considered to be a citizen. Citizenship was, mostly but not exclusively, a privilege of being born white.

This changed in 1868, with the passage of the Fourteenth Amendment, the first sentence of which reads "All persons born or naturalized in the United States, and subject to the jurisdiction thereof, are citizens of the United States and of the State wherein they reside." The amendment leaves little room for argument that African Americans were not citizens of the United States, so members of the sovereign citizen groups maintained that, while the Fourteenth Amendment did make blacks into US citizens, it also created two kinds of US citizens. Their theory creatively parsed the words to claim that, although the amendment guaranteed "citizenship" to all native-born persons, it did not make all native-born persons "Citizens" of an equal sort. (The capitalization of the word *citizens* came to be treated as incredibly important in their arguments.) Fourteenth Amendment citizens held a different, and lesser, form of citizenship than did persons who possessed citizenship prior to the passing of the amendment. This lesser "Fourteenth Amendment Citizenship" was created especially for blacks and was intended to provide them only with a short list of "rudimentary rights," not with the full civil rights of white citizens.

The racism in this argument is self-evident, and some modern proponents have transformed the argument of distinct forms of citizenship into something more compatible with sovereign citizen ideology. According to this revisionist interpretation, Fourteenth Amendment citizenship is still real and still distinct from constitutional citizenship, but the distinction is not race-based. Instead, it is a lesser form of citizenship created to strengthen government control over individuals. It's argued that ordinary citizenship carries with it rights that are guaranteed by nature or by the Constitution, whereas Fourteenth Amendment citizenship is a creation of the government and therefore carries only the protections that the government chooses.

THE CORPORATION OF THE UNITED STATES/ CORPORATE PERSONHOOD

Most intelligent people believe that the United States is a country. And that it's run by a federal government, and that the central controlling law for that government is the United States Constitution, ratified in 1787. But there are people who claim that in 1871 the United States of America was surreptitiously turned into a corporation, and that the US Constitution of 1787 was replaced with a *new* constitution that transformed all American citizens into government-owned corporate property. Congress did this, it is said, as part of a secret deal made with international bankers, such as the Rothschild family, a European banking dynasty. Post–Civil War America needed money, and so the country was magically transformed into a corporation, the controlling interests of which were then handed over to mysterious foreign elites. It sounds like a bizarre amalgam of anticorporate leftism and paranoid right-wing thought, and it's just one more of the many pseudolegal theories of the sovereign citizen movement.[15]

The entire conspiratorial theory is built around essentially just one quotation, ripped from its original context and misinterpreted by people who failed to remember either that thesauruses exist or that thesauruses must be complicit in the cover-up.

At the center of the "United States Corporation" claim is a very real congressional statute, the District of Columbia Organic Act of 1871. Article I of the Constitution established the creation of a district outside of state territory ("not exceeding ten miles square") that would be the seat of the new federal government, and for which the US Congress would provide legislation. The district was initially formed from one hundred square miles contributed from Maryland and Virginia, although in 1846, the Virginia portion was returned to that state and became Alexandria.

For some eighty years, the district included two cities with individual charters: the pre-Revolution city of Georgetown and the federal city of Washington, which was named for George Washington in 1791, during his first term as president. In 1871, following a decade of rapid growth, Congress reorganized the governance of the district. The city charters were repealed, and a new, singular charter was created for the District of Columbia. This was done in the aforementioned Organic Act, passed on February 21, 1871.

So how does an act reorganizing Washington, DC, turn the United States into a corporation owned by international bankers? Because the act refers to the district as "a body corporate for municipal purposes" that will "exercise all powers of a municipal corporation not inconsistent with the Constitution and laws of the United States."

The inclusion of the word *corporation* was all the sovereign citizens seem to have needed to build a conspiracy theory. The presence of the modifier *municipal* seems not to have affected them, even though American cities are commonly organized as "municipal corporations," without the inclusion of the word *corporation* to imply any sort of private ownership. The selective quotation they use here is so selective that they rarely even quote a full phrase, lest they be forced to acknowledge the inclusion of *municipal*. So references on sovereign citizens' pages typically just refer to the act by name, quote just the terms *corporation* and *Constitution of the United States*, and provide no further context.

The secret transformation of the United States from a free nation into a Rothschild-owned corporation is nefarious enough, but according to sovereign citizens, it gets worse. One of the core sovereign citizen beliefs—indeed, one of their beliefs that is most closely tied to the "sovereign citizen" name itself—is that this corporatization of America did not stop with the nation. Supposedly, individual Americans have also been assigned secondary corporate identities. These corporate shells, they say, are initially created through the issuance of a state birth certificate. The corporate shell is then sold by the federal government to international banking interests as collateral, presumably in some secret, underground, international birth certificate exchange.[16]

It is the person's corporate identity that is subject to tax laws, traffic laws, and the like, and sovereign citizens claim to offer a "cure" of sorts for this: the so-called redemption movement. Redemption theory claims that a person can slough off his corporate identity and reclaim his "true" identity through the filing of certain legal papers and the use of "sight drafts," which amount to little more than rubber checks.[17] Multiple leaders and participants in the redemption movement have been convicted of fraud and tax evasion because, for instance, the movement claims that Americans are not "citizens" and thus can avoid federal income taxes by reclassifying themselves as "non-resident aliens." Not only have courts rejected this approach, but the IRS has declared this scheme to be frivolous and subject to a $5,000 penalty.[18]

THE "MISSING" THIRTEENTH AMENDMENT

I was first introduced to the "missing" Thirteenth Amendment to the Constitution during the course of researching my earlier project on Birtherism. I was interviewing a Georgia computer repairman who had spearheaded the first "citizen grand juries" to indict Obama over his eligibility (a very posse comitatus-esque action), and he mentioned that lawyers were illegally serving in the federal government. Being a lawyer myself (though he did not know this), and having twice entertained myself by running for federal office against another lawyer, this was news to me. Here, I learned, was an entire constitutional conspiracy theory that I had never encountered before.

In contrast to the other examples in this chapter, the "missing" Thirteenth Amendment is firmly rooted in real events. Decades before the familiar Thirteenth Amendment was passed, outlawing slavery in post–Civil War America, there was an earlier, failed Thirteenth Amendment. It was passed by the US House and Senate in 1810, and read: "If any citizen of the United States shall accept, claim, receive or retain, any title of nobility or honor, or shall, without the consent of Congress, accept and retain any present, pension, office or emolument of any kind whatever, from any emperor, king, prince or foreign power, such person shall cease to be a citizen of the United States, and shall be incapable of holding any office of trust or profit under them, or either of them."[19]

This Titles of Nobility Amendment (sometimes abbreviated TONA) then proceeded to the states for ratification. Over several years, it was ratified by twelve states and rejected by five others. In 1818, secretary of state John Quincy Adams determined that the amendment had failed to receive the required number of ratifying votes and had thus failed to be adopted. Adams conducted this inquiry at the request of President James Monroe, precisely because there was some level of confusion during those early days of the Republic as to whether the amendment had passed. Although Adams found that it had not passed—and, although such early American legal experts as William Rawle and Joseph Story stated that it was never ratified by enough states—in the interim years, it had made its way into at least one substantive publication. The 1815 edition of the United States Statutes at Large included the amendment, noting that its status was unclear. The amendment was also included in copies of the Constitution that were provided to members of the Fiftieth Congress, and since a new edition of the United States Statutes at Large was not published until 1845, the Titles of Nobility Amendment was erroneously published and republished in various documents throughout the 1800s. It made its final appearances around the turn of the century.

The amendment disappeared into obscurity until 1983, when archival researcher David Dodge found it printed in an 1825 copy of the Maine Civil Code. Intrigued, Dodge researched further and discovered that the amendment had actually been passed by the requisite number of states, but (according to him) its passage was subsequently suppressed. Dodge's evidence for this conclusion was based on one particular publication of the amendment, in the 1819 Virginia Civil Code. Virginia had not responded to Adams's inquiry in 1818, and Dodge saw the inclusion of the amendment in the Virginia codebook as proof that the state had ratified it.[20]

In fact, the Virginia legislature had expressly rejected the amendment in 1811, and there is no record of the state ever considering the amendment again. When the Virginia Civil Code was revised and republished in 1849, the new book stated that the amendment's previous inclusion was a mistake. Even if Virginia had reconsidered the amendment anytime before 1819, there still was never a sufficient number of ratifying states at any moment to adopt the amendment. By the time the twelfth recorded state approved the amendment, a total of fourteen states were required.

None of this stopped Dodge, however, who took up the amendment as a personal crusade and is largely responsible for what meager support it has today. It should probably not come as a surprise that Dodge has a long history with the sovereign citizen movement. He fancies himself a constitutional scholar and has a reputation in his Maine hometown for hassling the local judicial system in the form of impersonating a lawyer for fellow sovereign citizens.[21]

Belief that the Titles of Nobility Amendment was passed and suppressed is not as widespread as most of the other pseudolaw beliefs described in this chapter. Yet even it has succeeded in gaining prominence in recent years. In 2010, the Republican Party of Iowa adopted a new platform that included a smattering of fringe thought, from opposing the nonexistent currency the Amero to endorsing the return of the gold standard. One plank, though, was odd enough to raise the eyebrows of even seasoned conspiracy watchers: "We call for the reintroduction and ratification of the original 13th Amendment, not the 13th Amendment in today's Constitution."[22]

What had long been a forgotten footnote in American history was suddenly spotlighted in the platform of a major political party. (One hopes that the wording of this plank is merely unfortunate, and that the Iowa GOP was not actually suggesting the repeal of the amendment banning slavery.) According to a party spokesman, its inclusion was in protest of President Obama's receipt of the Nobel Peace Prize.

The "missing" Thirteenth Amendment may be a fascinating bit of constitutional trivia, but that's all it is. And although it's included here with other pseudolegal claims—particularly because it's a favorite among sovereign citizens—the arguments made in support of it have much in common with pseudohistory, including claims of suppressed events, of books erased from existence, of old truths that were forgotten and must be rediscovered. And like so much other pseudo-scholarship, the evidence presented in defense of the argument is heavily reliant on anomalies: books that accidentally included the amendment or discrepancies in the states' record keeping.

But the pseudolaw is still there, dwelling on arcane procedural rules that it is said weren't followed to the letter, much like the ones tax protesters use in their treatment of the Sixteenth Amendment. There are also advocates who fall back on creative interpretations of the amendment's language, insisting that the prohibition against "titles of nobility" would necessarily forbid lawyers from holding elected office. Because, it is further argued, the term *Esquire* somehow carries with it the implication of loyalty to the British Crown, and it's common for lawyers to use the word *Esquire* after their names. Therefore, based on pseudolegal logic, all lawyers have foreign titles of nobility.

NATURAL-BORN CITIZENSHIP

Following the Birther movement in 2008, a brand-new pseudolegal theory was created and popularized. If, during the 2008 election or prior, you had asked a stranger to tell you who can be elected president, you almost certainly would have been told that the president must be born in the United States. Most scholars would say that the constitutional requirement of "natural-born citizenship" also extends to children born to American citizens while overseas, but the general rule is that if a child is born on US soil, he (or she) can grow up to be president.

This bit of common knowledge played a large role in the growing Birther movement in mid-2008, as critics began speculating that if Obama had been born outside the United States, then he might not be eligible to be president. Almost immediately, Birthers began spawning alternative theories of ineligibility, and the almost immediate production of Obama's birth certificate caused some critics to push forward with those theories instead.

The allegation was made very early on that Obama's mother was simply too young at the time of her son's birth for him to have been born a US citizen; this was the result of a misinterpreted statute involving foreign births to a single American parent. Around the time of the Democratic National Convention, the Obama campaign acknowledged that under British law, Obama had actually been born with a dual citizenship he inherited through his father, but which had expired when Obama was in his twenties. A new theory emerged, arguing that an individual born with dual citizenship cannot be elected president, even if that person has single citizenship at the time of the election.

These variations on a theme eventually culminated in what would become the Birthers' favorite pseudolegal theory: the two-parent definition of natural-born citizenship. Shortly after Obama won the presidential election, a growing number of Birthers began arguing that it was not enough for the president to be born in the United States. They claimed that in order to be considered a natural-born citizen, as required by the Constitution, the president must be born in the United States, *and* both of his parents must have been US citizens when he was born.

The argument originated with an actual attorney, albeit one who was no longer practicing law and who was, instead, making a living as a professional poker player. Leo Donofrio filed suit against the New Jersey secretary of state in the final days before the election, and when he appealed his denial, he began the workings of the two-citizen-parent argument. It first appeared almost as an afterthought in a filed brief, tossed off casually as a supposed fact but with no supporting evidence.

After Donofrio posted some of his pleadings online and did some interviews, other Birthers rushed to find anything they could construe as supporting evidence. Through legal research heavily reliant on Google®, the Birthers successfully crowd-sourced a handful of publications over the years that supported this view. A Swiss expert on international law. An 1896 newspaper column. A 1916 partisan attack piece. Even the racist Supreme Court decision of *Dred Scott v. Sandford* was cited.

It was promptly pointed out to the Birthers that this theory had a major historical flaw. Twenty-first president Chester A. Arthur was born to an Irish father, and in over 120 years, the question of his eligibility went unopposed. The Birthers' response? They declared that, like Obama, Arthur was also a usurper. He just got away with it.

Counterexamples were thus rendered useless in Birther eyes. Legal experts were discounted as being biased, ignorant, or paid off. Similarly unpersuasive were the numerous published definitions of presidential eligibility that said nothing about a parental citizenship requirement, or publications that overtly stated that the native-born child of aliens could become president.

This bit of pseudolaw began having an effect not only on the legal attitudes of its believers but on their memories as well. Birthers began backdating their theories, claiming that they remembered discussions of Obama's natural-born citizenship in 2007 and earlier, but they could never produce evidence of these discussions. They claimed to have witnessed a televised debate in 2004 during which Obama evaded a question from Alan Keyes about his presidential eligibility; Keyes's own campaign manager confirms this never happened. They swear they have memories of being taught the two-citizen-parent requirement in their school days, but none of the textbooks bear that out. Conveniently, no Birthers "remembered" these particular lessons before the election—all such "memories" surfaced only after Mr. Donofrio introduced the idea to them.

Donofrio repeated this trick in June 2011, when he wrote a blog post claiming that the Supreme Court had defined "natural-born citizen" in a case, and that it had done so in a way that expressly excluded President Obama.[23] The case, *Minor v Happersett*, was one that Birthers had cited in passing for years, arguing that the Supreme Court had never definitively ruled on the issue. But starting in June 2011, the armchair lawyers of the Birther world quickly made this one case the center of their legal arguments. When an administrative court in Georgia heard ballot challenges in January 2012 over the president's eligibility, all three lawyers relied almost exclusively on that one case for their constitutional argument.[24]

SPOTTING PSEUDOLAW

Now that we understand what pseudolaw is, how do we recognize a pseudolegal argument when it's presented? What features help to distinguish frivolous legal claims from potentially legitimate ones?

Armchair Lawyering

Just as pseudoscience is the playground of nonscientists and persons working outside their field of expertise, pseudolaw is, more often than not, the product of nonlawyers. In some cases, as with flag fringers and TONA proponents, nonlawyers have a conspicuous aversion to actual lawyers.

Almost none of the various pseudolegal theories described in the previous pages were developed by actual lawyers. The Birther movement's Leo Donofrio is one of the few mentioned who has a law degree, and even he had never filed a lawsuit prior to a pro se Birther case in 2008. Nevertheless, the fact that he had never worked as a lawyer did not stop him from presenting himself to his Birther brethren as a constitutional scholar.

It's the same fake-expert problem seen in the other pseudo-scholarships, only in pseudolaw, *every* person feels like he or she can be the equal of a Supreme Court justice. Being a crank scientist demands at least a rough understanding of the field and perhaps the ability to speak in jargon. But being a crank legal expert requires nothing more than reading the Constitution, remembering what you learned in fifth-grade civics, and suddenly proclaiming that you're as authoritative as one of the Founding Fathers.

If you find that the advocates of a questionable legal theory are all nonlawyers, that should raise questions. If you find that actual lawyers will reliably tell you that the theory is wrong, then that's further validation. And if you ask the advocates about where to find legitimate legal scholars who support their position, and they can't oblige, then you've all but confirmed that they're promoting bad legal advice.

Rejection of Established Precedent

The practice of law entails two equally important forms of source material. The first is the passed and published law itself: the plain text that was passed and approved by the legislative and executive branches, including statutes, regulations, even the Constitution. The second source is case law. Have earlier courts evaluated a particular law or tackled a similar issue? How did that earlier court interpret that law? Was it interpreted consistently in other cases? Have courts in other jurisdictions reached similar conclusions? How does the logic of those earlier decisions apply to a new case before the court? These earlier cases are used as precedent for deciding the new issue, helping to guarantee a certain level of consistency over time, even as judges change. The alternative is that any given interpretation of the law could continually change based simply on the judge occupying the bench at the time.

Pseudolawyers don't tend to give quite so much deference to precedential decisions. Rather, they may choose to ignore relevant precedent entirely. They may not be trained lawyers, but that won't stop them from declaring that their interpretation of the Constitution is correct, and that the Supreme Court's is wrong.

This attitude is an unsurprising outgrowth of the first commonality of pseudolaw: the prevalence of armchair lawyering. Trained lawyers understand and appreciate the importance of precedent, even when they disagree with it. A lawyer is capable of recognizing what the status of the law is, and if he wants to argue that an old decision should be overturned, he will craft arguments as to why the supposedly wrong decision is inconsistent with other accepted law. And those arguments will need to be compelling in their own right; simply declaring that "the judge was wrong!" and relying on stray quotes and novel interpretations of law isn't a recipe for success.

The rejection of precedent is central to pseudolaw because the defining characteristic of pseudolaw is its frivolousness. The arguments pseudolawyers advance have already been addressed by the courts, and they have been universally rejected. Judges have repeatedly found themselves faced with litigants who claim that flag fringe is important to jurisdiction, and those judges have all agreed that it's not. (One judge, when confronted with a party who said that the flag put the courtroom under maritime law, simply instructed the party to pretend he was on a boat.) Tax protesters have continually advanced their arguments as defenses to criminal and civil charges of tax evasion, and they've continually lost those battles.

These sorts of 100-percent-loss rates are strong indicators that a legal argument is frivolous. The judicial decisions behind them are, if not binding precedent, at least incredibly persuasive to any judge. When a Georgia administrative judge held that Birther arguments about President Obama's eligibility were baseless, he stated in his opinion that he found the arguments presented in an Indiana decision on the same subject to be persuasive.[25] Relying on the reasoning of another court (and especially on the unanimity of other courts) is something any judge can do; as expected, however, Birthers were furious that the judge would cite to a persuasive case, since it was not technically binding upon him.

Because of the pseudolegal focus on "binding" precedent, and because the American judicial system has both state and federal court systems with multiple appellate levels, pseudolaw has a ready-made system of goalpost moving to exploit. No matter what court has decided an issue, and no matter how many courts have agreed on that issue, Birthers can always complain that the issue hasn't been addressed by a *higher* court—and as a last resort, that it hasn't been addressed by the *Supreme* Court.

Pseudolawyers of all stripes love to argue that their particular theory of law has not been explicitly rejected by the US Supreme Court. And that is often true, because of the way the Court chooses its cases. The Supreme Court likes to hear cases that involve new and important unresolved questions or cases upon which lower courts have disagreed. By the nature of this selection process, the Court has no incentive to hear cases that concern arguments that all lower courts have agreed are frivolous. There's no need for the Supreme Court to weigh in and say that flag fringe is irrelevant or that people don't have corporate shells owned by foreign banks. The Supreme Court doesn't need to declare that Barack Obama is eligible to be president despite having a Kenyan father, anymore than it needs to declare that Hillary Clinton was eligible despite being a woman. It's universally accepted that those factors are irrelevant, and so there's no reason for the Supreme Court to state the obvious.

Appeals to Authority

The legal custom of citing to established precedent is itself a form of an appeal to authority, but its purpose is to keep our system of laws consistent over time. If courts were not bound by the earlier decisions of other judges, there would be inconsistent results galore, and the law would be unpredictable. However, that's not the sort of appeal to authority that pseudolawyers are often guilty of. Since actual precedent does not favor their arguments, they appeal to different, and less reliable, authorities.

These alternative authorities may be historical figures, political pundits, or military figures. They may have simply written a book or a blog on a pseudolegal subject and thus are treated as legal experts simply for having been published. By this latter method, pseudolaw-yers can become their own authorities.

Of course, a nonlawyer could advance a legal theory that a court finds persuasive and chooses to follow. And trained lawyers and judges regularly find themselves on the dissenting end of the law. But the final arbiter of what is and what is not authoritative law is the court system itself. If someone's cited authority is not a judicial decision or a legal expert who can detail the history of the law, but is instead a TV personality or a former soldier or an author who claims that he's right where all the judges are wrong, then there is good reason to doubt that he's giving solid legal advice.

Quote Mining

Quote mining, a favorite of other denialists and conspiracy theorists, is one of the primary tools used in pseudolaw. Nowadays, selective quotation is, to an extent, a staple of the practice of law. Opposing sides present the court with their competing interpretations of statutes and case law, citing particular quotes that support their positions. Judges do the same thing in their written opinions. In a split decision of the Supreme Court, for instance, the justices in the majority will single out the quotes that they believe support their conclusions, and the dissenting justices do the same with other quotes, whether from the same or different cases.

The distinguishing characteristic of real law is that, while there's a certain amount of selective attention given to favorable or unfa-vorable quotations and earlier opinions, attorneys and judges are expected to not misrepresent or ignore precedent that is unfavor-able to their arguments. If other appellate decisions are known to be unfavorable to an attorney's argument, the attorney is expected to at least acknowledge the existence of that precedent and to distin-guish it from his own case. Justices in a Supreme Court majority will write about why the dissenters' preferred quotes aren't controlling, and the dissenters will say that the majority fails to recognize the significance of case law that should result in a different holding. And, of course, it's naturally expected that quotations are not to be taken out of context or used in such a way as to actively misrepresent their original meaning.

Pseudolawyers are bound by no such codes of conduct. They will strip a quotation of all context, imposing their own spin on it by putting it in isolation. They will treat a court's unbinding dicta as if it were a court's official holding. They will cite to a dissenting opinion as soon as they'll cite to a majority one. They won't limit themselves to citing legal opinions or texts; they'll just as soon pull quotes from books or newspapers and treat them as the equal of a court decision.

In the discussion of flag fringe, I noted that advocates of that argument frequently cite to a 1925 attorney general's advisory opinion that did, in fact, discuss the presence of fringe on a US flag. But whereas fringers hold this up as support for their pseudolegal beliefs and will even quote at length from the opinion, they consistently misrepresent the actual stated conclusion of the attorney general, which was that fringe did not matter. If that's not bad enough, they then compound this exercise in quote mining by simply fabricating a completely fake quote and affixing it to the real quote from the opinion.

Birthers tried quote mining with the *Minor v. Happersett* case in 2011. The case did include discussion of who was a natural-born citizen, but it concluded its brief comments by saying that it was explicitly not resolving the question. Furthermore, the case was chiefly concerned with voting rights for women, not with citizenship. Birthers cherry-picked the sentence that, in isolation, supported their position and then attempted to explain away the contextual factors.

Spotting quote mining is difficult without research, because one naturally has to consult the source to see if it has been accurately represented. Using the techniques discussed in chapter 5 is a good start. The lack of a researchable citation may mean that the context has been lost in repetition or, worse, that the person repeating the quote wants to make it difficult to see the context. One should be wary of bold pronouncements made by prominent persons, especially when the words seem to be inconsistent with what's known of the individual. And whereas lawyers would want to quote from statutes and case law, the pseudolawyer is more likely to cite to quotes from nonbinding sources, like speeches or personal or published writings.

Regarding pseudolaw in particular, the use of suspiciously strong supportive quotations ought to be a warning bell to check the source material. Because the law is a matter of consensus, and because pseudolaw is fringe by definition, a purported quote from a respectable source endorsing a pseudolegal proposition is likely being misrepresented. Maybe it's taken out of context. Maybe it's from a dissent. Maybe the case was subsequently overruled. Or maybe it's not even a real quote.

Capitalization and Grammar

Supreme Court justice Felix Frankfurter once said that the three most important keys to interpreting a statute were (1) Read the statute, (2) Read the statute, and (3) Read the statute. Choice of words is important. Sentence construction is important. Even punctuation is important.

If you listen to sovereign citizens, you will soon start to hear that the use of capital letters is not just important but critical. Whether or not a particular term is capitalized can not only affect the interpretation of a statute; it can radically alter judicial process and even the course of national history.

Believers in the secret Rothschild-owned-corporation-of-the-United-States theory use this kind of argument as their grounds for claiming that the Constitution drafted by the Founding Fathers has been repealed and supplanted. Their reasoning? The 1871 Act says that the new municipal corporation will have all the powers "not inconsistent with the Constitution and laws of the United States."[26] This, they say, is evidence of the creation of a new document, because the Founders referred to the "Constitution *for* the United States" not "*of* the United States." And they contend this change of preposition reflects a complete reinvention of the US government.

According to those who say that there are multiple categories of US citizen, how are we supposed to know that the Fourteenth Amendment created a distinct form of citizenship? Capital letters. It is contended that pre–Civil War law referred to capital-C *Citizens*, whereas the Fourteenth Amendment guaranteed that all individuals born in the United States would be lower-case *citizens*.

In their efforts to attribute the inspiring motivation of the Founding Fathers to a deceased Swiss writer, Birthers have also attempted to fall back on a capitalization argument. Emmerich de Vattel's premiere work was an expansive treatise on international law titled *The Law of Nations*. Birthers say the Constitution itself proves that Vattel was an influence on its creation, arguing that his book is referenced by name in America's founding document. Their justification for this is based not just on making a flimsy capitalization argument but also by ignoring the context of their cherry-picked quote (from section eight of the Constitution) that Congress shall be empowered "To define and punish Piracies and Felonies committed on the high Seas, and Offenses against the Law of Nations." Not only is it textually improbable that the Constitution is referring to offenses against a book, but the argument ignores the fact that the Constitution capitalizes almost every noun.

Such examples aren't terribly significant among the sovereign citizen community, but one capitalization-related belief is central to a long line of frivolous judicial arguments, and it is intimately tied to the corporate citizenship theory. When the government creates one's corporate shell through the issuance of a birth certificate, the shell is given a new name. The appearance of the newborn's name in all-capital letters on the birth certificate signifies the new corporate entity, whereas the flesh-and-blood person's name is properly in uppercase and lowercase letters. To wit, my true name is Loren Christopher Collins, whereas my birth certificate reads LOREN CHRISTOPHER COLLINS.

But it doesn't stop there. The sovereign citizen would contend that only my corporate name is punctuation-free; my "true" name includes both a hyphen and a colon to signify my familial associations. So, if I were a sovereign citizen believer, I would write my name like this:

Loren-Christopher: Collins

It's silly, yes, but such distinctions are a blessing when it comes to spotting pseudolegal arguments. Whenever and wherever you see a person writing his name in that fashion, you can be certain that you're looking at frivolous pseudolaw. Lots of pseudolaw proponents *don't* use this technique, but for those who do, their own internalized nonsense has effectively branded them.

Sovereign Citizen

As discussed earlier in this chapter, there is an almost tautological relationship between pseudolaw in America and the sovereign citizen movement. There is no intrinsic reason why the majority of pseudolegal beliefs should be tied to a single movement, but they are. At the same time, virtually every novel legal position advocated by sovereign citizens could qualify as being labeled pseudolaw.

Even pseudolegal arguments that don't begin inside the sovereign citizen movement seem to grow in that affiliation over time. The earliest Birthers were not sovereign citizens; many were dejected Hillary Clinton fans. But over time, the movement began to display stronger sovereign citizen–esque qualities. Many Birthers eventually began disputing not only whether being native-born made a person eligible to run for president; they also began disputing that native birth guaranteed the person to any sort of US citizenship at all. When, in January 2012, Birthers finally succeeded in getting an opportunity to present their eligibility arguments before a judge, they presented zero evidence that the president was born outside Hawaii. But what argument was made at length, complete with visual aids? That the president is a mere "Fourteenth Amendment citizen," a lesser class of US citizen.

Consequently, any legal claims that one can recognize as coming from the sovereign citizen movement should be viewed with extreme suspicion. And indeed, much of the terminology associated with sovereign citizens is all but exclusive to them. The category of "Fourteenth Amendment Citizen" is almost never seen outside of sovereign citizen circles. The "Corporation of the United States" is a similarly unique phrase. The same goes for the use of the Uniform Commercial Code (UCC) for anything outside of contract law.

And, of course, the standard appeals to conspiracy are once again a red flag. The real practice of law doesn't cater to arguments about long-suppressed meanings or far-reaching cover-ups; seeing those sorts of arguments ought to be a warning that a solid legal argument is not going to follow.

CHAPTER 10

WHAT'S THE HARM?

A surprising obstacle when it comes to instilling the value of critical thinking is simply getting someone to care. What, they may ask, is the harm in believing in bogus claims or pseudoscience?[1] Even if the belief is wrong, what's the worst that could happen? Sometimes the harm is relatively obvious. Believing in pseudoscience, and particularly believing in bad medical information, can have dire consequences. If you believe that vaccines are dangerous and choose not to get vaccinated, then you're consciously taking the risk of contracting a disease. Maybe you don't fully appreciate the extent of that risk, and maybe you don't even acknowledge the efficacy of the vaccine itself, but it would be hard to not at least recognize that getting a contagious disease is a risk.

There may be no more straightforward example of the consequences of false belief than that of falling for a financial scam. Americans continue to lose millions of dollars a year to Nigerian e-mail scammers, even though that particular scheme has come to be known as shorthand for the most obvious kind of online fraud. Believing in mysterious African princes who randomly contact you by e-mail to offer you millions of dollars can, and does, lead to bank accounts being emptied and life savings being lost. Meanwhile, a simple familiarity with that one trope is enough to help a person avoid a much wider array of scams by providing a skeptical lens through which to look at the world.

But what of other forms of nonsense? What's the harm in believing in astrology? Or homeopathy? Or Ouija boards? What's the harm in denying evolution, or in believing that the moon landing was faked, or that the president was born in Kenya? In fact, there are numerous reasons to avoid small but silly beliefs. They're just not as obvious as having your savings account drained by the Honorable Joseph M'Butu of Ghudaza.

HEALTH CONSEQUENCES

Vaccine denialists may not fully appreciate the risks that come with not getting inoculated against diseases, but those risks are nonetheless experienced not only by denialists but also by others who suffer as the general public's herd immunity is eroded by the lack of widespread vaccination.

Former Playboy model Jenny McCarthy first began publicly denouncing vaccines in 2007, following her claim that her young son had been diagnosed with autism. McCarthy blamed the autism on the vaccines he had received, and then began encouraging parents to avoid vaccinating their children.[2] Between her books and her television appearances speaking out against vaccination, McCarthy has become the face of vaccine denial.

To help fight her message, TV producer Derek Bartholomaus created Jenny McCarthy BodyCount. The site's mission statement is to publish "the total number of vaccine preventable illnesses and vaccine preventable deaths that have happened in the United States since June 2007 when she [McCarthy] began publicly speaking out against vaccines." As of this writing, the site offers up the following numbers:

102,961—Number of Preventable Illnesses from June 3, 2007, to August 11, 2012

1,016—Number of Preventable Deaths from June 3, 2007, to August 11, 2012

0—Number of Autism Diagnoses Scientifically Linked to Vaccinations from June 3, 2007, to August 11, 2012[3]

The fates of these people aren't directly attributable to McCarthy; individual people made the decision to not get vaccinated. They may not have ever even heard of Jenny McCarthy. But they made medical decisions based on misinformation, and because of that, over one hundred thousand of them paid with their health, and over a thousand paid with their lives.

Medical misinformation doesn't have to come from celebrities; it can come from the government. South African president Thabo Mbeki publicly questioned AIDS research, and his Ministry of Health was actively hostile to the use of antiretroviral drugs (ARVs), calling them poison. Instead of proven drugs, South Africa promoted various "alternative" treatments for HIV that were not proven to be effective.

A 2008 study in the *Oxford Journals* looked at South Africa's HIV history for 1999 through 2007, contrasting the trends of the country as a whole against the nation's Western Cape province, where antiretroviral drugs were encouraged and supported. The study found that if all of South Africa had had the same positive approach to ARVs as the Western Cape did, then an estimated 171,000 HIV infections and 343,000 deaths could have been prevented during those nine years.[4] Half a million people suffered because their government didn't trust the science on HIV and AIDS.

In addition to the different types of medical denialism, there are also "alternative" medicines that advance unsupported modalities. Some are simply ineffective, but others are dangerous treatments, masquerading as helpful therapies.

Chelation therapy is a legitimate medical course of treatment for a particular ailment; namely, heavy metal poisoning. A chemical that binds to heavy metals (lead, mercury, cadmium) is injected into the patient's blood and helps to flush those metals out of the body through urination. For that purpose, it's proven and effective. But among advocates of alternative medicine, chelation therapy is touted as a cure for everything from cancer to diabetes to Alzheimer's. And while the injected chemical is helpful to persons suffering from heavy metal poisoning, it is potentially toxic to the average person. It is known to cause kidney damage and can also create heart problems. In 2005, a five-year-old Pennsylvania boy actually died of heart failure after his parents tried to use chelation therapy to treat his autism.

MISSING A SUPERIOR ALTERNATIVE— OPPORTUNITY COSTS

The risks of alternative medicine are not limited to direct physical harm. Nonscience-based medicine is not alternative because it's harmful; it's alternative because it hasn't been proven to work. Often, such treatments perform no better than a placebo under controlled circumstances and are thus viewed as simply ineffective.

Homeopathy is the best example of this, as homeopathic "medicine" is diluted to the point where it contains no trace of its own supposed active ingredient. Homeopathic drugs are just water pills, and they carry roughly the same level of medical risk or reward. Still, ineffective treatments carry a different sort of price, in the form of opportunity costs. A normal bottle of homeopathic pills costs about ten dollars. That's ten dollars that could be used to cover the co-pay for real medicine, or that could be put toward the cost of an effective treatment.

Money, though, is the simplest of the opportunity costs that are imposed by misinformation. Time and attention that is spent on bad or useless endeavors is time that cannot be spent pursuing more effective alternatives.

Peter Sellers was a renowned actor and comedian, best remembered for playing several roles in *Dr. Strangelove* and for his performance as Inspector Clouseau in the *Pink Panther* series. In real life, Sellers began suffering from heart attacks at age thirty-eight. His condition was not immediately fatal, and Sellers did manage to live another sixteen years. But he very likely could have lived longer. During those sixteen years, Sellers chose not to pursue accepted medical treatment for his heart condition and instead traveled to the Philippines roughly twice a year to undergo "psychic surgery." He finally consented to the implantation of a pacemaker following a heart attack when he was fifty-one, but he refused further surgery that was recommended, and he died of a final heart attack at age fifty-four.[5]

More recently, in 2011, Apple CEO Steve Jobs passed away after a bout with pancreatic cancer. Jobs's wealth could have paid for a hospital's worth of doctors, but following his diagnosis, he decided against having surgery to remove his tumor. For nine months, Jobs instead tried to treat his cancer with acupuncture, veganism, and herbal and other alternative treatments. Finally Jobs acceded to his doctor's wishes and had the tumor surgically removed; a few years later, he had a liver transplant. Neither successfully controlled the cancer, and Jobs eventually died from it. He was fifty-six.[6]

It cannot be said with any certainty whether Jobs's fate would have been different if he had opted for surgery immediately. According to his biographer, Walter Isaacson, it was a decision that Jobs regretted later in his life.[7] The nine months that Jobs invested in vegan diets and Eastern medicine didn't directly hurt him, but during those nine months his cancer continued to spread unchecked. Surgery may not have cured him even if it had been performed soon after his diagnosis, but at least it was a proven way to attack the problem; the "alternative" medicines he chose ultimately harmed him by diverting his attention and occupying his time.

In the same way, Peter Sellers's stubborn reliance on psychic surgery kept him from pursuing heart treatments that could have kept him alive past fifty-four. The psychic surgery itself was a magic trick, and as such never directly harmed Sellers. But Sellers's belief in psychic surgery may have cost him his life.

Opportunity costs are hardly limited to health. Time, effort, and money that are expended in the course of pseudoscience, conspiracy theories, or supernatural beliefs could similarly be put to better use.

Conspiracy theorists, for all their faults, do often operate from a commitment to a certain cause. They pride themselves as being agents of truth and are willing to expend years of their lives in pursuing their theories, even at the expense of their careers and relationships. They may be obsessive, but they're diligent in their obsessiveness. JFK-assassination theorists will examine videos frame by frame. Pseudolaw advocates will pore over old manuscripts for useful material. They all produce reams of treatises documenting their "findings," so much so that one of the most common fallacies they exhibit is the argumentum verbosium, or proof by verbosity.

All that energy spent on "proving" that the CIA murdered Kennedy or that President Obama was born in Kenya is energy that could be spent more constructively. One of the most common rejoinders to Birthers from Republicans themselves is that the president's opponents should focus on his policies, not on conspiracies about his birth. Birtherism is born out of a distrust of Barack Obama; its advocates are universally people who want him out of the Oval Office. But they don't spend their time advocating for conservative causes, or campaigning for candidates they support, or documenting the failings of the administration. Instead, they expend endless time on blogs and message boards, making dead-end attempts at litigation and promoting their own denialist beliefs about the president's citizenship status. It's such a waste of time and resources that some conservatives have postulated that the White House actually prefers that Birtherism refuses to die out, because it's preferable to have one's enemies occupied with silly nonsense than focusing on legitimate political weaknesses.

The industry of multilevel marketing actively exploits individuals' self-interest, selling the promise of future wealth in exchange for hefty commitments in the present. The pitch offers up a life of economic self-sufficiency, but to get to that point there are purchase commitments and sales quotas and books and CDs and seminars and so on. A few people do make money in these systems; though, more often than not, those who do make money are the people at the top. The others tend to find that after a few years, once they've deducted the money they've spent on motivational materials and product samples, they would have been better off simply earning a side income in a more traditional way, such as working a second job.

WASTED TIME AND RESOURCES

Closely related to the opportunity costs of time and effort are the outright waste of time and effort. The distinction between the two is slight, and a broad view of opportunity costs would easily include any form of waste. But for the sake of illustration, the difference here is that opportunity costs are often viewed as involving a common interest. Someone chooses to pursue a useless medical treatment instead of an effective one. Someone invests himself in exposing a nonsensical theory of corruption instead of shining the light on real infractions. Someone spends their nights on a scheme that isn't going to make them wealthy instead of using that time to increase their earnings in other ways. Any kind of waste can be viewed as an opportunity cost, just where the opportunity missed is not directly tied to the action taken. Other interests or hobbies that could be explored are instead neglected or are never discovered at all.

Having built up the slight positive side of conspiracy theorists— their willingness to commit their time and resources to a cause they truly believe in—it's time to cut them back down. When it comes to research, the stamina of conspiracy theorists is admirable in a way. They're willing to make sacrifices in the interest of some greater perceived public interest. On the flip side, conspiracy theorists aren't known for conducting research that's objectively good. They focus on anomalies, they see patterns where none exist, and they often consume all material through the heavy filter of their own biases. These tendencies, if simply transferred to other research projects, would not tend to aid in the production of promising research.

Such debates are frequently played out on conservative online forums like FreeRepublic. The site leans hard to the right; not only is support for President Obama a bannable offense; so, too, is the expression of support for more moderate Republicans like former New York City mayor Rudy Giuliani or former Massachusetts governor Mitt Romney. For the last few years, FreeRepublic has also been very friendly to Birthers, to the point where objection to Birther conspiracism has also become a bannable offense. And yet some of the most common objections to Birtherism seen on the site are from fellow diehard conservatives, who insist that Birtherism is meritless and that conservatives should focus instead on protesting the president's policies or on campaigning for his opposition. A straightforward opportunity cost of Birtherism is that there are other ways of removing the president from office that have more potential. But Birthers don't see it that way. It's not just an illegitimate means to an end; it's an illegitimate end.

As a result, more meritorious interests and hobbies are overlooked. An assassination-conspiracy theorist who invests years into "investigating" JFK's death could instead be doing more worthwhile research on some other aspect of American history. A 9/11 Truther could expend his energy instead on protesting anti-Muslim bigotry. Or it could be as simple as someone who stops listening to late-night conspiracy-theory radio shows and instead uses those hours for real education. There is no shortage of legitimate causes that need the involvement of committed people. It's a shame when motivated people instead spend their limited time and energy on illegitimate causes.

FINANCIAL LOSS

The 419 Nigerian e-mail scam (more properly known as "advance-fee fraud") may be the Internet's most infamous financial rip-off. The e-mails have even inspired parodies, both on television and in viral online media, which is not terribly common for such schemes. It is likely the absurdist nature of the scam that makes it so ripe for humor: an e-mail written in pidgin English supposedly by some powerful and influential foreign dignitary who has reached out to you, personally, for help in smuggling millions or billions of dollars into the country. And in exchange for using your bank account, he'll give you a substantial cut of the wealth. Of course, there is no dignitary and there are no millions of dollars. There's just a scam artist with an e-mail account, hoping that if he spams enough people, he'll get a response from someone who is the perfect combination of (1) wealthy and (2) gullible. Being greedy is probably a bonus as well.

And yet, despite the ubiquity of this hoax, it continues to find victims. Between 2006 and 2008, an Oregon woman lost over $400,000 to a scammer who claimed to have an inheritance from her grandfather. She overlooked the bad writing in fake letters from "President Bush" and ignored the advice of friends and family who told her she was being scammed.[8] A British man lost over £130,000 in 2009 to a Nigerian scam that used a MySpace® page where the scammer posed first as a romantic interest with a large inheritance, then as a fake FBI agent, and then as a fellow scam victim. Even after he had given up $100,000 to the scammer's initial persona, the victim's credulity allowed him to hand over another thirty grand when he thought he was being helped by the agent and other victim.[9] It is estimated that some 8,500 people in 152 countries were victimized by this particular scam in 2009. The total loss to the victims was $9.3 billion. Worse yet, that number represents a nearly 50 percent increase over the $6.3 billion lost to advance-fee fraud in 2008.[10] As infamous as the Nigerian e-mail scam is, it's still capable of finding those wealthy and gullible victims.

And the 419 scam is just one of the more well-known scams that preys on the unsuspecting "investor." Financial scams of all flavors have been around as long as finance itself. It's impossible to know them all, and that's why they continue to find victims. But financial scams tend to play some of the same tricks to win over their marks, and recognizing those tricks allows one to recognize which financial "opportunities" may deserve some extra scrutiny.

A classic warning sign is the promise of a high rate of return on your investment. As every first-year economics student learns, there is a dynamic between risk and reward. Low-risk investments like treasury bonds or bank CDs are safer but offer less of a return. Putting that money in the stock market or in a business opportunity may bring greater returns, but those are riskier investments, and they may lose money instead of gaining. Thus, it should raise suspicion when an offer promises to be both very safe and very profitable. I once encountered online ads for bank savings accounts with interest rates of 8 percent or greater; when the best CD rates were less than 5 percent, that seemed implausible. And indeed, the "banks" that were promoting these offers were offshore agencies that were not FDIC-insured. Private, close offers may promise even greater reward. Before his scandal went public, Bernie Madoff promised investors returns of 18 percent to 20 percent. Even his victims couldn't say, after the fact, how they had been so willing to believe such phenomenal returns could be guaranteed.

Another common element in financial scams is the requirement of an upfront payment. Nigerian 419 scammers say that they have hundreds of millions tied up, and so they need your financial assistance to pay for legal help or just to pay bribes. Even low-key but legal financial tricksters employ this tool. Sketchy modeling agents use this across the country. They'll advertise that they're seeing potential new clients at a local hotel or conference center, and then they charge parents who want to show off their cute kids in the hopes of breaking big. Except legitimate modeling agencies don't charge their clients; they earn their living by booking jobs. The demand of an upfront payment is a sign that something might not be on the level.

It's obvious, of course, that financial scams can result in lost money. But believing in misinformation can cost money in other ways. Birther attorney Orly Taitz has lost tens of thousands of dollars in pursuing dead-end conspiracy theories about President Obama's eligibility.[11] Individual Birthers have reportedly donated over a hundred thousand dollars to the website WorldNetDaily to promote Birtherism, and they have only some billboards to show for it. WorldNetDaily even collected thousands of dollars in donations for a "reward" that it said it would give to the hospital named on Obama's long-form birth certificate. When the president released his long-form birth certificate, did WND donate the money it had collected?

No. It simply erased the donation page and never accounted for the money it had collected for over a year, contrary to the promise it had made to donors.[12]

Alternative-medicine proponents like to rail against Big Medicine or Big Pharma, and complain about the profit interests of American medicine. But alternative treatments are themselves surprisingly expensive. It was mentioned above that homeopathic pills, despite being utterly useless, still cost at least ten bucks a bottle. Other alternative treatments cost far more than ten dollars. Visits with an acupuncturist or chiropractor can cost hundreds of dollars per visit, and courses of treatment may run for months. Outside the field of medicine, a feng shui analysis can cost hundreds of dollars.

The website Alternative Therapies sells psychic surgery "tours" to the Philippines that can cost upward of $1,300.[13] Such price tags go well beyond the cost of simple co-pays and take money that would be better spent on licensed physicians and legitimate procedures. Alternative-medicine practitioners are also fond of teaching their craft to others and charging for the instruction. Hundreds or thousands of dollars can be spent learning the completely useless practices of Reiki or reflexology.

It's all too easy for such practitioners to justify these sorts of charges. Just as chiropractors and reflexologists can legitimately take on the title of "doctor," virtually every other form of pseudo-scholarship and alternative medicine opens the door for someone to take on the title of "expert." And that presumed "expertise" allows exorbitant fees to be charged, even for worthless acts.

The Church of Scientology is infamous for its ability to extract money from followers' bank accounts, charging them for spiritual enlightenment and then increasing the costs of their various products and services as followers become more and more involved. The natural human response toward sunk costs is to keep spending rather than writing off earlier monies as a loss.

Helpfully, the law does sometimes step in to provide some consumer protection against misinformation. "Psychics" often can't practice without admitting upfront that their work is for entertainment purposes only. And if someone gets worthwhile entertainment value out of visiting a psychic or a tarot card reader, then that's hardly much worse than losing the same amount of money gambling or on cigarettes.

LEGAL CONSEQUENCES

The legal principle of *Ignorantia juris non excusat* is that "ignorance of the law excuses no one." Faulty beliefs encourage ignorance and sometimes, particularly in the case of pseudolaw, can result in direct conflict with law enforcement and the judicial system.

Tax protesters very effectively illustrate this type of faulty belief. They subscribe to unsubstantiated theories about US tax law and then pay the consequences, which can be both financial and legal. One of the most high-profile examples is blockbuster actor Wesley Snipes. Snipes was taken in by the tax theories of Eddie Ray Kahn, a long-time protester who had previously served prison time for tax evasion. In 2006, Snipes and Kahn were both charged with conspiracy, tax fraud, and failure to file tax returns. After years of pretrial efforts, Snipes was convicted of the misdemeanor failures to file and sentenced to three years in prison. Kahn was convicted of the felony charges as well and was sentenced to ten years.[14] Following his sentencing, Snipes insisted that he was not a tax protester, despite his infractions and associations; meanwhile, Kahn repeatedly insisted during sentencing that he did not "consent" to the court's jurisdiction over him.[15] This is a familiar refrain among tax protesters and sovereign citizens. Many a tax protester has been imprisoned for falling for the bogus legal theories of men like Eddie Ray Kahn. Wesley Snipes was unfortunate enough to be a millionaire celebrity when he made that mistake.

Apart from falling for bad legal theories, there are other ways to suffer legal consequences for being insufficiently skeptical. Terry

Lakin was a lieutenant colonel in the US Army, a military doctor, and surgeon with over fifteen years of active service. He was an educated man with a family and a respectable history in the armed forces. In 2009, Lakin began taking an interest in Birther theories about President Obama. He started filing complaints through military channels, demanding that he be provided additional proof that the president was born in Hawaii. When he was given orders to deploy to Afghanistan in the spring of 2010 as part of Operation Enduring Freedom, Lakin chose to side with conspiracy theorists instead of with comrades-in-arms, and he refused to deploy. Nor was he passive in his dissent; he promptly posted a video of himself to YouTube®, declaring that he would ignore his orders unless the president acceded to his demands.[16]

Needless to say, the president did not take orders from a soldier. Lakin stood his ground and soon found himself being court-martialed and facing formal charges of missing movement and disobeying direct orders. Lakin was found guilty in December 2010 and was sentenced to six months in military prison. He was dishonorably discharged from the army, losing both his pay and his pension. After his release, Lakin was denied the opportunity to even practice private medicine in Kansas, because the state medical licensing board found that his refusal to deploy to provide medical service to his fellow servicepeople constituted a "disregard for his professional duties and undermines the integrity of the medical profession," and that he "potentially jeopardized the health, safety and welfare of the military troops for which Applicant was employed to provide medical care."[17]

Birtherism is, by any measure, a remarkably silly variety of denialism, but Lakin's case illustrates the seriousness of falling for such foolishness. Lakin lost a career, a pension he was just a few years away from, and six months of his freedom. He was stripped of his rank, dishonorably booted out of the military, and, because of the nature of his infraction, he couldn't even rely on the ability to get work as a civilian doctor. And yet Lakin stubbornly stands by his decision to throw away a respectable military career in favor of a conspiracy theory, even after the very birth certificate he demanded was publicly released and dispelled all his doubts. To acknowledge his mistake, and to admit that his lack of critical thinking made him ruin his own life in a very direct way, seems to be more than he's capable of.

Lakin acted out in a way that hurt him personally, but false beliefs can cause legal harm in more circuitous ways. Paul Ingram was a Republican Party chairman in Washington State whose daughter, in 1988, suddenly accused her father of sexual and physical abuse, satanic worship, and even baby eating. Ingram insisted he had no memory of any such events, but he consented to undergo hypnosis in the event that such memories were repressed. While under hypnosis, Ingram began to confess to memories of his alleged atrocious conduct. Even though a physical examination of his daughter failed to find any evidence of the injuries she had claimed to suffer, Ingram still chose to plead guilty to six counts of rape. He subsequently tried to retract his plea but was denied by the courts. Paul Ingram was finally released in 2003, following the completion of his prison sentence.[18]

Ingram's family had belonged to a church that believed not only that Satan could take control of individuals and cause them to commit heinous acts against their will, but also that the devil could remove the memories of performing those acts. Along with the trust he placed in the hypnosis session, Paul Ingram was conditioned to believe that he might have feasted on babies and violated family members with no recollection of doing so. The consequence of those beliefs was that he spent fourteen years in prison, and even after his release, he is still a registered sex offender.

Paul Ingram suffered not only because of the beliefs he held as the accused, but also because his daughter carried the same satanic-possession beliefs. Ingram's case is unique in that he became convinced of his own guilt. Wrongful convictions are more often the result of misinformation on the side of those making the accusations.

Facilitated communication operates essentially as a human Ouija board. People who can't communicate through normal means, such as some autistic persons, have their hand supported by a "facilitator," and the aided hand then types messages out on a keyboard. It has been largely dismissed as a science, as most studies have found that it is simply the facilitator who is controlling the message, whether consciously or not. Since 1994, the American Psychological Association has taken the official position that facilitated communication is an unproven procedure with no scientific support.[19]

Science or not, criminal prosecutors have relied on claims supposedly made by autistic patients through facilitated communication as the grounds for pursuing sexual abuse cases against the family members of those patients. One case even resulted in a conviction. In 1992, a severely autistic eleven-year-old made accusations of sexual abuse against a caregiver via facilitated communication. The caregiver was criminally charged, and the Wichita, Kansas, judge not only allowed the admission of the facilitated statements but also allowed the child to offer testimony at trial through facilitated communication. The judge even denied a request by the defense to "blind" the facilitator during trial testimony (much like blindfolding a person using a Ouija board), a protocol that would have better prevented against the unintentional influence of the facilitator. On appeal, the Supreme Court refused even to apply the Frey test (a judicial standard created by the US Supreme Court to determine the admissibility of scientific evidence) to facilitated communication and instead approved the trial court's decisions and upheld the conviction.[20]

The Wichita case may be the only conviction based on facilitated communication, but other people have suffered varying levels of public embarrassment and even criminal charges because of it. Most of these cases occurred during the 1990s, but in 2007, Michigan prosecutors brought sexual abuse charges against the parents of an autistic fourteen-year-old girl based on accusations that emerged through facilitated communication. In that case, the charges were ultimately dropped, and the family subsequently sued the law enforcement agencies.[21]

It's important, however, to remember that in the case of something like facilitated communication, its failure to perform under rigorous testing conditions thus far does not mean that it cannot work. If a nonverbal person has the minimal intellect and muscle control, it may be a valid hypothesis that they could "speak" through facilitated communication. But here is where the application of critical thinking comes into play. It's not just about rejecting the idea outright but perhaps designing a test to remove outside influences. As the defense in the Wichita case requested, a facilitator can be blinded, and the act of facilitation with a particular subject can be evaluated. If the facilitator and the subject are shown different pictures, and the picture that is then described is the one that the facilitator saw and the subject never did, then facilitated communication has failed the test.

It's bad enough to suffer the legal consequences of falling for misinformation oneself. But it may be worse when it's the state that has been taken in by faulty facts. A gullible individual could be seen as bringing his fate upon himself, but when the state makes the mistake, that means that innocents are liable to suffer.

SOCIAL STIGMA

It almost goes without saying that misinformation can often be, for lack of a better word, silly—or rather, silly to anyone who doesn't believe. David Icke and his followers don't believe it's silly to claim that shape-shifting reptilians rule the world, but the rest of the world disagrees.

That's an extreme example, but it applies across the board. When you learn that a person is a Birther or a 9/11-conspiracy theorist, it makes you question that person's broader political philosophies. If you find that someone believes the world is only six thousand years old, you're liable to doubt their understanding of science. And if they tell you that the government is controlling our minds with fluoride in the water and chemical trails from airplanes in the sky, you'll probably just nod your head and think about how best to extract yourself from that conversation. (In that way, misinformation can actually serve as a helpful social cue, letting you know that this is someone you may not want to spend much time with.)

Our perceptions of others are built around the things they say and believe, and when those things are ridiculous, debunked, or impossible, their continued belief plays into how other people see them. As social harms go, it's not a big one. And from the point of view of the misinformed person, the world's ridicule is often taken as a bizarre form of validation. They see themselves as truth seekers in a world full of the deceived, and they're happy to suffer attacks or insults when they think their cause is just. They see ridicule as nothing more than an attempt to get them to give up, and so, rather than engendering doubt as to their beliefs, they become more entrenched in believing they're correct.

When researching his book *Among the Truthers,* Jonathan Kay found that it wasn't uncommon for 9/11 Truthers to allow their obsession to alienate them from their families and loved ones. In some cases, marriages were strained or even ended as a result of such beliefs. Some Birthers talk about how their families don't approve of their conspiracist hobby.[22] In these cases, it's hard to say whether the specific conspiracy theory ought to be blamed for the negative impact on a relationship. Obsession with a conspiracy theory, at least the type that ruins marriages, is likely more a function of the mind of the conspiracy theorist himself than the particular bogus theory he's come to believe.

CONTAMINATED THINKING

It's possible that many of the above risks may seem somewhat . . . obvious. Spending money can cause you to lose money. Believing in foolish legal theories can get you in trouble with the law. Espousing silly ideas can make people think less of you. But misinformation's least measurable harm is also its least obvious and, in many ways, its most insidious.

Misinformation doesn't affect the believer in a discrete and singular way. As with all information, it is incorporated into a person's worldview and contributes to how they process what they already know and what they learn in the future. Some people are simply predisposed to believing in conspiracy theories, and it's hard to say whether any amount of skeptical education can change that. Conspiracy theorists are an incredibly varied bunch, and they demonstrate little to no demographic trends, except one: a person who believes in one conspiracy theory is very likely to believe in multiple conspiracy theories.

It may be that that tendency is inborn, and that someone inclined to think in conspiratorial terms is simply prone to seeing sinister plots in many places. But the testimonials of some conspiracists and denialists, particularly recovering ones, do tend to suggest that the acceptance of one bogus theory can lead one down a rabbit hole of misinformation as one's introduced to new theories that make other wild claims.

Conversely, critical thinking contaminates one's thinking too, but in a positive way. Instead of being increasingly susceptible to erroneous claims and ideas, you find yourself applying that skepticism and weeding out the bad information before it becomes ingrained. It may be as simple as visiting Snopes® or FactCheck.org or Wikiquote to debunk a scurrilous rumor or false claim. Misinformation may be capable of spreading virally, but such resources mean that real misinformation might not be more than a single URL away. Knowing this could spare you an embarrassing "share" on Facebook when you're told that your latest political outrage was directed at an *Onion* article.

Or it might take more effort, like getting your doctor's opinion about an alternative-medicine claim or asking an attorney about a pseudolegal argument. Such arguments are also undoubtedly hashed out online, and the answers are there if you can distinguish the credible sources from the noncredible ones. It's not always immediately evident that "BIO-Complexity," the National Vaccine Information Center, and the Institute for Historical Review are, respectively, a creationist publication, an anti-vaccine advocacy group, and a Holocaust-denial organization. It can sometimes be hard to identify dishonest pseudo-scholarship if it's a new subject to you. That's when consulting a trusted source can be helpful.

During that process, and afterward, it's important to keep an open mind. Your conclusions are always going to be based on the evidence gathered thus far, and new and different evidence could make a difference; that's one of the central lessons of scientific experimentation. When new evidence presents itself, you need to consider whether it's compelling. If it is, then consider whether it's sufficient to alter your earlier conclusions. As little as I think of David Icke and his theory of shape-shifting reptilians, if I were to watch President Obama turn into a lizard-man during the State of the Union address, I would be forced to reconsider my previous stance.

This sort of reasoned approach can help prevent the mistake of allowing one's mind to be *too* open. Denialists, conspiracists, and pseudo-scholars all like to paint themselves as skeptics, rebelling against the conventional wisdom. They're skeptical of any source, any authority, and any evidence that tends to support the consensus opinion.

Real critical thinking is not so rote and simple. It requires spotting suspicious facts and sources, and knowing when to trust and when to investigate further. It requires being aware of the logical fallacies that our minds are susceptible to and resisting the easy answers that can come from falling into those traps. It demands a willingness to reconsider things you may already believe and to evaluate evidence neutrally. And while it may not lead you to answers that you like, at least you can be confident that it's leading you to answers that are true.

NOTES

INTRODUCTION

1. "Modern History Sourcebook: Alexander H. Stephens (1812–1883): Cornerstone Address, March 21, 1861," Fordham University, http://www.fordham.edu/halsall/mod/1861stephens.asp (accessed August 17, 2012).

2. Loren Collins, "The Truth in the Story of Secession," redandblack.com, April 30, 2003, http://redandblack.com/2003/04/30/the-truth-in-the-story-of-secession/ (accessed March 14, 2012).

3. Carl Sagan, *The Demon-Haunted World: Science as a Candle in the Dark* (New York: Ballantine Books, 1997), pp. 209–10.

4. Ibid., p. 216.

CHAPTER 1. BALONEY DETECTION

1. Robert Manning, "Hemingway in Cuba," *Atlantic* online, August 1965, http://www.theatlantic.com/past/docs/issues/65aug/6508manning.htm (accessed March 10, 2012).

2. I was the subject of one 2011 PolitiFact article, and my reviewed statement was ruled "True." See http://www.politifact.com/personalities/loren-collins/ (accessed August 6, 2012).

3. Michael Shermer, *The Believing Brain* (New York: Times Books, 2011), p. 60.

4. Ibid., p. 87.

5. Walter R. Fisher, "The Narrative Paradigm: In the Beginning," *Journal of Communication* 35, no. 4 (December 1985): 74–89.

6. Shermer, *Believing Brain*, p. 259.

7. Brendan Nyhan and Jason Reifler, "When Corrections Fail: The Persistence of Political Misperceptions," *Political Behavior* 32, no. 2 (2010): 303–30, http://www.dartmouth.edu/~nyhan/nyhan-reifler.pdf (accessed March 10, 2012).

8. "The Notorious Calaveras Skull," *Archaeology* online, http://www

.archaeology.org/online/features/hoaxes/calaveras.html (accessed March 10, 2012).

9. "Fossil Man," Center for Scientific Creation, http://www.creationscience.com/onlinebook/ReferencesandNotes26.html (accessed March 10, 2012).

10. Ron Polarik, *Obama's Forged Birth Certificate* (blog), December 18, 2008, http://bogusbirthcertificate.blogspot.com/ (accessed March 10, 2012).

11. "Answers," *Obama's Garden* (blog), February 18, 2011, http://www.obamasgarden.wordpress.com/2012/07/27/answers/ (accessed March 10, 2012).

12. James von Brunn, *Tob Shebbe Goyim Harog! (To Kill the Best Gentiles!)*, http://vho.org/aaargh/fran/livres9/vonBrunn.pdf (accessed March 10, 2012).

CHAPTER 2. DENIALISM

1. Stephen Jay Gould, "Fall in the House of Ussher," *Natural History* 100 (November 1991): 12–21.

2. Joseph Farah, "Why I Believe in Creation," WorldNetDaily, December 17, 2004, http://www.wnd.com/2004/12/28069/ (accessed March 10, 2012).

3. "Evolution, Creationism, Intelligent Design," Gallup, http://www.gallup.com/poll/21814/evolution-creationism-intelligent-design.aspx (accessed March 10, 2012).

4. Carl Sagan, *Broca's Brain* (New York: Random House, 1979), p. 64.

5. Mark Hoofnagle and Chris Hoofnagle, "What Is Denialism?" Denialism.com, http://www.denialism.com/2007/03/what-is-denialism.html (accessed August 23, 2012).

6. Ibid.

7. AmericaUnited, comment on Free Republic, http://www.freerepublic.com/focus/f-news/2030080/posts (accessed March 10, 2012).

8. RaceBannon, comment on Free Republic, http://www.freerepublic.com/focus/f-news/2030190/posts (accessed March 10, 2012).

9. Dr. Conspiracy, "WND Document Expert Says: Not Quite Accurate," *Obama Conspiracy Theories* (blog), July 28, 2011, http://www.obamaconspiracy.org/2011/07/wnd-document-expert-says-not-quite-accurate/ (accessed March 10, 2012).

10. "Testimony by Experts," Federal Rules of Evidence, Rule 702.

11. Stephen Jay Gould, *Hen's Teeth and Horse's Toes* (New York: W. W. Norton, 1983), pp. 254–55.

12. Loren Collins, "For Inauguration Day: A Birther Platonic Dialogue," *Barackryphal* (blog), January 20, 2009, http://barackryphal.blogspot.com/2009/01/for-inauguration-day-birther-platonic.html (accessed March 10, 2012).

13. Michael C. Labossiere, "Description of Fallacies," Nizkor Project, http://www.nizkor.org/features/fallacies (accessed August 8, 2012); and SGU Productions, "Top 20 Logical Fallacies," Skeptic's Guide to the Universe, http://www.theskeptics guide.org/resources/logicalfallacies.aspx (accessed August 8, 2012).

14. Complaint in Philip Berg v. Barack Obama, 2:2008cv04083 (E.D. Pa. 2008).

CHAPTER 3. CONSPIRACY THEORIES

1. Associated Press, "Former Atlanta Police Officer Admits Covering Up Botched Raid That Killed Elderly Woman," Fox News online, May 15, 2008, http://www.foxnews.com/story/0,2933,355796,00.html (accessed August 12, 2012).

2. Paul Martin, "Lincoln's Missing Bodyguard," Smithsonian online, April 8, 2010, http://www.smithsonianmag.com/history-archaeology/Lincolns-Missing -Bodyguard.html (accessed August 12, 2012).

3. Jonathan Kay, *Among the Truthers* (New York: HarperCollins, 2011), p. 49.

4. Michael Barkun, *A Culture of Conspiracy* (Berkeley: University of California Press, 2003), p. 6.

5. Loren Collins, "FDR Did NOT Say 'In Politics, Nothing Happens by Accident,'" *Loren Collins* (blog), September 21, 2009, http://www.lorencollins.net/ blog/?p=39 (accessed March 10, 2012).

6. Heather Childers, Twitter post, http://twitter.com/heatherchilders/ status/187227025642237952 (accessed August 14, 2012).

CHAPTER 4. RUMORS

1. "Hundreds of Israelis Missing in WTC Attack," *Jerusalem Post* online, http://www .web.archive.org/web/20050412040213/http://www.fpp.co.uk/online/02/10/ JerusPost120901.html (accessed August 19, 2012).

2. David Aaronovitch, *Voodoo Histories: The Role of the Conspiracy Theory in Shaping Modern History* (New York: Riverhead Books, 2010).

3. "The 4,000 Jews Rumor," USINFO.STATE.GOV, http://web.archive.org/ web/20050408072925/http://usinfo.state.gov/media/Archive/2005/Jan/14-2609 33.html (accessed March 10, 2012).

4. Orac, "Another Acupuncture Study Misinterpreted," ScienceBlogs, May 13, 2009, http://scienceblogs.com/insolence/2009/05/13/another-acupuncture -study-misinterpreted/ (accessed August 13, 2012).

5. The District of Columbia Organic Act of 1871 (41st Congress, 3d Sess., ch. 62, 16 Stat. 419, enacted 1871-02-21).

6. Alan Peters, "Obama's Half-Brother Confirms Obama Grew Up as a Moslem," *Anti-Mullah* (blog), June 14, 2008, http://noiri.blogspot.com/2008/06/obamas -half-brother-confirms-obama-grew.html (accessed March 10, 2012).

7. Alan Peters, "Obama's Birth Circumstances Review," *News Views* (blog), June 22, 2008, http://alanpetersnewsbriefs.blogspot.com/2008/06/obamas-birth -circumstances-review.html (accessed March 10, 2012).

8. Brian Deer, "How the Case against the MMR Vaccine Was Fixed," *British Medical Journal* 342 (2011), doi: c5347.

9. Kenneth Lamb, "Post, Tribune: Is Obama Really African-American?" *Reading between the Lines* (blog), February 14, 2008, http://kennethelamb.blogspot .com/2008/02/barak-obama-questions-about-ethnic.html (accessed March 10, 2012).

10. Ibid.

CHAPTER 5. QUOTATIONS

1. Megan McArdle, "Out of Osama's Death, a Fake Quotation Is Born," *Atlantic* online, May 2, 2011, http://www.theatlantic.com/national/archive/2011/05/out -of-osamas-death-a-fake-quotation-is-born/238220/ (accessed March 13, 2012).

2. Penn Jillette, Twitter post, May 2, 2011, 12:15 p.m., https://twitter.com/#!/ drbombay76/status/65178286015266816 (accessed March 13, 2012).

3. Simon Pegg, Twitter post, October 21, 2011, 3:10 a.m., https://twitter .com/#!/simonpegg/statuses/127325939934830592 (accessed March 13, 2012).

4. sbh, "David Barton's 'Unconfirmed' Quotations—The Current Score," *Rational Rant* (blog), November 14, 2011, http://rationalrant.blogspot.com/2011/ 11/david-bartons-unconfirmed-quotationsthe.html (accessed August 15, 2012).

5. William Hermanns, *Einstein and the Poet: In Search of the Cosmic Man* (Brookline Village, MA: Branden, 1983), p. 58.

6. Ben Patterson, *Waiting: Finding Hope When God Seems Silent* (Downers Grove, IL: InterVarsity, 1989).

7. James C. Humes, *Roles Speakers Play* (New York: Harper & Row, 1976), p. 208.

8. Earl G. Lockhart, *My Vocation, by Eminent Americans; or, What Eminent Americans Think of Their Callings* (Freeport, NY: Books for Libraries, 1972), p. 238.

9. Roger Babson, *Religion and Business* (New York: Macmillan, 1920), p. 89.

10. Roger Babson, *Storing Up Triple Reserves* (Whitefish, MT: Kessinger, 2003), p. 286.

11. Roger Babson, *Instincts and Emotions, Should They Be Suppressed or Harnessed?* (New York: Cosimo, 1927), pp. 58–59.

12. Bill Moyers, "On Receiving Harvard Medical School's Global Environment Citizen Award," Common Dreams, December 6, 2004, http://www.commondreams .org/views04/1206-10.htm (accessed August 19, 2012).

13. Glenn Scherer, "Christian-Right Views Are Swaying Politicians and Threatening the Environment," *Grist*, October 28, 2004, http://grist.org/politics/ scherer-christian/ (accessed March 13, 2012).

14. "U.S. Senate Debate Sponsored by the League of Women Voters in Illinois," Alan Keyes Archives, October 21, 2004, http://www.keyesarchives.com/transcript .php?id=370 (accessed August 19, 2012).

15. John Semmens, "Edwards Campaign Threatens Student Journalists," *Arizona Conservative*, October 27, 2007, http://web.archive.org/web/20080801043405/ http://azconservative.org/Semmens118.htm (accessed March 13, 2012).

16. Adam Gobin, "Israeli Influence Impedes Objectivity," redandblack.com, October 1, 2002, http://redandblack.com/2002/10/01/israeli-influence-impedes -objectivity/ (accessed March 13, 2012).

17. "Boxing Rings: Al-Jazeera's Talk Shows," *TBS Journal* 8 (Spring/Summer 2002), http://www.tbsjournal.com/Archives/Spring02/talkshows.html (accessed March 13, 2012).

18. Ibid.

19. Molly Ivins, "Mega-Un-Dittos from Here, Rush," *Fort Worth Star-Telegram*, October 12, 1993.

20. Molly Ivins, "Lyin' Bully," *Mother Jones*, May/June 1995, http://mother jones.com/politics/1995/05/lyin-bully (accessed March 13, 2012).

21. Ibid.

22. Gobin, "Israeli Influence Impedes Objectivity."

23. "Syndicated Columnist Georgia Anne Geyer Uses Fabricated Sharon Quote," CAMERA, May 20, 2002, http://www.camera.org/index.asp?x_article=34&x _context=2 (accessed August 15, 2012).

24. Thomas F. Schwartz, "Lincoln Never Said That," *For the People* 1, no. 1 (Spring 1999): 4–6, http://abrahamlincolnassociation.org/Newsletters/1-1.pdf (accessed March 13, 2012).

25. Wikiquote entry, "Mohandas Karamchand Gandhi," http://en.wikiquote .org/wiki/Mohandas_Karamchand_Gandhi (accessed August 15, 2012).

26. Nicholas Klein, *Proceedings of the Third Biennial Convention of the Amalgamated Clothing Workers of America* (1919), Google® e-book, p. 53, http://books.google.com/ books?id=QrcpAAAAYAAJ&dq (accessed March 13, 2012).

27. John Adams, letter to Benjamin Rush, April 4, 1790.

CHAPTER 6. HOAXES

1. "The Occidental Tourist," Snopes®, September 17, 2009, http://www.snopes.com/politics/obama/birthers/occidental.asp (accessed August 15, 2012).

2. Hudson Hongo, "Top Ten Facebook Reactions to the Onion of 2011, Part II," LiterallyUnbelievable, December 31, 2011, http://literallyunbelievable.org/post/15081148066/top-ten-facebook-reactions-to-the-onion-of-2011-part (accessed March 11, 2012).

3. Amy Kuperinsky, "Bon Jovi Not Dead; Rumor Was Twitter Fiction," NJ.com, December 19, 2011, http://www.nj.com/entertainment/index.ssf/2011/12/bon_jovi_not_dead_rumor_was_tw.html (accessed March 11, 2012).

4. Shelby Grad, "False Report of Bon Jovi Death Appears to Copy Times' Jackson Story," *Los Angeles Times* online, December 19, 2011, http://latimesblogs.latimes.com/lanow/2011/12/false-news-report-about-bon-jovi-death-appears-to-copy-times-story.html (accessed March 13, 2012).

5. Ki Mae Heussner, "Legend of Bigfoot: Discovery? Try Hoax," ABC News online, August 15, 2008, http://www.abcnews.go.com/Technology/story?id=5583488&page=1#.UCuOBKOwVb_ (accessed August 19, 2012).

6. "Bigfoot Hoaxers Say It Was 'Just a Big Joke,'" CNN online, August 21, 2009, http://www.edition.cnn.com/2008/US/08/21/bigfoot.hoax/ (accessed August 19, 2012).

7. Bob Keefe, "Bigfoot's a Hoax, California Site Reveals," ajc.com, August 19, 2003, http://www.ajc.com/eveningedge/content/metro/clayton/stories/2008/08/19/bigfoot_hoax.html (accessed August 19, 2012).

8. *Ulsterman's Untruths* (blog), http://ulster-man.blogspot.com (accessed August 19, 2012).

9. Ben Dimiero, "The Unbelievable Adventures of Ulsterman, Super-Journalist," Media Matters, May 4, 2011, http://mediamatters.org/blog/201105040021 (accessed March 13, 2012).

10. Matthew Goodman, *The Sun and the Moon: The Remarkable True Account of Hoaxers, Showmen, Dueling Journalists, and Lunar Man-Bats in Nineteenth-Century New York* (New York: Basic Books, 2008), p. 277.

CHAPTER 7. PSEUDOSCIENCE

1. L. Rosa et al., "A Close Look at Therapeutic Touch," *Journal of the American Medical Association* 279, no. 13 (April 1, 1998): 1005–1010.

2. P. S. Blackawton et al., "Blackawton Bees," *Biology Letters* 7, no. 2 (April 23, 2011): 168–72.

3. Brendan O'Neill, "Do They Really Think the Earth Is Flat?" BBC News online, August 4, 2008, http://news.bbc.co.uk/2/hi/uk_news/magazine/7540427 .stm (accessed August 23, 2012).

4. Christine Garwood, *Flat Earth: The History of an Infamous Idea* (New York: Thomas Dunne Books, 2008), pp. 1–14.

5. Ibid.

6. William Carpenter, *One Hundred Proofs That the Earth Is Not a Globe*, 4th ed. (Baltimore, MD: self-published, 1885).

7. Ibid.

8. Cornelia Dean, "Scientific Savvy? In U.S., Not Much," *New York Times* online, August 30, 2005, http://www.nytimes.com/2005/08/30/science/30profile .html?pagewanted=all (accessed March 14, 2012).

9. Alissa de Carbonnel, "Third of Russians Think Sun Spins Round Earth?" Reuters, February 11, 2011, http://www.reuters.com/article/2011/02/11/us-poll -education-odd-idUSTRE71A4OI20110211 (accessed March 14, 2012).

10. "Galileo Was Wrong: The Church Was Right," *Galileo Was Wrong* (blog), http://www.galileowaswrong.com/galileowaswrong/ (accessed March 14, 2012).

11. Phil Plait, "Geocentrism? Seriously?" *Bad Astronomy* (blog), *Discover* online, September 14, 2010, http://blogs.discovermagazine.com/badastronomy/ 2010/09/14/geocentrism-seriously/ (accessed March 14, 2012).

12. The Non-Moving Earth and Anti-Evolution Web Page of the Fair Education Foundation, Inc., http://www.fixedearth.com/ (accessed March 14, 2012).

13. Gen. 1:1–10, New International Version.

14. Gen. 2:7–8 (NIV).

15. Jean-Baptiste Lamarck, *Hydrogeology* (Champaign: University of Illinois Press, 1964), p. 75.

16. Dan Gilgoff, "Survey: U.S. Protestant Pastors Reject Evolution, Split on Earth's Age," *Belief* (blog), CNN online, January 10, 2012, http://religion.blogs .cnn.com/2012/01/10/survey-u-s-protestant-pastors-reject-evolution-split-on-earths -age/ (accessed March 14, 2012).

17. "Students' Perceptions of Earth's Age Influence Acceptance of Human Evolution," ScienceDaily, March 11, 2010, http://www.sciencedaily.com/releases/ 2010/03/100310162833.htm (accessed March 14, 2012).

18. Philip Henry Gosse, *Omphalos: An Attempt to Untie the Geological Knot* (London: J. Van Voorst, 1857).

19. Steve Bradt, "Mice Living in Sand Hills Quickly Evolved Lighter Coloration," *Harvard Gazette*, August 27, 2009, http://news.harvard.edu/gazette/ story/2009/08/mice-living-in-sand-hills-quickly-evolved-lighter-coloration (accessed August 19, 2012).

20. "Peer-Reviewed & Peer-Edited Scientific Publications Supporting the Theory of Intelligent Design (Annotated)," Center for Science & Culture, Discovery Institute, February 1, 2012, http://www.discovery.org/a/2640 (accessed August 19, 2012).

21. Michael Shermer, "Show Me the Body," *The Work of Michael Shermer* (blog), http://www.michaelshermer.com/2003/05/show-me-the-body (accessed August 19, 2012).

22. Richard Black, "'New Mammal' Seen in Borneo Woods," BBC online, December 6, 2005, http://news.bbc.co.uk/2/hi/science/nature/4501152.stm (accessed March 14, 2012).

23. Carl Sagan, *The Demon-Haunted World: Science as a Candle in the Dark* (New York: Ballantine Books, 1997), p. 64.

24. Ibid., pp. 109–10.

25. Juliet Lapidos, "Elf-Detection 101," Slate, March 10, 2009, http://www.slate.com/articles/news_and_politics/explainer/2009/03/elf_detection_101.html (accessed March 14, 2012).

26. Stephanie Messenger, *Melanie's Marvellous Measles*, sidebar on Nature Matters! http://naturematters.info/ (accessed March 14, 2012).

27. "Homeopathy," CVS Pharmacy online, http://health.cvs.com/GetContent.aspx?token=f75979d3-9c7c-4b16-af56-3e122a3f19e3&chunkiid=38314 (accessed March 14, 2012).

28. Trine Tsouderos, "Federal Center Pays Good Money for Suspect Medicine," *Chicago Tribune* online, December 11, 2011, http://www.chicagotribune.com/health/ct-met-nccam-overview-20111211,0,3391775.story (accessed March 14, 2012).

29. "Potential Roles of the Placebo Effect in Health Care," National Center for Complementary and Alternative Medicine, June 27, 2011, http://nccam.nih.gov/research/results/spotlight/051711.htm (accessed March 14, 2012).

30. "Time Cube 4ce," http://www.timecube.com (accessed August 19, 2012).

31. Neal Adams, "Heck's a Poppin!" *Neal Adams Science* (blog), http://www.nealadams.com/index.php/science/read-watch-learn (accessed August 19, 2012).

32. Erik D. Andrulis, "RNA Metabolism and Life," Case Western Reserve University, Molecular Biology and Microbiology, http://www.case.edu/med/microbio/andrulis.htm (accessed August 19, 2012).

CHAPTER 8. PSEUDOHISTORY

1. Richard Thornton, "Ruins in Georgia Mountains Show Evidence of Maya Connection," Examiner.com, December 21, 2011, http://www.examiner.com/architecture-design-in-national/massive-1-100-year-old-maya-site-discovered-georgia-s-mountains (accessed March 14, 2012).

2. Maggie Koerth-Baker, "No. Nobody Found Mayan Ruins in Georgia," *Boing Boing* (blog), December 23, 2011, http://boingboing.net/2011/12/23/no-nobody-found-mayan-ruins-i.html (accessed March 14, 2012).

3. Thornton, "Ruins in Georgia Mountains Show Evidence of Maya Connection."

4. Ned Potter, "Mayan Ruins in Georgia? Archeologist Objects, Debate Breaks Out Online," ABC News online, January 5, 2012, http://abcnews.go .com/Technology/mayan-ruins-georgia-archeologist-objects-web-story-viral/story?id=152 91662#.UDaxbaPNk-o (accessed August 24, 2012).

5. Fender Discussion page, http://www.fenderforum.com/forum.html?db =&topic_number=769048 (accessed August 24, 2012).

6. Stanley Wells and Michael Dobson, eds., *The Oxford Companion to Shakespeare* (New York: Oxford University Press, 2001), p. 220.

7. P. Callahan, "Computerized Analysis Helps Researchers Define Shakespeare's Work Using 'Literary Fingerprint,'" Phys.org, September 27, 2006, http://phys.org/news78593028.html (accessed August 20, 2012).

8. Peter Millican, "The Story of an Unlikely Hypothesis (and a Fine Book)," PhiloComp.net, http://www.philocomp.net/humanities/dreams (accessed March 14, 2012).

9. Gary Langer, "John F. Kennedy's Assassination Leaves a Legacy of Suspicion," ABC News Poll, November 16, 2003, http://abcnews.go.com/images/pdf/937a1JFKAssassination.pdf (accessed August 24, 2012).

10. Taylor Branch, *At Canaan's Edge: America in the King Years 1965–68* (New York: Simon & Schuster, 2006), p. 770.

11. "Sirhan Bishara Sirhan Trial: 1969—A Murder Plan," Law Library, American Law and Legal Information, http://law.jrank.org/pages/3182/Sirhan-Bishara -Sirhan-Trial-1969-Murder-Plan.html (accessed August 20, 2012).

12. "Civil Case: King Family versus Jowers," King Center, http://www.theking center.org/civil-case-king-family-versus-jowers (accessed March 14, 2012).

13. "MLK's Family Feels Vindicated," CBS News, February 11, 2009, http://www.cbsnews.com/2100-273_162-73745.html (accessed March 14, 2012).

14. "Atlantis," *Wikipedia*, http://www.en.wikipedia.org/wiki/Atlantis:_The _Antediluvian_World (accessed August 23, 2012).

15. Ignatius Donnelly, *Ragnarok: The Age of Fire and Gravel*, 1883, Internet Sacred Text Archive, http://www.sacred-texts.com/atl/rag/rag03.htm (accessed August 23, 2012).

16. "Immanuel Velikovsky's *Worlds in Collision*," Skeptic's Dictionary, http://www.skepdic.com/velikov.html (accessed August 22, 2012).

17. I. S. Shklovskii and Carl Sagan, *Intelligent Life in the Universe*, transl. Paula Fern (San Francisco: Holden-Day, 1966).

18. Thornton, "Ruins in Georgia Mountains."

19. Felipe Fernandez-Armesto, quoted in Tim Castle, "Columbus Debunker Sets Sights on Leonardo da Vinci," Reuters, July 29, 2008, http://www.reuters.com/article/2008/07/29/us-britain-book-leonardo-idUSL242804420080729 (accessed March 14, 2012).

20. George Orwell, "As I Please," *Tribune*, February 4, 1944.

21. Jack Cashill, *Deconstructing Obama: The Life, Loves, and Letters of America's First Postmodern President* (New York: Threshold Editions, 2011), p. 159.

CHAPTER 9. PSEUDOLAW

1. "Pseudolaw," RationalWiki, http://rationalwiki.org/wiki/Pseudolaw (accessed March 14, 2012).

2. "Sovereign Citizen Movement," American Defamation League, http://www.adl.org/learn/ext_us/scm.asp?xpicked=4 (accessed August 22, 2012).

3. "The Posse Comitatus," Wesley Swift Library, http://swift.christogenea.org/book/export/html/1321 (accessed March 14, 2012).

4. "Benjamin Franklin," Wikiquote, http://en.wikiquote.org/wiki/Benjamin_Franklin (accessed August 24, 2012).

5. "16th Amendment," Legal Information Institute, Cornell University Law School, http://www.law.cornell.edu/constitution/amendmentxvi (accessed August 24, 2012).

6. Daniel B. Evans, Tax Protester FAQ, http://evans-legal.com/dan/tpfaq.html (accessed March 14, 2012).

7. "Frivolous Tax Arguments in General," IRS online, February 16, 2012, http://www.irs.gov/taxpros/article/0,,id=159932,00.html (accessed August 24, 2012).

8. "Get That Gold Fringe Off My Flag!" American Patriot Friends Network, http://www.apfn.org/apfn/flag.htm (accessed March 14, 2012).

9. "Flags, Guidons, Streamers, Tabards, and Automobile and Aircraft Plates," Army Regulation 840-10, Army Publishing Directorate, November 1, 1998, http://www.apd.army.mil/pdffiles/r840_10.pdf (accessed August 24, 2012).

10. J. Krim Bohren, "The Gold Fringed Flag," Controversial & Banned Books, http://www.banned-books.com/truth-seeker/1994archive/121_5/ts215b.html (accessed March 14, 2012).

11. "Get That Gold Fringe Off My Flag!"

12. "About the Gold Fringe on the American Flag," Army Study Guide, http://www.armystudyguide.com/content/army_board_study_guide_topics/flags/about-the-gold-fringe-on-.shtml (accessed August 24, 2012).

13. *McCann v. Greenway*, 952 F. Supp 647 (W.D. Mo. 1997).

14. "Sovereign Citizen Movement."

15. Lisa Guliani, "The United States Isn't a Country—It's a Corporation!" Serendipity, http://www.serendipity.li/jsmill/us_corporation.htm (accessed August 22, 2012).

16. "Sovereign Citizens Movement," Southern Poverty Law Center, http://www.splcenter.org/get-informed/intelligence-files/ideology/sovereign-citizens-movement (accessed August 22, 2012).

17. "His 'Straw Man' Free, a Scammer Finds the Rest of Him Isn't," *Intelligence Report* 118 (Summer 2005), Southern Poverty Law Center, http://www.splcenter.org/get-informed/intelligence-report/browse-all-issues/2005/summer/patriots-for-profit (accessed August 22, 2012).

18. 26 U.S.C. 6702.

19. "Titles of Nobility Amendment," *Wikipedia*, http://en.wikipedia.org/wiki/Titles_of_Nobility_Amendment (accessed August 24, 2012).

20. Much of the information in this section comes from Jol A. Silversmith, "The 'Missing Thirteenth Amendment': Constitutional Nonsense and Titles of Nobility," *Southern California Interdisciplinary Law Journal* 8, no. 577 (April 1999), ThirdAmendment.com, http://www.thirdamendment.com/missing.html (accessed August 24, 2012).

21. Ibid., citing Geoff Davidian, "Sovereign Citizens Defy Law," *Maine Sunday Telegram*, August 7, 1988.

22. "Our Platform," Republican Party of Iowa, http://iowagop.org/platform.php (accessed March 14, 2012).

23. Leo Donofrio, "*Minor v. Happersett* Is Binding Precedent as to the Constitutional Definition of a Natural Born Citizen," *Natural Born Citizen* (blog), June 24, 2011, http://naturalborncitizen.wordpress.com/2011/06/24/minor-v-happersett-is-binding-precedent-as-to-the-constitutional-definition-of-a-natural-born-citizen (accessed August 24, 2012).

24. Snopes® entry, "Georgia on My Mind," http://www.snopes.com/politics/obama/birthers/georgia.asp (accessed August 24, 2012).

25. "Office of State Administrative Hearings, State of Georgia," Scribd, http://

www.scribd.com/doc/80422088/2012-02-03-Decision-From-Malihi-GEORGIA-ALJ-Obama-is-NBC (accessed August 24, 2012).

26. "An Act to Provide a Government for the District of Columbia," Library of Congress, http://Memory.loc.gov/cgi-bin/ampage?collId-llsl&filename-016/llsl016.db&recNum=0454 (accessed August 24, 2012).

CHAPTER 10. WHAT'S THE HARM?

1. The title of the chapter is taken from the website What's the Harm? (http://www.whatstheharm.net), which collects stories of people who were measurably hurt by pseudoscience and misinformation.

2. Jenny McCarthy, *Louder Than Words: A Mother's Journey in Healing Autism* (New York: Dutton, 2007).

3. Jenny McCarthy Body Count, http://JennyMcCarthyBodyCount.com (accessed December 17, 2011).

4. Nicoli Nattrass, "AIDS and the Scientific Governance of Medicine in Post-Apartheid South Africa," African Affairs, *Oxford Journals* 107, no. 427 (2008): 157–76, http://afraf.oxfordjournals.org/content/107/427/157 (accessed March 14, 2012).

5. Dave Gamble, "The Pointless Death of Peter Sellers," *Skeptical Science* (blog), January 3, 2011, http://www.skeptical-science.com/critical-thinking/pointless-death-peter-sellers (accessed August 24, 2012).

6. David Gorski, "Steve Jobs' Cancer and Pushing the Limits of Science-Based Medicine," *Science-Based Medicine* (blog), October 10, 2011, http://www.sciencebasedmedicine.org/index.php/the-death-of-steve-jobs (accessed August 24, 2012).

7. Ibid.

8. Anna Song, "Woman Out $400K to 'Nigerian Scam' Con Artists,'" KATU.com, November 11, 2008, http://www.katu.com/news/34292654.html (accessed August 24, 2012).

9. "Postman Loses £130,000 Savings to Nigerian Internet Scam after Being Duped by a Friend He Met on MySpace," *Daily Mail* online, January 16, 2009, http://www.dailymail.co.uk/news/article-1116067/Postman-loses-130-000-savings-Nigerian-interest-scam-duped-friend-met-MySpace.html (accessed August 24, 2012).

10. Jacqui Cheng, "Suckers Victims Lost $9.3 Billion to 419 Scammers in 2009," Ars Technica, January 29, 2010, http://Arstechnica.com/security/2010/01/victims-lost-93-billion-to-419-scammers-in-2009/ (accessed August 24, 2012).

11. David Weigel, "Orly Taitz Sanctioned for $20,000," *Washington Independent* online, October 13, 2009, http://washingtonindependent.com/63558/orly-taitz-sanctioned-for-20000 (accessed August 24, 2012).

12. "$10,000, No $15,000 for Proof of Obama's Birth Hospital," January 9, 2010, WorldNetDaily, http://www.wnd.com/2010/01/121395 (accessed August 24, 2012).

13. Alternative Therapies, http://www.therapies.com/ (accessed August 24, 2012).

14. "Wesley Snipes Gets 3 Years for Not Filing Tax Returns," *New York Times* online, April 25, 2008, http://www.nytimes.com/2008/04/25/business/25snipes .html (accessed August 24, 2012).

15. Transcript of Wesley Snipes sentencing hearing, FraudsandScams.com, April 4, 2008, http://www.fraudsandscams.com/SnipesTax/Sentencing%20 Transcript.pdf (accessed August 24, 2012).

16. Terry Lakin Action Fund, http://www.terrylakinactionfund.com (accessed August 24, 2012).

17. Mike "No Man" Navarre, "Former LTC Terrence Lakin Denied Medical License," *NIMJ Blog-CAAFLOG* (blog), February 6, 2012, http://www.caaflog.com/ ?s=lakin+denied+medical+license (accessed August 24, 2012).

18. Carl Sagan, *The Demon-Haunted World: Science as a Candle in the Dark* (New York: Ballantine Books, 1997), pp. 161–63.

19. Alice Gomstyn, "Not Just the Wendrows: Sex Abuse Cases Dismissed after Facilitated Communication," ABC News online, January 7, 2012, http://abcnews. go.com/Health/wendrows-sex-abuse-cases-dismissed-facilitated-communication/ story?id-15274276#.Twj7tfLNns6 (accessed August 24, 2012).

20. *State v. Warden,* Supreme Court of Kansas, March 10, 1995, Find a Case, http:// ks.findacase.com/research/wfrmDocViewer.aspx/xq/fac.19950310_0042072. KS.htm/qx (accessed August 24, 2012).

21. Gomstyn, "Not Just the Wendrows."

22. Jonathan Kay, *Among the Truthers* (New York: HarperCollins, 2011), p. 155.

INDEX